Critical Psychology

The International Journal of Critical Psychology

Issue 13

Critical Professionals

Guest Editor
Jane Selby

Collection as a whole © Lawrence & Wishart 2005
Individual articles © the individual authors 2005

The authors have asserted their rights under the Copyright, Design and Patents Act, 1998 to be identified as the authors of this work. All rights reserved. Apart from fair dealing for the purpose of private study, research, criticism or review, no part of this publication may be reproduced, stored in a retrieval system, or transmitted, in any form or by any means, electronic, electrical, chemical, mechanical, optical, photocopying, recording or otherwise, without the prior permission of the copyright owner.

ISSN 1471 4167
ISBN 1-905007-10-8

Cover design E-Type
Cover image © Kate Paxman
Typeset by E-Type, Liverpool, UK
printed by Biddles Ltd, King's Lynn, UK

Critical Psychology is published three times per year by
Lawrence & Wishart
99a Wallis Road
London E9 5LN
United Kingdom

Editor
Valerie Walkerdine (University of Cardiff)
Email: WalderdineV@cardiff.ac.uk

Editorial Assistant
Theophilus Gokah
IjcP@cardiff.ac.uk

Individual subscriptions £40
Institutional subscriptions £120

For advertising information contact
editorial@lwbooks.co.uk

Contents

Editorial: Subjectivity as a critical fulcrum: professional practice as dilemma
Jane Selby   5

Features

Pippa Dell and Irina Anderson
Practising critical psychology: politics, power and psychology departments   14

Bronwyn Davies and Eva Bendix Petersen
Intellectual workers (un)doing neoliberal discourse   32

David Harper
The critical professional and social policy: negotiating dilemmas in the UK Mental Health Act campaign   55

Kerry Frizelle
Negotiating identity within the politics of HIV/AIDS: developing interventions for young South Africans   76

Lise Bird, Sue Cornforth, Duane Duncan, and Shirley Roberson
Professionals becoming researchers: collective engagement and difficulties of transformation   96

Jane Callaghan
Playing the game: Professionalisation and depoliticisation   117

Paula M. Smith
Distinguishing myself in hysteria   139

Sally Denshire
'This is a hospital, not a circus!': Reflecting on generative metaphors for a deeper understanding of professional practice   159

Reviews

Laura Miller
Let's theorise it better: A review of two introductions to critical (social) psychology   179

Notes on Contributors   188

Book Reviews Editors
Dr Lisa Blackman
Dept of Media and Communications,
Goldsmith's College, University of London,
London SE14 6NW. UK
Email: coa01lb@gold.ac.uk

Associate Editors
Australasia
Ben Bradley (Charles Sturt University)
Ann Game (University of New South Wales)
Nicola Gavey (University of Auckland)
John Kaye (University of Adelaide)
Sue Kippax (University of New South Wales)
Isaac Prilleltensky (Victoria University)
Jane Ussher (University of Western Sydney)

UK
Lisa Blackman (Goldsmiths College, University of London)
Stephen Frosh (Birkbeck College, University of London)
Wendy Hollway (Open University)
Ian Parker (Manchester Metropolitan University)
Ann Phoenix (Open University)
Jonathan Potter (Loughborough University)
Lynne Segal (Birkbeck College, University of London)
Couze Venn (Nottingham Trent University)

North America
Tod Sloan (University of Tulsa)
John Broughton (Columbia University)
Betty Bayer (Hobart and William Smith Colleges)
Kum Kum Bhavnani (University of California, Santa Barbara)
Kareen Malone (University of West Georgia)
Michelle Fine (The City University of New York)

International Editorial Board
Erika Apfelbaum (CNRS, Paris)
Erica Burman (Manchester Metropolitan University, UK)
Teresa Cabruja (University of Girona, Spain)
Michael Cole (University of California, San Diego, USA)
Heidi Figueroa Sarriera (University of Puerto Rico)
Angel Gordo-Lopez (Universidad Complutense de Madrid)
David Ingleby (University of Utrecht, Netherlands)
Ingrid Lunt (University of London, UK)
Wolfgang Maiers (Free University of Berlin, Germany)
Amina Mama (University of Cape Town, South Africa)
Janet Sayers (University of Kent, UK)
Corinne Squire (University of East London, UK)

Editorial: Subjectivity as a critical fulcrum
Professional practice as dilemma

Jane Selby

In the mid 1800s Thomas Huxley, an eminent empirical scientist specialising in marine invertebrates, spearheaded a hard-fought battle against the well-endowed 'privileged, old-boy network' of clerics and their aristocratic allies (Desmond and Moore, 1991, p.431) whose rule of the scientific roost was based on Christian dogma. A point of struggle was to wrest the Presidency of the Royal Society from the clergymen's camp and into the hands of *professional* scientists. Charles Darwin, one of modern psychology's trailblazers, served as a paragon for this 'new tightly knit, highly regulated "profession"' (op cit, p. 432), a man whose scientific laurels had been won over years of meticulous research. His public eminence in science owed nothing to privilege or natural theology.[1]

No less ardently than Huxley, psychologists have long embraced the status of professional scientist. This has mixed consequences. As Cahan and White (1992) describe, psychology was first envisaged in the 1700s as *the* strategic science of the Enlightenment. It would not only define the basis and limitations for all other sciences, but would map out the kinds of knowledge necessary to make social and political progress towards a juster, more democratic world. By identifying with the professional sciences, modern psychology has gained social status as being objective and value-neutral. At the same time, it has lost any obvious foundation in political commitment to promotion of the common good. 'There is nothing in the definition of psychology that dedicates our science to the solution of social problems' as APA President George Miller (1969, p.1063) once famously observed. Like the oldest profession, prostitution, psychologists buy a reputation for even-handedness at the cost of foregoing any political agenda. To the good professional, all comers are served, all questions are catered for – however attractive or unattractive to the individual psychologist providing the service – provided clients can afford the going rate. This means most often that the profession conceives the problems it investigates and the people it studies in terms that suit those who benefit socially and financially from maintenance of the status quo, not those who would benefit from political change (Ingleby, 1974; Rose, 1999). As Steve Reicher (1996, p.237) puts it: 'The ultimate irony is that we have bought our own autonomy as academics at the cost of denying autonomy to those that we study. To risk a poetic allusion: we have bought our own freedom at the cost of everyone else's soul – a truly Faustian contract'.

Reicher's antidote to professional psychologists' pact with Mephistopheles is political organisation. But the tragedy of Faust's dissatisfaction with the barrenness of academic achievement is first and foremost an 'internal' one, a tragedy of lost souls, played out vicariously for Faust through his doomed relationship with his inamorata, the beautiful, virtuous and hard-working Gretchen (Goethe, 1996). Unprotected by Mephistopheles's magical powers, Gretchen's love for Faust brings upon her social stigmatisation, imprisonment, moral ruin and personal wretchedness.

It is the 'internal' subjective dramas of the professional that this issue explores. Critical psychologists are all familiar with the 'external' consequences of the Faustian contract represented by allegiance to the role of professional scientist: complicity with the agendas of the powerful at the expense both of raising voices for the powerless and of living out the 'calling' to help others that is central to the recruitment of so many who join the discipline.[2] Hence we find contradictions similar to those in psychology in more obviously vocational professions which may be new to the academy, like nursing, teaching and policing. Professionals of many different stripes live out these conflicts 'subjectively'; that is, in their intimate dealings with colleagues, clients and their own identities (Selby, 1985). In this issue I take it that these subjective struggles require the attention of critical psychologists just as much as the better-known political contradictions of the profession: attention which requires us to acknowledge personal psychological struggles and the articulation of such struggles as central to any serious rethinking of the discipline.

These 'internal' contradictions are compounded by others. Not only does such professional work support the political status quo, but professionals themselves now form elites. To train as a professional continues to require substantial financial resources and continues to be accessible, mainly, to children of the wealthier. Indeed, Gandhi, one of the last century's greatest moralists and political leaders (Gandhi, 2001, pp 163-4) recognised, living under a more extreme form of colonisation, that to educate his children at good schools and at university would be reinforcing privilege, and so he denied them this education.

This issue (and articles by Fullagar and Gibb with the same theme, in a forthcoming issue) calls upon the notion of professionals, because its connotations catch the dilemmas and urgency of issues that are shared across the boundaries of disciplines both practice-based and scholarly. First we examine the different ways in which our experiences hold conflict and dilemmas which few, if any, training and research programmes prepare us for. In our work, we find we need critical and conceptual clarity to validate the processes of resistance to and reflection upon the (inter)personal subjectivities constituted through our professional lives. So we can find ourselves, in making explicit our experiences as professionals, pondering an inherently psychological set of concerns around struggle, burnout, tolerance, creativity, change and satisfaction. In so doing we need to forefront the inevitability of subjective complexity in good, innovative practice.

The second main concern has been with the overall political and cultural contexts of training and organising within professions and scholarship. We can identify issues of governmentality intrinsic to the regulation of practice and undermining of, as well as enabling of, professional and scholastic autonomy. What, for example, are the links between macro-issues of policy-making and training schedules and the curtailment of liberatory practices in social and political change (Harper, this issue, and Frizelle, this issue)?

The traditions taken up here in addressing these concerns have included Foucauldian foci on power and governmentality (Rose, 1999) and Risk Theory's account of science and expertise as having lost their claim to certainty by producing risks and uncertainties of their own (Gibb, see forthcoming IJCP issue; Bradley and Morss, 2002; Beck, 1997). These perspectives lead us straight into the heart of subjectivity and experience as a locus both for change and the articulation of knowledge. In accounts of subjectivity there is a need to develop insights into the ordinary and extraordinary processes of individual identity and intersubjective construction of knowledge. For this need social constructionism comes to the fore with its emphasis on relational forms as the unit of analysis for the understanding of psychological processes (Gergen, 1994). In addition we can employ psychoanalytic understandings of interpersonal processes which find both emotional life and irrationality at the heart of human endeavour (Selby, 1993).

More generally, what emerges as the crux of this issue is emphasis on how to struggle, how to manage 'righteous' anger, how to tolerate and even use discomfort and pain in processes of change. What can be missing is a way of taking up inklings from our own experience about organisational structure and group process – 'They will say I'm doing this all wrong ...', 'The ring of the phone lurches me into anxiety ...', 'If I could annihilate you ... if only'. There is the counter-transferential evidence of resentment and cynicism: 'The senior administrator's exhilaration in undermining those he cannot outdo ...', 'I can't believe they would do this ... and get away with it'.

Many of the papers in this issue are experimental, in that what is written about and how it is written has required the authors to spotlight problems while grappling with *how to* spotlight, and so bring out some vision or perspective of value to their readers (Denshire, this issue; Petersen and Davies, this issue). Thus we find Harper seeking to express how it is to be caught up in a labyrinth of engagements both professionally and personally felt, pinioned by incompatibilities, coerced by compromise. Callaghan struggles to cast light on circumstances in which even the critical psychologist cannot avoid conforming, the best of his/her resistance perforce covert, damned to a subjectivity fraught by compromise. Smith mulls over what from one perspective is a 'breakdown' marked by ill health and petty aggressions towards a colleague, seeking for insight to endow those painful years with more adequate meaning by linkage to patriarchal oppression, devout vows, and the needs to challenge inequities in our cultures. In such and other ways the papers provide pioneering reflection on everyday, even commonplace, dilemmas for professionals and academics who, while 'critical' and thirsty for change, wrestle to dress experiences constituted by current organisational structures in ill-fitting theoretical clothes. By so doing the papers published here challenge all of us to cultivate a sometimes painful gaze that dwells on the darker corners of our professional lives rather than fleeing without further ado into the comfortable numbing embrace of theoretical or methodological orthodoxy. The seductiveness of such flight was copiously documented for the social sciences many years ago by George Devereux (1967; cf. Bordo, 1989).

By insisting we need soberly to reflect upon the way we take up into theory our professional discomforts and anxieties, and our fears into narrated coherence, the papers in this collection give a new psychological relevance to the daily trials and tribulations of our working lives. How can we conceptualise the processes of internalising and identification, the ways we take on board the power structures which at once hail us and constrain us as 'experts'? How do we move from doing something 'willingly' to being genuinely willing (Peterson and Davies, this issue)? What does it take to convey a 'positive uncertainty' (Frizelle, this issue) when engaged with people at serious risk? What do we mean by and how are we to think about the 'messy bits' caught up in a given job's 'contradictory imperatives' (Bird et al, this issue, Harper, this issue)? What resources are required to persevere with derided interventions within the heartland of medicine (Denshire, this issue)? How long can we live out forms of resistance experienced as 'hysterical' without any alternative narrative (Smith, this issue)?

What makes the papers here critical is best conceptualised through the way 'the professional' stands at odds with 'the academic'. While in practice the contradictions involved may be sewn or stapled together (e.g. Petersen and Davies, this issue), the seam is always pulling and liable at any moment to open again into a running sore. In Plato's (1961, p.879) *Theaetetus*, Socrates sagely observes that 'philosophers' embody values that make them a laughing-stock for the streetwise smart-alecks whom Socrates epitomises as 'lawyers' because the lawyer is supremely well-versed in the busy commerce of the day-to-day, glorying in personal scandal, cunning rhetoric and worldly achievement. The philosopher, in contrast, has no truck with such ephemeral preoccupations, 'what lies at his feet or is before his eyes, what his next-door neighbour is doing' … timekeeping, form-filling, administrative deadlines, corridor gossip and one-up-manship. The philosopher is interested in deeper questions: what being human is, the meaning of justice. Likewise the ideal academic, the image at the back of our minds of the person who informs and inspires, has all the time in the world to dwell on the 'deep' concerns and great debates that raise us high above the quotidian. So, as academics we wish to work and 'profess' in freedom from the thousand irksome strings of Lilliputian bureaucracy. But as professionals our daily business is to work incrementally within or despite bureaucracies, thereby to make better the non-ideal worlds which seek out our knowledge and care. It is thus that, for critical psychologists, academics and professionals alike, we cannot help but live and breathe both sides of a conflict that grows up 'inside' us: the stronger the practical pressures get to develop and change the everyday workings of the disciplines we are committed to, the more we need freedom to think, write, practice and work in the light of an understanding that rises 'above' and so makes sense of subjectivities steeped in ennui and anxiety.

The papers here include two which focus on clinical psychology in different ways – one in terms of training and professionalism in South Africa (Callaghan), the other addressing the professional dilemmas of trying to change mental health policy (Harper). While the psychologists who contribute take up recognisable themes of critical psychology, Dell et al focus explicitly on the challenges and constraints on critical psychologists during these times of university shifts towards entrepreneurialism. Others also focus on contemporary university life, Bird et al documenting and reflecting on an interdisciplinary group as they grapple with the nature of transforming their disciplinary research practices, while Petersen and Davies develop ways to represent both the experience of dilemmas for apparently successful academics and how the macropolitical forces become internalised. Fullagar (in press) reports on research which makes overt the implicit contradictions facing vulnerable youths and the professionals who are positioned to help their depression and self-harm. Gibb (in press) provides a clear and incisive perspective on how managerialism and neoliberalism directly impact on nursing professionals, undermining traditionally complex practices of care for patients. Denshire represents the work of occupational therapists by developing general methods of metaphor analyses and autobiography in reflecting on and validating important clinical work. Also autobiographical is Smith's multiple account of incidents over decades and the importance of continuing to develop perspectives which allow us to think about psychological disruption and distress in resistance to oppression.

The Southern hemisphere dominates, with six papers from Australasia and two from South Africa. The other two are from the UK. Strikingly the papers may refer to local and specific politics and cultural concerns, but each allows general engagement with the challenges of transformation, its representations and our individual roles in them.

Finally, and predictably in an institutional world dominated by the finance-based hierarchies of the new managerialism, the project which produced this issue – aspiring to build a trans-disciplinary scholarship that thinks subjectivity in the same space as professionalism – has drawn considerable flak. The grouping of academic-professionals who first came up with the idea for the issue had met in a creative atmosphere afforded by an open and supportive debate. No sooner formulated as a coherent enterprise, however, than the project drew forth the wrath of senior University managers who judged that this particular grouping had no right to forge an unsolicited investigation into professionalism. Far from receiving support for the initiative in the name of valuable scholarly inquiry, they were castigated for not recognising that the project needed to have been vetted by management to ensure it did not threaten any part of the intellectual territory presided over by the Office for Research. The ensuing attacks played their part in a drama which led to the resignation of a key academic within the institution, who concluded she could only find a semblance of intellectual freedom outside the 'scholarly' community.

The issue is for Sally Denshire, Simone Fullagar, Agnes MacMillan and Michelle Ortlipp. Thanks to Ben Bradley for helping me through the historical literature.

Notes

1. The public perception did not tell the whole story, however. Darwin's father and grandfather had also been Fellows of the Royal Society. Charles Darwin's father Robert appears to have gained his fellowship purely on nepotistic grounds (Desmond and Moore, 1991, p.10), but Charles's grandfather, Erasmus, made many significant scientific discoveries. In fact, Charles Darwin's election was probably as much on nepotistic grounds – that is, on the strength of his family history and his connections with the current scientific elite (and perhaps the materials he had returned to British scientists from his voyage on *HMS Beagle*) – as in acknowledgement of any startling discovery. He was elected to his fellowship on 24 January1839, long before he had caught the public eye or published any significant scientific findings.
2. The term 'professional' has a range of connotations. Its origin is rooted in professions of religious faith, when to be 'professed' was to take the vows of a religious order (Little et al, 1973 p. 1681), while later a profession

becomes 'The occupation which one professes to be skilled in and to follow', specifically the 'three learned professions of divinity, law and medicine' (op cit). The connotations here are of seriousness, scholarship and authority, connotations we retain when we argue for someone's 'professional' attitude. Then there is the concept of the 'professional' rather than the 'amateur' sportsman, with a history of its own complexity: part of which, however, may lend itself to another connotation – that of disparaging one who 'makes a trade' of a high calling (op cit).

References

Beck, U. (1997). *The reinvention of politics*. Cambridge: Polity.

Bordo, S. (1989). *The Flight to Objectivity: Essays on Cartesianism and Culture*. Albany: State University of New York Press.

Bradley, B.S. and J.R. Morss (2002). 'Social construction in a world at risk: Towards a psychology of experience'. *Theory and Psychology* 12: 509-531.

Cahan, E.D. and S. H. White (1992). 'Proposals for a Second Psychology'. *American Psychologist* 47: 224-35.

Desmond, A. and Moore, J. (1992). *Darwin*. Harmondsworth: Penguin Books.

Devereux, G. (1968). *From anxiety to method in the behavioural sciences*. The Hague: Mouton.

Fullagar, S. (in press). 'The Paradox of Promoting Help-Seeking: A Critical Analysis of Risk, Rurality and Youth Suicide'. *International Journal of Critical Psychology*.

Gandhi, M. K. (1927/2001). *An autobiography, or the story of my experiments with truth*. Ahmedabad: Navajivan Publishing House.

Gergen, K.J. (1994). *Realities and Relationships: Soundings in Social Construction*. Cambridge, MA: Harvard University Press.

Gibb, H. (in press). 'Risk rationality and the emergence of a new professionalism in nursing'. *International Journal of Critical Psychology*.

Goethe, J. W. von (2000). 'Faust, Part One' (translated by R. Jarrell). Harmondsworth: Penguin Books.

Ingleby, D. (1974). 'The job psychologists do'. Armistead, N. (Ed.).*Reconstructing Social Psychology*. Harmondsworth: Penguin.

Little, W., H. W. Fowler and J. Coulson (1973). *The Shorter Oxford English Dictionary On Historical Principles*. Oxford: Oxford University Press

Miller, G.A. (1969). 'Psychology as a means of promoting human welfare'. *American Psychologist* 24: 1063-75.

Plato (1961). *The collected dialogues of Plato, including the letters*. Hamilton, E. and H. Cairns (Eds). Princeton: Princeton University Press.

Reicher, S. (1996). 'The reactionary practice of radical psychology'. Parker, I. and R. Spears (Eds). *Psychology and Society: Radical Theory and Practice*. London: Pluto Press.

Rose, N. (1999). *Governing the Soul: The Shaping of the Private Self*. London: Free Association Books. (Second edition).

Selby, J.M. (1993). 'Psychoanalysis as a critical theory of gender'. Mos, L., W.

Thorngate, B. Kaplan and H. Stam (Eds).*Recent trends in theoretical psychology* 307-318. New York: Springer Verlag.

Selby, J.M. (1985). 'Feminine Identity and Contradiction: Women Research Students at Cambridge University'. *PhD thesis*. University of Cambridge, UK.

Practising critical psychology
Politics, power and psychology departments

Pippa Dell and Irina Anderson

In this paper we discuss some of the discursive practices in place that delimit, constrain and simultaneously produce psychology as a predominantly scientific (or mainstream/traditional) discipline. We will also focus on how these practices police and regulate sites of resistance such as are offered up by alternative epistemologies, for example critical psychology. The politics of these discursive practices, what Foucault (1977; 1980) has described variously as the power/knowledge nexus and the microphysics of power, will be considered in relation to: First, how the positioning of critical psychological research as potentially problematic and destructive in relation to other research aspects of the discipline is made manifest through modern economic imperatives. Second, how critical psychologists in psychology departments are themselves positioned as 'other', 'different' and 'difficult', and in ways that more mainstream psychologists don't necessarily encounter. Third, we will consider some of the consequences for the student experience of engaging with critical psychologies: the implications, both positive and negative, of deconstructing and de-centring the subject (the individual and psychology); the politicisation of their everyday life; and the implications the critical psychologies have for students' future practices as professional psychologists.

Introduction
Adopting an approach to psychology which questions its social construction as an academic discipline and which articulates the

diverse disciplinary practices that act to maintain the scientism of psychology is self-evidently a difficult academic stance to take. The power of scientific discourse is well documented and indeed, is so firmly imbricated within psychology, that to offer alternative understandings of what psychology might be or even become is to almost automatically engage its full disciplinary strategies – that is those social practices that legitimate particular truths about the nature of psychology and seek to discipline those that do not concur (Henriques, Hollway, Urwin, Venn and Walkerdine, 1998; Rose 1985; 1989). Most critical psychologists, at some time in our careers, will have experienced some of these social practices which seek to constrain and exclude us. Obvious examples include the dearth of explicitly critical posts being advertised, the constant surveillance and questioning of our research and indeed our persons by colleagues, and the difficulties we experience in developing courses that have an explicitly critical curriculum. We have become better versed at strategies of resistance to these hegemonic practices. For example, advertising for academics to teach qualitative methodologies and/or conceptual issues rather than critical psychology *per se*;[1] honing our rhetorical skills and becoming expert at exposing epistemological assumptions underpinning mainstream research; importing critical approaches into courses with innocuous sounding titles. As a consequence of developing such strategies of resistance, however, we would argue that the disciplinary regimes we have to deal with in our academic life have become more insidious and thus harder to resist.

One such disciplinary regime is associated with what might be called the 'economic imperative' or more precisely, a set of historically specific economic discourses[2] and discursive practices that do *more* than limit the ways in which psychology can be practised through, crudely, the allocation of funding by centralised bureaucracies. Rather, following Foucault (1977) we would argue that these economic discourses and social practices are productive, meaning that they legitimate particular forms of authority, construct particular truths about the nature of psychology and position and constitute people as proper psychologists. Whilst these are powerful effects, they are not absolute truths but rather are 'historically produced within certain specific conditions of possibility' (Walkerdine, 1986: 64) that function to constitute and simultaneously set up spaces of resistance to a 'field of knowledge' (Foucault, 1977: 27). Moreover, these discourses (and discursive practices) are about power:

[Not] a sovereign power, a fixed possession of particular individuals. [Rather Foucault (1977)] reconceptualises power in terms of a 'microphysics of power' as an aspect of the regulative function of knowledge itself' ... Discourses regulate and discipline by constituting fields of knowledge, instituting truths, constituting subjectivities in particular ways, positioning people within discourses and subjecting them to normalising judgements ... so that power relations although unevenly distributed, are everywhere (Malson, 1998: 29)

It is precisely how (some of) these micro-physics of power operate in psychology departments in the UK that we are interested in exploring in this paper, or more particularly how the wider socio-historic and cultural contexts within which we practice psychology both constitute and regulate us professionally and personally and how we might, by identifying these discursive regimes, start to resist their hegemonic practices.

Critical psychology and the economic imperative

In a recent chapter entitled *'Practising Critical Psychology within a British Psychology Department'* Hollway (2000) describes some of the power-knowledge-practice relations that many critical psychologists are encountering in the academy today. Whilst these social practices are nothing new (present debates about the nature of psychology after all have an iterative history: Rose, 1989), of particular relevance to the economic imperative are the external bureaucratic procedures imposed by the government that have 'huge power to influence [universities'] income' and which generate 'practices at both university and departmental level that profoundly influence the production of knowledges' (Hollway, 2000: 42). Arguably the most pernicious of these in the current economic climate are related to student funding arrangements and research income.

With respect to student funding, in the UK, the Higher Education Funding Councils currently pay universities more to train science students than arts students. Funding falls into four categories: Band A, the most expensive, for fields such as clinical medicine, to band D for classroom based subjects such as the arts and humanities. Psychology is currently funded (2003-2004) as a laboratory-based subject in band B. However, this funding is predicated on the careful construction of psychology as a science and the support of powerful lobbies.[3] Indeed, in 1995/1996 funding arrangements for UK psychology departments were reviewed to ensure that psychology curricula included a certain proportion of laboratory and related science teaching to justify band B funding. In the context of possible loss of income (and thus of academic jobs and concomitant increased teaching loads for those who remain in post) not unsurprisingly a climate of adherence to the scientific tenets of psychology became more overtly manifest, irrespective of the 'increasingly influential critiques of such a stance' (Hollway, 2000: 40).

Indeed, as we write, this funding debate has re-emerged, as have the now-familiar strategies to science psychology. Specifically, in August 2003 the Higher Education Funding Council for England (HEFCE) launched a consultation process to discuss its proposals to develop the ways in which it planned to allocate funding for university teaching, widening access and improving student retention. As part of this radical redevelopment of student funding, which also incorporated the advent of variable tuition fees, yet again the funding of psychology was called into question. This time, it was proposed that psychology should be reassigned to band C (intermediate-cost subjects) from 2004-2005, a potential loss of up to £600 per full-time student per annum. We have recently heard (January 2004) that this proposal now has been accepted, although the actual financial costs of this re-banding to individual psychology departments are still to be finalised.

Not unexpectedly, this re-banding has excited considerable debate within the psychological community. It is predicted that it will have 'considerable detrimental effects on the discipline' (*The Psychologist*, 2003: 656). The initial proposal in August 2003 to re-band psychology resulted in a powerful lobby group, the Joint Committee (of the British Psychological Society, the Experimental Psychology Society and the Association of Heads of Psychology Departments) for Resources in Higher Education (JCRHE) to write to the chief executive of HEFCE to protest at the proposed changes. As well as outlining the financial impact of such a funding change, this carefully crafted letter highlights very clearly the continuing construction of psychology as a science in the UK. As reported in *The Psychologist*, this letter 'emphasised the increasing use of neuroscientific techniques and the provision of experimental skills training, and pointed out that the proposed cut in funding would inevitably lead to a "de-sciencing" of the discipline' (*The Psychologist*, 2003: 657).

This explicit linking of certain types of psychology, namely those that require expensive laboratories and equipment and which train students in experimental methods, to enhanced funding has had a detrimental consequence for those of us teaching critical psychology. Specifically, it has positioned certain types of psychologists, those that 'do science' within the discipline, as being more valuable to a department's finances. Whilst the recent changes in funding could reduce such discrimination, in practice we believe the opposite to be more likely. With a reduction in central funding from government, psychology departments will be forced to seek alternative sources of income to maintain their staff-student ratios (and thus Graduate Basis for Registration with the British Psychological Society); one obvious source being to increase the number of grant applications to the science research councils.

Against this economic imperative, it will become increasingly difficult to counter the notions that more critical approaches are not only *'worth less'* financially, but *'worthless'* academically. Indeed some critical psychologists reluctantly have already played the game and invested in, for example, specialist observation rooms and expensive videoing facilities to assist focus group or interview based research (equipment to aid and simultaneously technologise and thus 'science' qualitative research), or submitted proposals to the funding bodies to conduct research that is tangential to their main interests. This compromise, which we believe will become increasingly necessary, has several pernicious implications for those engaging with critical psychology.

First, and most obviously, it has done little more than bolster those practices that sustain and reproduce the superior status of scientific psychology and its concomitant orthodox knowledges (Hollway, 2000: 40). Second, it places critical psychologists in a difficult moral position: play the game and ensure that you don't lose your department funding (and thus jeopardise jobs) but live with the dilemma of having in some sense sold out. Third, it acts as a useful disciplinary strategy – divide and rule – those that don't play the game within this economic imperative being further marginalised and excluded, deemed to be problematic and destructive when compared with their more docile critical peers.

Similarly, with respect to the allocation of research income, in recent years the UK university sector has been subjected to four research assessment exercises (RAE), the purpose of which, purportedly, is to measure the quality of British research in order to differentially allocate research funding. As part of this bureaucratic exercise, units of assessment had to be defined. Despite, as Hollway (2000) has noted, 'intellectual and institutional trends in the direction of inter-disciplinary work' the eventual units of assessment employed were based on disciplinary boundaries immediately disadvantaging (and even excluding) many critical psychologists whose work is located within disciplinary interstices. Furthermore, within psychology (unit of assessment 13; www.rae.ac.uk) the criteria chosen to measure quality (or more realistically the chances of your department being awarded a 5* or a 6* – the highest rankings available and thus the maximum amount of research money [op cit]) in the most recent RAE exercise in 2001 included: four peer refereed publications (preferably in good international journals, of which the impact indices mention few that are explicitly critical in orientation); number of PhD students supervised and within a specified timeframe (this tends to suit more experimental rather than theoretical theses); and external grants awarded (useful for those who require research assistants and laboratory equipment, but less so for those whose methodologies require active engagement of the researcher in the data collection or indeed for those wanting to write more theoretically oriented books).

The implications of these criteria for reinforcing scientism in psychology and dictating the future direction of psychology are obvious. More subtle, however, have been some of the social practices that these criteria warrant. First, the imposition of this economic imperative has taken on a guise of neutral agency within psychology departments. The RAE criteria are used to justify departmental research strategies that govern which categories of research are permissible and which are not, whilst simultaneously absolving the individuals concerned in these decisions of any blame: comments such as 'it's not our fault, it's the requirements of the RAE' become increasingly commonplace. Second, through a process of reification, the RAE criteria not only become benchmarks for excellence but also become separated from the very human power/knowledge processes involved in their design. Third, resisting these criteria, questioning their construction and indeed relevance, invokes strong disciplinary procedures that limit and delimit the research you can do. For example, not receiving a fair share of any research money because your work might not contribute to the next RAE; being excluded from the RAE submission itself and thus deemed research inactive, with all the implications this has in terms of career progression; and being required to take on more administration and teaching as your fair contribution to the wealth of the department.

Some of us have countered this 'bastion of positivism (where experimental cognitive neuroscientists reign supreme)' (Ussher, 2000: 15) by performing at a high level both within mainstream and critical camps simultaneously. However, this often comes at a considerable personal price, and is ultimately unsustainable. As Ussher (2000) describes in her admirably honest chapter 'Critical psychology in the mainstream: A struggle for survival', which details her time working in one of the more prestigious psychology departments in the UK (as evidenced by their RAE score), adopting this strategy can become overwhelming:

> [o]n the one hand, I was writing critical feminist work that came from the heart, and attempting to develop and grow academically in this sphere drawing on psychoanalytic theory, cultural theory, art history, in my teaching, my graduate supervision, and in a book I was writing on women's sexuality (Ussher, 1997b), at the same time I was running three major empirical research grants, having to publish in mainstream refereed psychology journals, running weekly graduate seminars, conducting my undergraduate teaching, and sole supervising six full-time and two part-time PhDs. In retrospect it was madness – few could keep up that level of work for long. But at the time it seemed the only way to survive. I wanted to make a niche for critical feminist work in a highly respected psychology department ... My mission was to make feminist psychology part of the mainstream map – whether they liked it or not. I did for a while, but at a cost (ibid, 2000: 15).

This cost of adopting what we might term a dual-mode strategy had consequences for Ussher's health in terms of the stress of overwork and, as she admits, ultimately contributed to her decision to resign from this post.

On a more positive note however, there are some strategies of resistance that we can adopt that are arguably less personally damaging. For example, some critical psychologists enter their research into other more appropriate units of assessment. Indeed, in our own case, it was decided that the critical psychology group at our university should go into unit of assessment 47: sociology – with the understanding that any thus accrued research monies should follow the researchers concerned. In our case, this resulted in a considerable proportion of our school's research money being derived from this strategy. Whilst this allowed us to be research active and thus valuable, and indeed to conduct the type of research we felt was most worthwhile, it was still a compromise. We consider ourselves to be psychologists rather than sociologists, and wanted to be recognised as such.

Second, at the time of writing, it seems that the next RAE units of assessment are changing from sixty-eight discipline-based units to approximately fifteen to twenty larger main panels and seventy sub-panels whose relationship to the previous discipline based units are still to be finalised but will be based on 'cognate disciplines' (Roberts, 2003; HEFCE, 2004: 5). Our rather naïve hope is that there will be genuine discussion as to the constitution of these multi-disciplinary main panels, due to be 'finalised in consultation with the research community in 2004' (HEFCE, 2004: 3); that there will be a fluid system that will allow any pairings of subject areas, as is implicitly suggested by the HEFCE document's support for 'the principles that the assessment process should be designed better to recognise excellence in applied and practice-based research, in new disciplines, and in fields crossing traditional discipline boundaries' (ibid, 2004; 5); and that inter-disciplinary research itself is more explicitly included, whether or not it constitutes the aforementioned new disciplines or fields. Indeed, *now* (Spring 2004) is the time for critical psychologists to get involved in these decision-making processes and at the RAE panel level – where we must be represented. There may still be time to get involved in the consultation process and indeed in putting forward names for panel membership. But we must do it soon, before the next set of RAE criteria become fixed and thus fixing.

Critical psychologist: Other, different and difficult?
As has become clear, the economic imperative and its institutionally based social practices have real consequences for people, rendering those who do not conform as 'other' (Kitzinger and Wilkinson, 1997) and potentially worth-less. However, this positioning within an economic discourse is not the only subjectification (cf Foucault, 1982) we encounter whilst practising critical psychology within the academy. There are other dividing practices put in place that act as modes of manipulation that seek to socially exclude us. These take the form of both the overt and hostile disparagement of our research, which some colleagues unfortunately still face, and the more subtle but no less

pernicious feminisation (and thus disempowerment) of our work and indeed our personhood.

Some examples of both of the above points include the following. Qualitative methodologies which are frequently used by critical psychologists are often described as a 'soft option' by our colleagues when compared with the more scientifically 'hard-nosed' statistical methods. We are also more likely to be asked to justify the inclusion of certain materials in our curricula than our more mainstream contemporaries. Finally, on a more personal level, we have been described as 'irrational' and 'emotional', for example, when we quite rationally and unemotionally question the epistemological assumptions underpinning positivist scholarship. Indeed one colleague once asked why it was that critical psychologists were 'always so difficult?'. In part this reflects ignorance of what it is exactly that we do (deconstruction after all is not synonymous with destruction, although this might surprise some of our peers). However, it is also part of the processes of normalisation at work within psychology. As Rabinow (1991, p21) has noted, 'an essential component of technologies of normalisation is the key role they play in the systematic creation, classification and control of anomalies in the social body'. Critical psychologists, by the nature of their work, are rendered visible, and can thus be identified and then classified as different, and potentially uncontrollable; the latter being often considered synonymous with dangerous. Processes of control such as the feminisation of our work (for example in describing our methodologies as 'soft') and the hystericisation of our persons (by describing us as 'irrational' and 'emotional') can then be brought to bear on us to correct and normalise, or at least render us invisible and powerless.

Identifying the ways in which we are positioned is one thing, countering them is quite another. Whilst discourses and their attendant practices produce the individual in particular ways and, as Foucault (1979: 96) argues, simultaneously produce their own 'plurality of resistances to power', how we can marshal strategies to resist these 'far-reaching, but never completely stable effects of domination' (ibid: 102) is less clear.

For some of us being positioned as 'radical', 'other' and 'potentially threatening' (Ussher, 2000: 12) proffers a place of enunciation that has considerable power to provoke and disturb by violating the authorised codes of what constitutes psychology, and in doing so, expose its social construction. Indeed, some thirty years ago Wilden (1972) valorised the mainstream as a necessity for the 'negative academic' who is dependent on there being an orthodoxy to critique. However, as we have seen, adopting this very visible position can invoke well-rehearsed disciplinary strategies for dealing with any potential threat to the status quo.

Alternatively, we can draw on the experiences of other minorities to counter these hegemonic practices. Of course critical psychologists are not oppressed in quite the same way as other minorities (we are still overwhelmingly white, middle-class and well-educated). However, this does not preclude us from drawing on others' experiences and resisting oppressive strategies through processes of liberation (Prilleltensky and Nelson, 2002). This not only involves identifying the ways in which 'marginalised populations gain awareness of oppressive forces in their lives and of their own ability to transform them' (ibid: 16) but of applying this critical consciousness to our own practice as critical psychologists. Whilst we have no simple solutions to offer, we see critical education as one way forward. As academics, we can practice criticality by educating our colleagues so that we start to deconstruct the myths surrounding critical psychology. We can also educate students to produce more critical psychologists and encourage them to participate in our social movement. And finally, we can educate the general public so that our approach becomes part of their understanding of psychology.[4]

Critical psychology and the student experience

The epistemological assumptions underpinning critical psychologies, which deconstruct and decentre the subject (both the individual – academics and students alike – and the discipline of psychology) and make visible the humaneering project of psychology (Rose, 1989; Curt, 1994) not unexpectedly also impact on the student experience. As part of the process of being encouraged 'to participate in, even challenge, established intellectual authority' (Aronowitz, 2000: 143) and to 'interrogate the values implicit within psychology and to consider the values that *should* underlie theory, research and practice' (Prilleltensky and Nelson, 2002: 42 italics in original) students find both the subject matter and the pedagogical methods of critical psychology deeply unsettling, both intellectually and personally. Often, in our experience, their long-held beliefs and indeed everyday lives are decentred and deconstructed and in unexpected ways. We know that all education should come with a health warning. This is particularly true for students on critical psychology courses who find themselves questioning not only their intellectual antecedents (the nature of psychology) but also their everyday existence, the wider socio-economic systems that produce and sustain such existence, and their own relationship with activism.

This questioning results in both positive and negative aspects within students' experiences of critical psychology courses and impacts on those of us teaching critical psychology and in ways that are rarely voiced within the academy. Indeed, most other authors writing about pedagogical practices surrounding critical psychology mainly focus on the favourable aspects of this process. For example, drawing on the insights of critical pedagogy (Freire, 1970, 1994) and feminist and anti-racist education practices (hooks, 1994; Mukherjee, 1992), Prilleltensky and Nelson (2002) discuss how these traditions' 'common focus on analysing oppression and using participatory approaches to create social change' (ibid, 2002: 40) can be successfully employed in teaching critical psychology. In their work, they detail how a complex matrix of key outcomes and processes of education can be delivered such as to engage students at a personal, relational and collective level. Moreover, their approach emphasises reflexivity and consciousness-raising, rather than individual achievement and acceptance of the status quo – these latter processes being more typically associated with mainstream psychology teaching methods. Indeed, they discuss how their critical psychology graduate programmes often transform their students into positive agents of social change and/or reinforce their students' personal identities as critical thinkers. They also report positively on their student-centred rather than teacher-centred approaches to teaching, which results in students having 'some say over what they want to learn and how they want to learn it' (Prilleltensky and Nelson, 2002: 45).

We concur with many of these positive experiences of critical pedagogy, as they mirror our own experiences of teaching critical psychology at a British university. For example, students taking our critical psychology module in their third year often find their engagement with the material to be a personally transformative and liberating experience, enabling them to pose questions about, and challenge the assumptions underpinning, mainstream psychology and society. They also seem to gain, both intellectually and personally, from choosing to adopt more critical methodologies in their third-year projects, a fact that other researchers have also noted (e.g. Gough, Lawton, Madill and Stratton 2003). However, we have also encountered some negative aspects to teaching critical psychology. These emerge in part from a lack of process-oriented training that should accompany, and indeed be a precursor, to the ways in which we teach. After all, the main goals of critical pedagogy are concerned not only with the content of courses, but with how the teaching gets done. That is, a move away from the nutritionist model, where students are passively fed the truths about the world discovered by experts (Herman, 1995), to a model encouraging personal reflection, relational development and collective praxis. Whilst we are dealing with issues of transformation and change we should also acknowledge that these often come at a high price, for students and lecturers alike.

For example, it is clear that the aims of our courses achieve their goals, which are to encourage students to become critical thinkers and agentic in issues of social change, as evidenced by student feedback, assessment of students' work and our external examiners' comments. However, as teachers of critical psychology who are at the forefront of delivering these transformations, we are often less well prepared to deal with the difficulties that students' personal journeys often raise for them, and indeed the often strong emotional reactions that accompany such transformations and which can be played out (or acted up) in the classroom context. With regards to the emotive aspects of teaching critical psychology, how, for example, can we deal with students who come to question their previously deeply held beliefs – for example students who now view religion as just another discourse, with the emotional consequences that accompany such a loss of faith? Or, how do we deal with students who may have directly encountered some of the issues, such as racism or sexism, that are deconstructed on the course, and are angry, saddened, and even disempowered by such an analysis? And what about those who get disillusioned with psychology itself, not realising that critical approaches are asking *how* we should do psychology, not *should* we do psychology?[5]

Whilst in an ideal world we should follow the advice of those who advocate training in group facilitation (Ivey, Ivey and Simek-Morgan, 1997), mentoring, and co-teaching (Prilleltensky and Nelson, 2002) to support us in our ability to critically educate our students, in practice this type of staff development is either difficult to obtain and/or requires other critically oriented academics from whom to learn – often a scarce commodity. And what about the impact of these students' responses on the staff themselves? How do *we* cope emotionally, practically, and indeed morally, with the effects our curricula and teaching practices have on our students? For example, as we know from our own undergraduate days in predominantly mainstream departments, there are unspoken but generally acknowledged rules for giving or attending a formal academic lecture, a seminar, or indeed a tutorial. To deliberately disrupt these rules through our teaching methods, even if this disruption is made explicit and visible, can destabilise the space within which our teaching occurs and decentre power structures in ways which both staff and students may find difficult.[6] Finally, what about the consequences of our critical teaching methods on our students' experiences of the rest of their course? If we have been successful in empowering them to have a voice, and to use it to question the assumptions underlying more mainstream research presented in their other modules, will they, like us, encounter the disciplinary strategies discussed above? We don't have easy answers to these questions but rather want to raise these issues as part of the wider debate about putting critical psychology into practice – in this instance, within the academy.

Lastly, the power assigned to scientific psychology, and imbricated in the economic imperative of the current academic climate in the UK, has a significant effect on one further issue related to the student experience of critical psychology courses. This issue has to do with difficulties stemming from the lack of a critical mass of critical psychologists. First, and as Hollway (2000) has noted, in the teaching arena having too few critical psychologists in a department makes issues such as the assessment of work that the students produce a potential minefield for teachers of critical psychology. For example, if there are not enough critical psychologists in a department, then who will second-mark what is taught on critical courses? Given the lack of critical psychologists in most psychology departments in the UK, psychologists from the traditional branches of psychology often end up second-marking students' work. However, the resultant epistemological clash between the individualistic, highly cognitively-orientated traditional psychology and the anti-cognitive, anti-boundaried stance of critical psychology is more than likely to produce disagreements between markers which cannot be resolved in any obvious or easy way. How many of us have found agreeing marks yet another exhausting arena in which, yet again, we have to resist the broader hegemonic practices of mainstream psychology? Thus, the importance of a critical mass of psychologists in UK (and other) university departments cannot be underestimated.

Additionally, what about the destinations of students who have undertaken critical psychology courses? Although more and more postgraduate critical courses and degrees by research are being introduced into the UK higher education system, and the possibility of a critical mass of psychologists practising criticality in their work is becoming an attainable vision, there are still too few outlets for our students to enter with their learned skills. Indeed, the boundaries created by the 'economic imperative' evident in the higher education system and the prevalence of the scientism and experimentalism of psychology continue to ensure that the students who choose to explore and practice criticality in their research and indeed in their future professions as, for example, clinical or educational psychologists, are disadvantaged by too few opportunities and a generalised lack of enthusiasm for critical pedagogy. Issues (and compromises) pertaining to the practice of critical researchers and critical professionals are beyond the remit of this paper (but see Ahmed, 1996; 1999; Harper, 2003). However, as teachers of critical psychologies, understanding these wider contexts within which our students will have to work are essential, as we have a duty to our current students to prepare them both intellectually and politically for their future as critical psychologists.

A final thought

As Foucault has argued, disciplinary regimes imply a set of strategies, procedures and ways of behaving that are associated with certain institutional contexts and which then permeate ways of thinking and behaving in general. What we hope to have demonstrated in this paper is the fruitfulness of employing this type of analytical framework to explore how wider socio-historic and cultural contexts provide the conditions of possibility for the production and regulation of knowledges within which our profession and indeed scholarship are organised. As critical psychologists working in the academy we, and our students, are subjected to these regimes and often positioned in ways that are disempowering. However, by identifying these discursive strategies we can start to address the ways in which they impact on our practice as critical teachers and researchers and develop our dialogue(s) of resistance. Indeed, one goal of this paper has been to open up a space to encourage and validate the processes of reflection on our professional praxis, strategies of resistance and further research. This we hope will have positive effects not only on our professional lives but also on our personal subjectivity.

Whilst there may still be compromises to make in order to survive in the academic jungle, we think if we can educate both critical psychologists (to be better prepared emotionally and politically – which must be included in any training of academic psychologists) *and* our non-critical colleagues (both within the academy and in the wider general public) the future for the practice of critical psychology in the academy has the potential to be a more liberating and less subversive endeavour for all concerned.

Notes

1. The strategy of advertising for qualitative and theoretical posts to attract critical psychologists can backfire of course: positivist but non-experimental methodologies can be defined as qualitative, and theoretical approaches need not be critical in orientation. Recently (December 2003) explicitly critical posts have started to be advertised in *The Times Higher Education Supplement* – whilst these are still few and far between we welcome this more explicit advertising and would like to encourage it wherever possible.
2. The term 'discourse' emerges from post-structuralist theory. Rather than viewing language as reflecting an always-already existing meaning, discourse implies 'the more active labour of making things mean' (Hall, 1982: 64). Furthermore 'a discourse is not simply a set of linguistic practices. The concept of discourse includes discursive practices; it consists of a whole assemblage of concepts, objects, events and activities ... [that have] powerful "real" effects' (Malson, 1998: 28).
3. For example, as reported in *The Psychologist*, December 2003 'in the 1995/1996 review of funding the Joint Committee (of the British Psychological Society, the Experimental Psychological Society and the Heads of Psychology Departments) for resources in Higher Education (JCRHE) was successful in negotiating with HEFCE to adopt a split-band funding arrangement (between Bands B and D)' (p 656).
4. However, as one of the manuscript reviewers has pointed out, we also need to acknowledge that in this case as in many other spheres, the burden of 'proof' is on the 'oppressed'. In other words, the onus of responsibility for education and acceptance falls on those very factions who are themselves excluded: here, the critical psychologists.
5. Whilst these types of responses might be particular to undergraduate programmes, where students' expectations of what constitutes educational methods might preclude an engagement with more reflexive work (when compared, for example, with a critical masters course where such personal involvement is seen as part of the political agenda) we note that these are also concerns for professional training courses. For example, Harper (2004) describes recent changes made to the curriculum of the professional doctorate in clinical psychology which he teaches, whereby the course team

have implemented a personal and professional module to directly address these kinds of issues.
6. See for example Thomas (2003) for a discussion of the behavioural consequences of teaching more critical material in a traditional undergraduate sociology programme.

Acknowledgements

Ideas discussed in this paper were first presented at the International Conference of Critical Psychology, University of Bath, 27-31 August 2003. The authors would like to thank members of the Critical Psychology Group at the University of East London, Dr Jim Hough and two anonymous reviewers for their encouragement and support in the preparation of this work. We would also like to thank Dr David Harper for his insightful comments on an earlier draft of this manuscript.

References

Ahmed, B. (1996). 'Reflexivity, cultural membership and power in the research situation: Tensions and contradictions when considering the researcher's role'. *Psychology of Women Newsletter* 17: 35-40.

Ahmed, B. (1999). 'Feminism in psychology and professional contexts: Debates in theory and method'. *Educational Child Psychology* 16: 54 – 61.

Aronowitz, S. (2000). *The knowledge factory: Dismantling the corporate university and creating true higher learning.* Boston: Beacon Press.

Curt, B. (1994). *Textuality and tectonics: Troubling social and psychological science.* Buckingham: Open University Press.

Foucault, M. (1977). *Discipline and punish: The birth of the prison.* New York: Pantheon.

Foucault, M.(1979). *The history of sexuality. Volume 1: An introduction.* London: Penguin Books.

Foucault, M (1980). 'Prison talk'. Gordon, C. (Ed.), *Power/Knowledge*, Brighton: Harvester.

Foucault, M. (1982). 'The subject and power'. Drefus, H. and P. Rabinow (Eds), *Michel Foucault: Beyond structuralism and hermeneutics.* Chicago: University of Chicago Press.

Freire, P. (1970). *Pedagogy of the oppressed.* New York: Continuum.

Freire, P. (1994). *Pedagogy of hope.* New York: Continuum.

Gough, B., R. Lawton, A. Madill and P. Stratton (2003). *Guidelines for the supervision of undergraduate qualitative research in psychology.* LTSN psychology: Report and evaluation, Series No. 3. [http://ltsnpsy.york.ac.uk/LTSNASP/mini projectsdetails.asp?id=11].

Harper, D. (2003). *Compromise or collusion, contradictory or critical? Reflections of one critical clinical psychologist's involvement in UK Mental Health Act campaigns.* Paper presented at the International Conference of Critical Psychology, University of Bath, 27-31 August.

Harper, D. (2004). 'Introducing social constructionist and critical psychology into clinical psychology training'. Pare, D. and G. Larner (Eds), *Collaborative practice in psychology and therapy*. Binghamton, NY: Haworth Press.

Henriques, J., W. Hollway, C. Urwin, C. Venn and V. Walkerdine (1998). *Changing the subject: Psychology, social regulation and subjectivity*. London: Routledge, second edition.

Herman, E. (1995). *The romance of American Psychology: Political culture in the age of experts*. Berkeley, CA: University of California Press.

HEFCE: Higher Education Funding Council for England, Scottish Higher Education Funding Council, Higher Education Funding Council for Wales, and Department for Employment and Learning Northern Ireland (2004). RAE 2008 research assessment exercise: *Initial decisions by the UK funding bodies*. Ref: RAE 01/2004. http://www.rae.ac.uk/pubs/2004/01/ [Accessed: February 2004].

Hollway, W. (2000). 'Practising critical psychology within a British psychology department'. Sloan, T. (Ed.), *Critical psychology: Voices for change*: Basingstoke: MacMillan Press, pp 34-45.

hooks, b. (1994). *Teaching to transgress: Education as the practice of freedom*. New York: Routledge.

Kitzinger, C. and S. Wilkinson (1997). (Eds). *Representing the other: A Feminism and Psychology reader*. London: Sage.

Malson, H. (1998). *The thin woman: Feminism, post-structuralism, and the social psychology of anorexia nervosa*. London: Routledge.

Mukherjee, A. (1992). 'Education and race relations: The education of South Asian youth'. Ghosh, R. and R. Kanungo (Eds). *South Asian Canadians: Current issues in the politics of culture*. Montreal: Shastri Indo-Canadian Institute. p.145.

Prilleltensky, I. and G. Nelson (2002). *Doing Psychology: Critically making a difference in diverse settings*. Basingstoke: Palgrave MacMillan.

Rabinow, P. (1991). 'Introduction'. P. Rabinow (Ed.), *The Foucault reader: An introduction to Foucault's thought*. St Ives: Penguin Books.

Roberts, G. (2003). *The joint consultation on the review of research assessment*. Bristol: Higher Education Funding Council for England.

Rose, N. (1985). *The psychological complex: Psychology, politics and society in England 1869-1939*. London: Routledge and Kegan Paul.

Rose, N. (1989). *Governing the soul: The shaping of the private self*. London: Routledge.

Editor of *The Psychologist* (2003): 'Funding under threat'. *Editorial* published in *The Psychologist*, December 2003, 16:12, 656-657.

Thomas, H. (2003). *The body, dance and cultural theory*. Basingstoke: Palgrave MacMillan.

Ussher, J. (1997). *Body talk: The material and discursive regulation of sexuality, madness and reproduction*. London: Routledge.

Ussher, J. (2000). 'Critical psychology in the mainstream: A struggle for survival'. Sloan, T. (Ed.) *Critical psychology: Voices for change*: 6-20. Basingstoke: MacMillan Press.

Walkerdine, V. (1986). 'Post-structuralist theory and everyday social practices: The family and the school'. S. Wilkinson (Ed.), *Feminist social psychology*. 57-76, Milton Keynes: Open University Press.

Wilden, A. (1972). *System and structure: Essays in communication and exchange*. London: Tavistock.

Intellectual workers (un)doing neoliberal discourse

Bronwyn Davies and
Eva Bendix Petersen

In this paper we explore how academics make sense of their current work conditions and in particular how they have been subjected, and have subjected themselves, to neoliberal discourse. Inspired by Richardson (1997), we present an interview with an academic about the impact of neoliberalism on her intellectual work, using poetic representation. We analyse the poetic representation by drawing on several conceptual technologies from poststructural theory, including the idea that power induces rather than merely represses. The paper explores the ambivalent take-up and refusal of neoliberal discourse through an analysis of the 'infinitesimal mechanisms' at work on the embodied subject, each with 'their own history, their own trajectory, their own techniques and tactics' in subjecting individuals (Foucault, 1980:99). We examine how 'the mechanisms of power have been – and continue to be – invested, colonised, utilised, involuted, transformed, displaced, extended etc' (Foucault, 1980:99) through the subjection of individuals in today's universities.

Key words: Neoliberal discourse, governmentality, subjectification, intellectual work, universities, critique, dissent.

Introduction
That neoliberal discourses have been thoroughly established in Australian universities over the last decade is reasonably well docu-

mented (Biggs and Davis, 2002; Coady, 2000a, 2000b; Connell, 2002; Ellis, 2001; Marginson and Considine, 2000; and Macintyre, 2001). The 'Enterprise University' and the signifying practices that come with it are, it seems, everywhere apparent – although its inevitable affects on academic work and day-to-day practices, and on academic identities, has yet to be adequately researched (Marginson, 2000). Put briefly, within neoliberal discourse it is taken for granted 'that the higher education system is a market in which private clients purchase private goods for private benefit' (Marginson, 2002:19). In our own analyses of neoliberalism in academic settings we have found that there are tensions between, on the one hand, the ways that the prevailing neoliberal discourse constitutes 'value' and 'success' and, on the other, the intellectual work that academics believe to be of value and what they believe to signify success in intellectual work (Davies, 2003a and 2003b; Davies, forthcoming, Davies and Petersen, submitted).

Universities have been manipulated by successive governments' withdrawing of funds followed by a conditional, partial and competitive re-allocation tied to the adoption of various neoliberal technologies (Connell, 2002). These technologies are designed to produce in individuals higher levels of flexibility, productivity, and co-operation with national economic objectives for the economic benefit for the nation. They provide mechanisms to facilitate the necessary change in individuals. They are a superficial set of governing practices, not intended to enter and change the soul of academic workers, to undermine their passion for and commitment to their work, but to improve some of their working practices and to make them more useful and relevant. But as Gordon (1991: 42) points out, the actual personal shift that the implementation of the technologies brings about may be massive: the individual subjects envisaged as the products of neoliberal reconstructions are subjects for whom 'the whole ensemble of individual life is to be structured as the pursuit of a range of enterprises'. As Rose (1999:138) elaborates, within neoliberalism 'a person's relation to all his or her activities, and indeed to his or her self, is to be given "the ethos and structure of the enterprise form"'. Within neoliberal regimes, he continues, 'all aspects of social behaviour are now reconceptualised along economic lines' (Rose, 1999:141). The new 'performance paradigm' within the academy, with its 'personal key performance indicators' is an example of the implementation of neoliberal self-enterprise technologies.

In light of this major shift (Apple, 2001; Apple, 2004) in the institutional practices of universities, we ask in this paper: how do academics get caught up, emotionally and in terms of their subjectivities, in neoliberal discourse? How is it, given that neoliberal discourse can so easily be constituted as monstrous and absurd (for example, valuing intellectual work in dollar terms), that academics appear to have engaged in relatively little systematic or widespread resistance and critique of it, given their overt commitment to resistance and critique as a way of life? And how has neoliberalism become an apparently viable, even normalised set of signifying practices through which academics control, regulate and report on their own work and on the work of others?

In order to develop our discussion of these questions we will draw on one academic's talk about herself as a worker and as a neoliberal subject. This interview is one of a series of interviews with twenty-five academics from Australia, New Zealand, Sweden and the US. The interviewees were from universities varying in status and size, in both major metropolitan universities and regional universities. They were selected for this diversity, but only from among those who were known by their peers as successful and dedicated academics. Their status ranged from Senior Lecturer to Professor and many currently had or had had major administrative responsibilities. The interviews were undertaken by the first author, and were an exploration with the interviewees of the impact of neoliberal management practices on their intellectual work. What we set out to do here, in this paper, is to analyse one of the interviews (it could, perhaps, have been any one of them), to try to identify the relations between individual subjectivity and neoliberal forms of government and power in academic workplaces.

The strategy of focussing on one interview might be thought of in terms of the logic of a 'case study' (Stake, 2000). As such it can be taken as a representation and exploration of those signifying practices that begin to become evident in the larger body of data. We have identified neoliberal discourses as being prevalent in Australian universities, and presume that we will find their trace in the talk of all participants. At the same time, by looking at the detail of one interview we will be able to tease out *how* engagement in and struggle with neoliberal discourse and its technologies manifests itself in all its complexity and ambivalence in the embodied subject. In working with this particular interview in the way that we have done, we will attempt to unfold the detail of how the take-up of neoliberal discourse takes place – not in terms of why the various institutions around the globe have taken them on board, since they have been given no real choice about this, but how individual subjects have taken them up. In doing so we take up the challenge Butler gives us in *The Psychic Life of Power* when she says:

> 'Subjection' signifies the process of becoming subordinated by power as well as the process of becoming a subject ... Although Foucault identifies the ambivalence in this formulation, he does not elaborate on the specific mechanisms of how the subject is formed in submission ... [Power] in this double valence of subordinating and producing remains unexplored. Thus if submission is a condition of subjection, it makes sense to ask: What is the psychic form that power takes? [...] The form this power takes is relentlessly marked by a figure of turning, a turning back upon oneself or even a turning *on* oneself. (Butler, 1997: 2-3)

The active turning of the subject of power on herself, often producing a passionate attachment to the specific form of subordination, does not, Butler argues, make the subject individually responsible for the specific nature of her subordination. Rather, she argues that the 'attachment to subjection' is the working of power on the individual psyche and is 'one of the most insidious of its productions. If ... the subject is formed by a will that turns back upon itself, assuming a reflexive form, then the subject is the modality of power that turns on itself; the subject is the effect of power in recoil' (Butler, 1997: 6).

By looking at neoliberal discourse as a form of power, and by engaging in detail with an individual's turning of that power on herself, we hope to learn more about the insidious production by neoliberalism of active subordination to its terms, a subordination that is experienced, at least in part, as voluntary and as desirable. Academics' desire to critique and to *undo* some aspects of neoliberalism are intricately enmeshed with their *doing* of neoliberalism – and so with becoming the neoliberal subject.

Neoliberalism as governmentality

Rose uses the term 'governmentality' to elaborate the ambivalence of those processes through which we are governed and through which we govern ourselves. He suggests that we look at neoliberalism not as a type of society or as a political philosophy but from the perspective of governmentality (1999:20-24). As political rationalities, he suggests, governmentalities are to be analysed as practices for governing nations, populations, economies, citizens, and individuals – indeed, as practices that 'govern the soul' (Rose, 1990). The concept of governmentality rests on Foucault's analytics of power (1980), which suggests that power should not be analysed in terms of 'who possesses it', or who controls and directs it, but as something which circulates, something that is employed and exercised through networks. 'The individual is an effect of power, and at the same time, or precisely to the extent to which it is that effect, it is the element of its articulation. The individual which power has constituted is at the same time its vehicle' (Foucault, 1980: 98).

Foucault suggests that we begin with the 'infinitesimal mechanisms' of the work of power in order to arrive at an understanding of forms of global domination:

> One must conduct an *ascending* analysis of power, starting, that is, from its infinitesimal mechanisms, which each have their own history, their own trajectory, their own techniques and tactics, and then see how the mechanisms of power have been – and continue to be – invested, colonised, utilised, involuted, transformed, displaced, extended etc, by ever more general mechanisms and by forms of global domination. (Foucault, 1980:99)

Neoliberalism, in this sense, can be read as a form of global domination, and in this paper we begin with the 'infinitesimal mechanisms' at work on everyday lives, in order to make sense of its working. Like Dean, we are interested in how the capacities and liberties of individual actors are formed by the practices of government:

> To ask 'how' questions of government, then, is also to ask what happens when we govern or are governed. Crucial to the resultant power relations are the capacities and liberties of the various actors and agencies formed in practices of government. To ask how governing works, then, is to ask how we are formed as various types of agents with particular capacities and possibilities of action. (Dean, 1999: 29)

To the extent that academics read the impositions of government as coercive and as, at most, only superficially shaping their actions, they are unlikely to read those impositions as constitutive of their identity as academic workers. But as Dean says, what is taken to be true and inevitable in global patterns of power and government shapes how individuals conduct themselves, how they shape their own conduct.

Studies of government and of governmentality are studies of the 'relation between the forms of truth by which we have come to know ourselves and the forms of practice by which we seek to shape the conduct of ourselves and others' (Dean, 1996: 220). In conducting our own lives we are involved in being governed and in governing, not just through superficial performances of ourselves, but through governing our own souls, bodies and desires.

Power induces rather than merely represses

Neoliberal discourse is not just a new set of words to describe old practices. That a university, for example, presents and congratulates itself for being 'A world-class *enterprise*' (our italics) is not merely a question of rhetoric, of reinscribing itself in fashionable terms. Rather as a signifying practice it is arguably a formative, even constative, practice (Butler, 1993:11) entering into the very production of what is intelligible and valuable:

> Discourse is not merely spoken words, but a notion of signification which concerns not merely how it is that certain signifiers come to mean what they mean, but how certain discursive forms articulate objects and subjects in their intelligibility. In this sense 'discourse' is not used in the ordinary sense ... Discourse does not merely represent or report on pregiven practices and relations, but it enters into their articulation and is, in that sense, productive. (Butler, 1995:138)

We will assume, in this analysis of the 'how', of the 'infinitesimal mechanisms', that neoliberalism has not simply been imposed through some powerful being or beings who are clever at manipulating academics, or at controlling them – though we will also assume that neoliberalism is not without power to control and manipulate. Rather we ask how neoliberal discourse, in Foucault's (1980: 99) terms, has 'traversed' us, how it has 'invested, colonised, utilised, involuted, transformed, displaced, extended' us in producing the kind of work we now do, even given us pleasure? How does it act upon our actions and desires? Power does not 'only weigh upon us as a force that says no but traverses and produces things, it induces pleasure, forms knowledge, produces discourse' (Foucault, 1980: 119). In that formation and production it makes us act and speak in particular ways: 'How light power would be' he says, 'and easy to dismantle no doubt, if all it did was to observe, spy, detect, prohibit, and punish; but it incites, provokes, produces. It is not simply eye and ear: it makes people act and speak' (Foucault, 2000a: 172). Neoliberalism does have, as one of its major mechanisms, technologies of surveillance which might be characterised as spying, detecting, prohibiting and punishing (Schmelzer, 1993). It seems evident, if we accept Foucault's analysis, and if we concede the extent of its take-up, that neoliberalism must also incite, provoke and produce. It must have been taken up, not just by government and by managers and auditors with a will to control us, but also 'willingly' by us.

In order for Foucault to come to terms with the way power produces us, he introduced, in *The Will to Knowledge* (1978), the concept of *subjectification*, through which he understood power not to be merely subjugating and repressive, but also to be enabling and life-giving. Becoming a subject, Butler writes, 'consists precisely in [the] fundamental dependency on a discourse we never chose but that, paradoxically, initiates and sustains our agency' (Butler, 1997: 2). It is this process through which power works not only as a line of force acting upon individuals from outside of themselves, but as a line of force turning the self upon the self that we are pursuing here in this paper.

Deleuze, in writing about Foucault, elaborates this idea of the folding of the line of force both in the context of resistance *and* of creating and recreating the possibilities of life, not only in subordination or submission to existing forces, but with the possibilities of something new – a new aesthetic – emerging:

> It's all very well invoking foci of resistance, but where are such foci to be found? ... Foucault doesn't use the word 'subject' as though he's talking about a person or a form of identity, but talks about 'subjectification' as a process, and 'Self' as a relation (a relation to oneself). And what's he talking about? About a relation of force to itself (whereas power was a relation of force to other forces), about a 'fold' of force. About establishing different ways of existing, depending on how you fold the line of forces, or inventing possibilities of life that depend on death too, on our relations to death: existing not as a subject but as a work of art. He's talking about inventing ways of existing, through optional rules, that can both resist power and elude knowledge, even if knowledge tries to penetrate them and power to appropriate them. But ways of existing or possibilities of life are constantly being recreated, new ones emerge, and while it's true that this dimension was invented by the Greeks, we're not

going back to the Greeks when we try to discern those taking shape today, to discern in ourselves an artistic will irreducible to knowledge and to power. (Deleuze, 1995: 92)

This capacity for invention and reinvention, through action upon the self, this invention of new ways of existing, may enable the subject to 'eclipse the conditions of its own emergence' (Butler, 1997: 14; Davies 2000:167-171), to go beyond what is contained in and envisaged by the discourses through which the subject is made a subject. But the changes may not always generate a more liberated or ethical life. The invention may take place through the take-up of a newly available discourse, such as neoliberalism, which promises to make things better, but at a cost to individuals and with many of the so-called improvements too costly in its constitutive effects.

The poetic representation

The particular subject we have chosen to focus on here was at the time of the interview a Senior Lecturer, in Australia, and was intending to apply for promotion to Associate Professor (equivalent to full professor in the US). She was later successful in gaining that promotion. She is therefore, in the interview, at a point where she is perhaps more than usually aware of the institution's definition of 'success' at that level. She is therefore arguably particularly vulnerable to the operations of power at work in the institutions, that vulnerability heightening her perception of the way it is working on her.

Inspired by Richardson (1997:131ff), we have transformed the interview transcript into a narrative poem using only the interviewee's own words and syntax. We selected key phrases and points that seem to us to evoke the complex positioning of the interviewee in relation to the university and to her current work practices. The poetic form allows the tensions and contradictions in her position to be made more starkly visible than they are in the interview: the joy in her work and the pain of it can be starkly juxtaposed thus opening up the 'infinitesimal mechanisms' to close inspection and analysis. The poem is written with the aim of making visible the whole range of discursive strategies with their coercive power.

What became more visible to us in the process of writing the poem was the subject's willing take-up of neoliberal discourses and her simultaneous joyful escape from those same discourses into the new/old pleasure of intellectual work. These ambivalences are not articulated through clearly separate discourses, but are presented in the interview as part of a closely woven fabric of self, riddled with tensions and contradictions – a painful joyful immersion in work that she is passionate about and from which she constantly envisages escape. In the interview the tensions and contradictions constantly slide away from our grasp through the elaborate and detailed rationalisations through which the life of the intellectual is normalised and made liveable. We found ourselves in reading the interview transcript inside an Escher drawing where we were never able to see where we had arrived. The poetic form allows us to stand back, to see and appreciate the drawing and to comprehend the multi-directionality of each moment.

I'd have to say that I feel uneasy about the entrepreneurial spirit
of the new University. But I can't say
that I hanker after the old days either –
When I came to University there was just as much problem
with the kind of male liberalism
I confronted

In fact because of my improved status and ability to negotiate
and because of the nature of entrepreneurialism, I feel
I have certainly gained in ways I wouldn't have otherwise –
I enjoy the challenge of seeking research funding, yeah
I've been successful – I'm sure it has made me a better researcher
Because of the opportunities

I always ask about my research, does it make a difference?
It's about the excitement of new ideas
Playing in your brain –
The whole thing for me is about being creative
If I didn't do that
I wouldn't still be here

I teach ten times more than I ever did
I do my assignment marking at 4 in the morning
The only time I'm not interrupted –
Some things are going to
drop off the edge
I have to accept being flaky

I think if study leave
   got taken away
   I would resign

I don't feel guilty for just reading instead of writing
I feel amazed that I get time to do it
If I ever do –
Because of time I've developed fast reading strategies
A blow-torch job
I think we probably all have

But I probably would feel guilty
   If I just sat and read every word
   And just enjoyed it as a reading

I don't think we're highly intimidated
I think demoralised or squashed –
There's a vital lack of funding
Funding cuts year after year after year after year –
Pretending that we can still do the job
when we can't anymore

I don't think universities should be corporate money-making
      organisations
selling research to industry and education to fee-paying students
Of course –
But I do think we have to be pragmatic
We do have to sell –
We do have to raise money to fund what we want to do

I usually hear *what* decisions are being made
But I never feel a part of
how they're being made –
Decisions come down from on top:
What is our current workload going to be?
What are we going to be punished for next?

I'm very, very good at strategising and that's something
   I really enjoy, I know how to play those games
   I know how to do it

intellectual workers (un)doing neoliberal discourse

Seems to me that if you have a whole-hearted kind of rejection of the
    current values
You can't play the game
You have to, to a certain extent, be pragmatic –
I have to strategise
Or I'll just be trampled on
You learn to play the game

You learn to share it with people who need it
    I haven't met a single guy that needed my help to learn to strategise
    But many women

I could drop it all tomorrow, the game
I don't see it as in my core somewhere
It's just something that you learn to do –
Like if you're playing mah-jong
Or if you learn any game
You learn the tricks of the trade

I still think that Australian universities have a huge amount to offer
    because of the toughness and resilience and the persistence
    of Australian academics. They still have a huge amount to offer

To me joy and happiness in your work
are the most fundamental things in terms of remaining well
You might as well forget everything else –
That's number one. Ask yourself
What's the thing that makes you passionate
and that you value above all else?

I set aside a day a week to do my research and writing
I love it –
I do that at a certain cost
Not only to myself, working the extra hours –
But other things fall off the agenda
So it's a cost to others as well

But if I don't do that I might as well have nothing
I might as well chuck the whole thing in –
There's no point

going through all this
to keep myself healthy for a job
I've lost my faith in

This year, for the first time
I actually nominated time off –
I kind of fudged it, I still had some things I had to do
But I was actually away and not available –
I'm starting to realise that that's essential
to my ongoing health

To actually have time out
from being continually available
from people who put deadlines on me –
Just saying to them:
'Sorry, I've had a really hard year
You have to find someone else'

When I went to the beach I took a book with me
Just going away and veging out –
A 400 page book, a novel, was just in another world
I did a little tiny bit of work: setting up a research project, finishing
    my paper –
The book was just fabulous – a fictional and creative coming to terms
With exactly the same issues as my research

I'm never afraid or unwilling to state my own views
I sometimes don't because I'm too busy
I think I must follow up, I must say something –
I don't because I don't get around to it
It's a good way to keep people quiet
Keep them so busy that they can never get their heads above the daily grind

I mean I just think it's an incredible privilege
    to be able to do this sort of work
    to have it as my work

One way I'm privileged is that my family's grown up
Someone who's got a family, trying to juggle what I'm doing at the
    moment

Would simply not be possible –
I basically don't socialise at all much. If I socialise I do it at work
Having to fit that into sleeping and doing all this work
I mean they're things everybody knows

Some of the processes and procedures and quality assurance
and all that
has actually made our work better –
But it has also given us a huge amount more work
incommensurate with the improvement in quality
that we've got out of it

Non-stop proliferation of administrivia
The enormous amount of housekeeping work
generated out of current systems –
A lot of the time I think that I am a bit out of my body
I want to be really efficient, get through all the shit so I
don't have to spend any more time at it than I have to

Like chewing a tea-bag instead of making a cup of tea
Frenetic activities. I do allow myself
to get quite stressed and adrenalin filled –
What I'm interested in is what rationalisations you make
to make yourself not look after yourself
I mean it's always going to be a balancing act

If you just lie down and rest you wouldn't be any better off
In the long run than if you work very hard –
I get a huge amount of satisfaction out of
flogging myself and working really hard –
Probably it's a really stupid way to live
but I'd rather live like that

You're going to die anyway
    I'm not saying that justifies making yourself sick
        But all life is to do with balancing, the using up and replenishing

I am actually getting heart arrhythmias
because I am really stressed –
Knowing that I had to stop, knowing how to do it even
But not feeling in the position to stop –

I did actually negotiate with myself a time when I would stop
I did stop more or less completely for three weeks

The current system loves workaholics and
loves people who get a buzz out of working really hard
because they can push them right to the very, very edge –
So it's recognising when it's gone further than you want it to
Being able to stop that
That, I think, is the difficult thing ...

Knowing that you still have choice
But at the end of last year
It felt very much out of my control ...
The work had to be done and that was it
Even then things were left undone, and things
Fell off the edge

Not sleeping is so horrible
The other night I marked half a dozen 8000 word reports until latish
And then I don't sleep –
And I thought well I'm not going to do that
I'll only do that under desperate circumstances
And only one-off

I knew I wasn't
   going to sleep
   And it was horrible

You don't have time to actually stop and think
And you often don't have time to speak about it
but I do think it happens in a very insidious way –
and I do try to resist it – hugely
But I think it is happening all the time
Surveillance at the heart of things

Reinforcing a police state; fascism, conformity
That amounts to a huge sea change in what it all means
while we don't even realise that it's happening –
That's what's so scary about it
And the university is just part of the technology for managing a
   police state
And I don't know what to do about it.

Living neoliberalism in the academy

The poetic representation is a way of 'working amongst the ruins' of social science following 'the crisis of representation' (St. Pierre and Pillow, 2000). In what follows, we engage in a reading of our poem, understanding that the interview itself was already a reading of the impact of neoliberalism on the subject, a reading produced by the interviewer and the subject of the poem. The production of the poem was another act of reading, this time by the authors, of what had been said in the interview. And in what we write below, we read again and in light of the theoretical work we began the paper with, in order to extend our understanding in relation to the questions we have asked. We approach the analysis of the poem not as an empirical revealing of the truth, but as our own work of art through which we make visible the tensions and contradictions of the constitutive representation that the subject is engaged in within this particular historical, neoliberal moment.

We began the poem with an expression of ambivalence. Our subject confronted/ was confronted by the 'old male liberal' discourses. While she may be 'uneasy' about neoliberal forms of government, she does not long to go back. The present unease is weighed against the less than perfect past. Moreover (and 'in fact') the new present has opened up individual pathways to success in the shape of new opportunities and challenges, which she enjoys. The re-constitution of herself as one who is in 'pursuit of a range of enterprises' (Gordon, 1991: 42) is not *all* bad, therefore. She resists the binary division of the world into the appalling present and the glorious past (Gordon, 2002), saying she is a better researcher because of the new opportunities. Further, the 'process and procedures and quality assurance', she says, have 'actually made our work better'. Thus, in contrast to 'the old', the new system is constituted here as a better alternative. This should not be taken to mean that she has taken herself up as a neoliberal subject in any total kind of way. She is not, or not merely, an entrepreneurial subject: she holds dear the idea that research is 'about the excitement of new ideas'. She insists on talking about her research, not in terms of economic gains but in terms of it 'making a difference'. 'The whole thing', she says, is about 'being creative', about 'playing in the brain'. In fact, the creative edge of intellectual life is constituted as so important that if it were no longer possible, she would no longer be there. The entrepreneurial work can be constituted as a 'game' to play, and not without its pleasures. Yet, the intellectual work is what is 'real'; it constitutes 'the core'. The entrepreneurial game in itself would not be enough to sustain her in her work. Our subject thus constitutes herself as caught up in two contradictory discursive rationalities, two forms of governmentality. She manages them by locating one as the core of academic work – and the core of who she is – and the other as a superficial game; one that must be played but held at arm's length. One discourse constitutes her as an entrepreneurial subject, and the other, that constitutes her core, constitutes entrepreneurialism as not enough, as not valuable in itself, even anathema to the 'core' business of academic work/life – it 'overruns' or 'invades' what she constitutes as her academic *raison d'être*. She constitutes neoliberalism as having 'invested, colonised, utilised, involuted, transformed, displaced, extended' (Foucault, 1980, p. 99) her intellectual core. It is understood as having improved and facilitated her work, and yet at the same time as something that must be held at bay for fear it will displace, overtake, undo what it is that really matters to her. The take-up of neoliberal discourse could perhaps be compared to the old classical contract with the devil: the pursuit of what is seen as meaningful, as what 'it is all about', comes at a cost, a giving in to, a playing of the superficial 'game'. The devil, however, to continue our metaphor, is smart – it begins with the erosion of her body ('I am actually getting heart arrhythmias').

She talks about the increase in her teaching load and how she has had to accept becoming a subject 'who lets things drop off the edge', because of the long hours. She says that she has had to accept being 'flaky'. Not only that, but she has changed her relationship to the pleasure of reading – if she 'just sat and read every word' she'd feel guilty. She naturalises the new blow-torch job, with the observation that 'we probably all have' started to do the same thing. She stands back from herself and sees herself engaged in new practices, practices that are not pleasurable, and that do not necessarily support the 'core' work, but that are necessitated by having bought into the will (the necessity) to be productive in neoliberal terms. The devil, we might say, to continue our metaphor, has no work to do, since she governs herself, she conducts her own conduct, and she does so in terms of the game that she constitutes as not the real game. One of the things that intrigue us, here, is how hard it is for her to catch herself doing it. At first she denies that there is a problem: she does not feel guilty if she reads; it is just, when she thinks about it, surprising to get time to do it. But as she mulls over the idea, and thinks about how rarely she now gets to read, she makes an account of her new practices, of everyone's new practices, circling round, eventually, to the recognition that guilt now interferes with the most basic of pleasures in her work.

Our subject constitutes her ambivalence between 'core business' and the increased 'housekeeping work' as something that has to be managed: 'a balancing act' she calls it. She is fascinated by the rationalities that she produces to make what she does acceptable. She talks about how she has to 'get through all the shit' so that she doesn't have to spend any more time at it than is absolutely necessary. The game she has bought into has some less than savoury aspects to it, it is really just 'shit', yet there is so much of it, it takes over, it is hard to carve out any time for the real work, the core business that keeps her there. She even takes a perverse pleasure in 'flogging' herself to get it all done – even though it *can* never all be done. She sets aside a day a week to do her research and writing, and this is what she loves. But that day comes at a price, of long hours, of threatening illness, of increased stress in the rest of her work-life. She never loses sight of the fact that without that core work, there would be no point being there.

The equation is shaky: the work of the new university is 'something that you learn to do', but which does not, must not, touch 'the core'. The protection of the core is riddled with caveats: the life that she leads would not be possible if … in fact it is not possible … she must get through this shit in order to … the core is getting smaller and smaller, the periphery larger and larger, she is sick, and stressed. But she loves to flog herself, she believes she can do it, she is passionate about her work. And the system loves her:

> The current system loves workaholics and
> loves people who get a buzz out of working really hard
> because they can push them right to the very, very edge

But the system will not pull her back from that edge. The deal with the devil is that she has to be the one (in the name of individual responsibility) who balances her 'attachment to subjection' (Butler, 1997: 6) with the recognition that the system she is subjected to will always push her too far.

The voluntariness of this process does not make it acceptable. Rather as Butler (1997: 6) points out, it is precisely the voluntariness that makes the power of this particular form of subjection all the more insidious. Furthermore our subject's love of her work, and the institution's love of her for being a good neoliberal subject, makes her vulnerable at the most elemental level. Butler analyses the child's formation as in part a dependency on love, and her analysis is perhaps not irrelevant to the psychic formation and re-formation of the academic subject:

> Let us consider that a subject is not only formed in subordination, but that this subordination provides the subject's continuing conditions of possibility ... [If the subject] is to persist in a psychic and social sense, there must be dependency and the formation of attachment: there is no possibility of not loving, where love is bound up with the requirements for life ... No subject can emerge without this attachment, formed in dependency, but no subject, in the course of its formation, can ever fully afford to 'see' it. (Butler, 1997: 8)

This point may be central to our entire analysis – the necessary invisibility of the dependence on being attached.[1] But there are other conditions that she can see that have a silencing effect. She is too busy to speak up, even on points she finds important. She does not explain her lack of resistance as due to being too intimidated, or too fearful. She is never afraid or unwilling to state her views, she says. However, she observes that she is often too busy; that she doesn't get round to it, even when she feels it is something she ought to get round to. Furthermore, she speaks of how she does not feel part of the decision-making process; that decisions come down from the top as unnegotiable directives to do with working more, to do with punishment for not conforming to some aspect of the managerial agenda. She describes an impossible workload that precludes acting ethically through critical engagement in her place of work. That workload is combined with the continual re-shaping of the workplace to become yet more demanding, yet more punitive. And how does she feel about this?

> I think demoralised or squashed –
> There's a vital lack of funding
> Funding cuts year after year after year after year –
> Pretending that we can still do the job
> when we can't anymore

The neoliberal agenda requires universities to 'prove' they are doing their job well in order to continue to receive funding. Academic subjects know they cannot afford to admit they can't do their work under these new conditions, since that would be the basis on which their institution lost its funding. They are caught in a fabrication that says they can do what is impossible, a fabrication that could constitute outspoken critique as a form of betrayal. The competition among institutions for funding, the individualisation of workers combined with the weakening of unions, means there is no powerful collective voice with which resistance can be articulated. Rather they are caught in the strategy of 'keep(ing) them so busy that they can never get their heads above the daily grind'. The lack of critique comes from a lack of time, from the danger of speaking the truth, and, looping back to our earlier points, from the way the institution loves the one who flogs herself, an unwillingness to define the past as more desirable, and a recognition that some of the changes do actually bring improvements in the quality of what is done.

Further, the excesses of neoliberalism can be accommodated in a discourse of pragmatism and survival, *and* the will to keep doing the 'real work'. As our subject says, she does not want 'us' to become corporate money-making organisations, 'of course', but 'we' must be pragmatic and raise funds to do what 'we want to do'. If we want to do something, of course, we must find the money for it. Desire for outcomes that are better than is possible on the ever-more limited government funding dictates individual and collective action to find the money to ensure the work is well done. Although in other parts of the conversation she constitutes neoliberal discourses as 'outside' her, as something 'invading' intellectual life and work, by invoking pragmatism she can take up entrepreneurial practices as her own. The discourses continually circulated by university administration and government could be said to invest, colonise, utilise, involute, transform, displace and extend her (Foucault, 1980:99). And 'of course' we cannot expect just to be funded if we want to do something: of course, naturally, we must raise the funds ourselves. 'Of course' we must sell our commodities as any other business in the global market place. It is a pragmatic truth – not ideal but pressing in terms of the possibilities of continuing the core agenda that she believes in. In order to do the core work, she must bend to the discourse of the periphery. Of course. To do otherwise would be not only to lose credibility, but to lose the power to get on with the core work – the work that keeps you there in the first place. And in submitting to this discourse, and in becoming good at doing what it is that brings in the money, there is the ever present danger that the discourse becomes so normalised that the need for critique is no longer visible.

The love of work, both the work that is her core and the peripheral work, give her 'a huge amount of satisfaction out of flogging [herself] and working really hard'. Others might find that a 'stupid' way to live, she says, but she has come to 'like' living like that. Working, and working hard and many hours, is therefore not only something she is forced to do, rather she constitutes it as central to who she is as a person. She has become who she 'is' by taking up this way of life. It has become so central to who she understands herself to be that 'the difficult thing' is 'being able to stop' even when she knows how to and that she is at risk if she does not. The flaw in all of this is that so much of this hard work is 'the enormous amount of housekeeping work generated out of the current systems'. The housekeeping systems have become the work, they have become the basis for institutional survival, they become the normalised, stress-filled everyday life of academe with 'the real work' squeezed into the spaces – leaving no time or energy or space for critique.

In conclusion

By looking at the detail of one interview we have teased out *how* engagement in and struggle with neoliberal discourse and its technologies manifests itself in its complexity and ambivalence in the embodied subject. Can we say with Rose (1999:138) that within neoliberalism 'a person's relation to all his or her activities, and indeed to his or her self, [has] "the ethos and structure of the enterprise form"'? Our subject enters into that ethos and structure and takes pleasure in her competence to do so at the same time as she keeps her distance from it. She takes responsibility for juggling neoliberalism and intellectual work, for taking up what is good in each and withstanding what is bad. She is deeply committed to a reading of herself as inventing herself and her life both within and outside the dominant presence of the neoliberal regime. She keeps alive the passion for the work that goes beyond that which is already known even while she dismisses the past that informs such ideals, as romanticised, not something she wants to go back to. She is, in this way, the artistic subject Foucault envisages who invents ways of existing 'through optional rules, that can both resist power and elude knowledge, even if knowledge tries to penetrate them and power to appropriate them' (Deleuze, 1995: 92). She is at the same time appropriated. She is caught up in a process of both doing and undoing neoliberal discourse, in a painful, risky, passionate attachment to her work/life, seeing herself as free, seeing herself harm herself and take care of herself, seeing the engagement with neoliberalism as necessary, pleasurable and dangerous, and seeing the danger as manageable because she constitutes herself as a rational, choosing subject in control of her own life, a subject who can maintain the core of her intellectual work free of the superficial intrusions of neoliberal subjection. This sense of individual power to choose and to resist lies at the heart of our answer to the three questions posed at the outset about how and why neoliberal technologies have managed to take hold.

As subjects make meaning of themselves and of what they do through current readily available, popular or institutionalised discourses, or through theoretically sophisticated and complex discourses, it is not possible to step outside those discourses to see what invisible baggage they carry and naturalise, or to see the ways those discourses might bind them in ways they could not have predicted. Such subjects, which include ourselves, are each embedded in history, in the discourses through which the world is being spoken and written into existence, and through which it is made meaningful, through which practices are understood and valued. The liberal discourses through which individual subjects are constituted suggest that we can stand outside history, outside discourse, and rationally choose how we will take up this or that aspect of it as if we were not already embedded in it, already establishing and re-establishing history through constituting ourselves within it. The subject both exceeds and succumbs in the same act:

> To claim that the subject exceeds [its subjection] is not to claim that it lives in some free zone of its own making. Exceeding is not escaping, and the subject exceeds precisely that to which it is bound. In this sense the subject cannot quell the ambivalence by which it is constituted. Painful, dynamic, and promising, this vacillation between the already-there and the yet-to-come is a crossroads that rejoins every step by which it is traversed, a reiterated ambivalence at the heart of agency. (Butler, 1997: 17)

Notes

1. As Butler unfolds in *the Psychic Life of Power* (1997) this dependency on being attached is not a pre-discursive 'psychological need' as some psychoanalytic theories might suggest. For a further elaboration of this point see Butler (1997).

References

Apple. M. W. (2004). 'Creating Difference: Neo-Liberalism, Neo-Conservatism and the Politcs of Educational Reform'. *Educational Policy* 18:12-44.

Atkinson, E. (2004). 'Thinking Outside the Box: An Exercise in Heresy'. *Qualitative Inquiry* 10:111-129.

Biggs, J. and R. Davis (Eds) (2002). *The Subversion of Australian Universities.* Wollongong: Fund for Intellectual Dissent.

Butler, J. (1993). *Bodies that Matter – on the discursive limits of 'sex'*. New York: Routledge.

Butler, J. (1995). 'For a careful reading'. Benhabib, S., J. Butler, D. Cornell, and N. Fraser (Eds), *Feminist contentions. A philosophical exchange.* New York: Routledge. pp :127-143

Butler, J. (1997). *The Psychic Life of Power.* Stanford: Stanford University Press.

Coady, T. (2000a). 'Introduction'. Coady, T. (Ed.) (2000b), *Why Universities Matter. A conversation about values, means and directions*: 3-25, Sydney: Allen and Unwin.

Coady, T. (Ed.) (2000b). *Why Universities Matter. A conversation about values, means and directions.* Sydney: Allen and Unwin.

Connell, R.W. (2002). 'Rage against the dying of the light'. *The Australian*, October 24:30-1.

Davies, B. (2000). *(In)scribing body/landscape relations.* Walnut Creek Ca: AltaMira Press.

Davies, B. (2003a). 'Death to critique and dissent? The policies and practices of new managerialism and of "evidence-based practice"'. *Gender and Education* 15: 89-101.

Davies, B. (2003b). 'Dissemination, or critique and transformation?' Francis, B. and C. Hughes (Eds). *Disseminating Qualitative Research*: 110-122, London: Open University Press.

Davies, B. (forthcoming). 'The (im)possibility of intellectual work in neoliberal regimes'. *Discourse.*

Davies, B. and E.B. Petersen, (submitted). 'Intellectual workers in neoliberal organisations: are they 'traumatised'?'. *Learning and Teaching in the Social Sciences.*

Dean, M. (1996). 'Foucault, government and the enfolding of authority'. Barry, A., T. Osborne and N. Rose (Eds). *Foucault and political reason. Liberalism, neo-liberalism and rationalities of government*: 209 -229, London: UCL Press.

Dean, M. (1999). *Governmentality: Power and rule in modern society.* London: Sage.

Deleuze, G. (1995). *Negotiations 1972-1990.* New York: Columbia University Press.

Ellis, B. (2001). 'The day the music dies'. *HQ* August/September: 41-43.

Foucault, M. (1978). *The Will to Knowledge. The History of Sexuality vol 1.* London: Penguin.

Foucault, M. (1980). *Power/Knowledge. Selected interviews and other writings.* Brighton: The Harvester Press.

Foucault, M. (2000). 'Lives of infamous men'. Faubion (Ed.), J.D., Foucault, M. *Power*: 155-175. New York: The New Press.

Gordon, C. (1991). 'Governmental rationality: an introduction'. Burchell, G., C. Gordon, and P. Miller (Eds). *The Foucault Effect: Studies in Governmentality:1-52.* Hemel Hempstead: Harvester Wheatsheaf.

Gordon, G. (2002). *Universities. The Recovery of an Idea.* Thorverton: Imprint Academic.

Macintyre, S. (2001). *'Funny you should ask for that': Higher Education as a market. The idea of a university: enterprise or academy?* Conference organised by The Australia Institute and Manning Clark House, *ANU*, 26th July.

Marginson, S. (2000). 'Rethinking Academic Work in the Global Era'. *Journal of Higher Education Policy and Management.* 22:23-35.

Marginson, S. (2202). 'Postgraduate training in the social sciences: knowledge, engagement, vocation'. *Journal of Australian Studies* (74): 7-46.

Marginson, S. and M. Considine (2000). *The Enterprise University. Power, Governance and Reinvention in Australia.* Cambridge: Cambridge University Press.

Richardson, L. (1997). *Fields of Play. Constructing an Academic Life.* New Brunswick NJ: Rutgers University Press.

Rose, N. (1990). *Governing the soul: the shaping of the private self.* London: Routledge.

Rose, N. (1999). *The Powers of Freedom.* Cambridge: Cambridge University Press.

Schmelzer, M. (1993). 'Panopticism and postmodern pedagogy'. J. Caputo, and M. Young. (Eds). *Foucault and the Critique of Institutions*: 127-136, Pennsylvania: The Pennsylvania State University Press.

St. Pierre, E. A. and W. S. Pillow (Eds) (2000). *Working the Ruins: Feminist Poststructural Theory and Methods in Education.* New York: Routledge.

Stake, R. E. (2000). 'Case Studies'. Lincoln,Y. S. and N. K. Denzin (Eds). *Handbook of Qualitative Research.* London: Sage Publications, pp: 435-454.

The critical professional and social policy
Negotiating dilemmas in the UK Mental Health Act campaign

David Harper

he critical professional psychologist wishing to influence social policy is faced with a number of competing imperatives. Through the means of a case study of UK government proposals to reform mental health legislation, I describe some of the dilemmas encountered and my attempts to address them. I review the rationales and evaluate the effects of interventions in professional and non-professional networks. Rather than being primarily theoretical, my aim is to provoke discussion and debate about the position of the critical psychologist who also occupies a position as a professional.

Introduction

Thirty years ago Ingleby argued that the goals of professionals employed by the State were bound up in the 'efficient regulation and protection of a particular political structure' (1974: 322). He saw the unwritten contract of psychologists as the maintenance of the status quo of society: 'adaptation of people to the social structure is our yardstick, not the adaptation of social structure to people' (1974: 322). Barely a decade ago, Reicher was both echoing and updating Ingleby's critique of psychology. He saw the contract of psychologists as a Faustian one: academic psychologists could say whatever they wanted provided this remained divorced from practice or activism.

Of course, the contradictions which psychologists subjectively face in their everyday work are intimately related to the historical forces which created the conditions for the psychological complex itself (Rose, 1985). However, whilst both Ingleby's and Reicher's chapters end on a relatively optimistic note arguing that it is possible for psychologists to work for social change, they write only in very general terms about how psychologists might actually go about things differently. In general, much academic critical psychology has been better at describing these contradictions and tracing their historical roots than in identifying how to grapple with them though there are notable exceptions (e.g. Ahmed, 2003; Dell and Anderson in press; Paré and Larner, 2004; Prilleltensky and Nelson, 2002).

As a clinical psychologist influenced by critical psychology, I have tried to work in ways which seek to avoid pathologising people with mental health problems, for example through using Narrative Therapy approaches and by conducting research which attempts to deconstruct clinical categories. However, I am constantly aware of the wider injustices which people with mental health problems experience, for example the inequalities inherent in how the mental health system operates and the pernicious influence of multinational drug companies (Johnstone, 2000). In addition, mental health service users[1] are routinely portrayed in the media in a negative light (Philo, 1996) and face discrimination in a wide range of spheres of life including employment, parental rights, housing, immigration, insurance, health care and access to justice (Sayce, 1998). One particular form of discrimination is that, in contrast to the area of physical health where people are generally free to refuse treatment if they wish to, mental health service users can, in most countries, be compulsorily detained in a psychiatric hospital and forced to have psychiatric medication.

Action to influence these broader issues requires change at the level of social policy. The opportunity to change legislation governing compulsory psychiatric treatment does not come round very often: it last changed in the UK in 1983 and, before that, in 1959. Thus when the Labour government announced plans to reform mental health law in 1998 it was important to respond. However, the professional wishing to influence social policy is immediately faced with two key challenges: can one work within professional structures whilst trying to avoid the attendant dangers of the expert discourse; and can one work collaboratively with other groups and manage the negotiation of the compromises which are inevitable when bringing different groups together?

The expert discourse: its possibilities and dangers
Those wishing to bring political and social change argue that it may be tactically useful, at certain times, to appeal to an expert discourse as part of those struggles. As Kitzinger puts it, 'for psychologists wanting to change the world, the rhetoric of traditional mainstream psychology is a very important piece of legitimation' (1997: 214). Whilst this may lead to short-term political success, she notes that traditional assumptions about psychological knowledge and the role of psychology are thus reinforced. In other words, there is an ever-present danger of psychologists colluding with the status quo.

However, psychologists exist in contexts 'in which things are always already going on or being done' (Willig, 1998: 96) and clinical psychologists are already involved, for better or worse, in particular kinds of actions like psychotherapy. Indeed, as Burton and Kagan (2005) have argued, there is a case for psychologists to be less concerned with the internal problems of psychology and, instead, to focus on serving the needs of oppressed groups. Willig (2003) has argued that it 'seems impossible to engage with the world as we find it without perpetuating some of its less desirable features. However, in order to change the world, we must engage with it'. The question then becomes not whether but, rather, *how* to act. But how are we to judge which actions are better than others?

Mental health rarely reaches the top of the public policy agenda and, with a parliamentary majority of 171, the government were in a strong position to push its proposals forward regardless of protest. Attempts to influence it therefore needed to be both co-ordinated and collaborative in order that maximum political pressure was exerted.

The challenge of collaborative work
Until recently, there has been relatively little written by critical psychologists about the process of doing collaborative work. Paré and Larner (2004) explicitly focus on this topic and the contributors to their book describe ways of collaborating in the separate domains of therapy, supervision, teaching and research. However, the work I will describe here cuts across such traditional categories. For example, within professional networks, whilst I drew on research in trying to influence policy I did not see my role primarily as a researcher and so models of collaborative research (e.g. Willig and Drury, 2004) or of influencing social policy through research (e.g. Prilleltensky and Nelson, 2002b) were of limited help. Moreover,

within non-professional networks my role was primarily as an activist.

If 'praxis is what lies between what is desirable and what is achievable' (Prilleltensky and Nelson, 2002a: 158) then it is important to try to develop ways of judging which alliances and compromises are necessary and which are beyond the pale. As Willig (2003) notes, 'the need to form alliances, to create a "United Front" with those whose views diverge from ours, in the interests of a specific strategic goal, exerts pressures which are not always easy to negotiate. Equally, the decision of where to draw the line and who not to work with, perhaps on principle, is a difficult one to take'. An even more complicated issue is where there are different views within groups as well as between them. It is more straightforward to join with the oppressed when there is agreement about key objectives. However, within groups of psychiatric survivors, as we will see below, there is often disagreement about key issues like the role of compulsory treatment. Should one work towards consensus or not? How can this best be managed?

In this paper, I will present a case study of work to influence mental health policy. I have generally found it more helpful to read examples of practice than the broad theoretical generalisations privileged within the academy but such accounts are generally more messy and complex. It is one thing to state one's allegiance to a set of abstract principles, but how to realise them? In what ways do the dilemmatic subject positions set up for us by the contradictions inherent in psychology come into play and how might we best address them?

I will give examples of some of the activities I conducted in work both within professional structures and in collaboration with other social movements for change. My focus will be both on the broader processes which come into play when one attempts to work critically as a professional and on my subjective experience of them. My aim is not to present what I think are the 'right' answers but to describe some of my actions, their rationale and my documentation and evaluation of them. Through this I hope that other critical applied psychologists might develop working models which enable them to balance priorities, engage in flexible and tactically-aware interventions and evaluate them.

Reforming the Mental Health Act

In the UK the number of all psychiatric in-patients who were compulsorily treated doubled between 1992 and 2000, with the percentage rising from 9.2 to 13.5 (Salize and Dressing, 2004). There were a total of 46,900 compulsory detentions in England in 2002-2003 (Department of Health, 2003). This treatment is governed by the 1983 Mental Health Act (MHA) and, in 1998, the Labour government announced that they planned to reform mental health legislation.

The government stated that changes to the Act were required because it was outdated as a result of the increasing shift from hospital-based to community care (Department of Health, 2000). It was also in need of reform to bring it in line with the 1998 Human Rights Act in which the European Convention on Human Rights was incorporated into British law. Indeed, a number of human rights-based legal challenges have recently been lost by the government (Blindman et al, 2003). The government also claimed that the general public had lost confidence in mental health services as a result of a 'tragic toll of homicides and suicides involving such patients' (Department of Health, 2000: 1). In the absence of any evidence of such a lack of confidence it seems clear that the government was motivated by other factors including concern about tabloid news headlines exaggerating the risk posed by people with mental health problems (Harper, 2004; Laurance, 2003).

The path to legislative change, especially contentious areas of social policy like mental health, is a long one. Since 1998 the government have published: a review by an expert committee (Department of Health, 1999a); two government green papers (Department of Health, 1999b, 1999c); a white paper (Department of Health, 2000); and a draft bill (Department of Health, 2002). A further draft bill was published at the time of writing in September 2004 for pre-legislative scrutiny (Department of Health, 2004).[2]

Contentious issues in the proposals

A detailed analysis of the proposals is beyond the scope of this paper and the reader is referred elsewhere for a more comprehensive discussion (e.g. Cooke et al, 2001, 2002b; Parliamentary Office of Science and Technology, 2003). In order to provide a context for issues touched on later, I will briefly outline five main areas of concern: definitions and criteria; compulsory treatment in the community; the clinical supervisor role; the notion of personality disorder; and preventive detention.

a) Definitions and criteria
Currently, doctors and a social worker can order compulsory psychiatric treatment under a number of sections of the Act (being given such

treatment is known informally as 'sectioning') if a person is considered a risk to themselves or others as a result of 'mental disorder' which is defined in relation to psychiatric categories seen by many as problematic (e.g. Hare-Mustin and Maracek, 1997).

Both the white paper and draft bill included a very broad definition of 'mental disorder'. To the extent that this reduced reliance on a flawed psychiatric diagnostic system, this was a positive move. However, this was not accompanied by stringent criteria which would provide clear limits on the circumstances in which treatment could be given compulsorily. The absence of such limits could lead to an increase in the number of people treated compulsorily especially at a time of increasingly defensive professional practice (Laurance, 2003). The expert committee had argued that compulsory treatment should only take place when a person lacked – perhaps only temporarily – the capacity to properly give or withhold consent because of their mental health problems. However, the government did not include capacity to consent as a criterion in their proposals.

b) Compulsory treatment in the community

Currently, compulsory psychiatric treatment can only take place in a hospital. For the vast majority the main intervention they receive is psychiatric medication which can have many negative side effects (Johnstone, 2000). Both the draft bill and the white paper had noted that compulsory treatment was to be extended into the community – in other words a person would no longer need to be a hospital in-patient to be 'sectioned'. This led many psychiatric survivor groups to fear that they would be forcibly injected at home and that there would be no escape from unwanted treatment. An increasing number of in-patient beds have been occupied by those treated compulsorily and some have argued that the total number of beds available acts as an informal upper limit on the numbers of people who can be 'sectioned' at any one time. Given that compulsory treatment was to no longer rely on a person being an in-patient (and therefore the number of beds available), it is possible that this move could fuel a continued increase in the number of people being treated compulsorily.

c) The clinical supervisor role

Currently the person with legal responsibility for compulsory treatment is the service user's consultant psychiatrist. Both the white paper and draft bill proposed replacing this role with that of a 'clinical supervisor' who would probably be the professional most involved in planning their care. The white paper also proposed that this role could be fulfilled not only by psychiatrists but also 'consultant psychologists'. Thus under these proposals, some clinical psychologists could soon have the powers to detain people for compulsory treatment.

d) Personality disorder
The white paper placed a lot of emphasis on public protection with a whole section of proposals aimed at 'high risk patients' which included what it called 'dangerous people with severe personality disorder' – variously referred to in policy documents and discussions as 'DSPD' or 'D and SPD'.

There were two concerns in relation to DSPD. Firstly, the use of the concept of personality disorder was disquieting because of its circular definition: this person behaves violently because they have a personality disorder; we know they have personality disorder because they behave violently. Secondly, policy documents were often ambiguous about the relationship between dangerousness and personality disorder. In the white paper the focus was on people who were felt to be dangerous as a result of their personality disorder. However psychiatric survivors with a diagnosis of personality disorder feared that they would be more likely to receive compulsory treatment under the proposals. Moreover, the difficulties with the reliability and validity of personality disorder are notorious and the judgement of whether a person's 'dangerousness' arose from 'it' or not is no less problematic. This led to concern that the government was attempting to address issues of public protection through mental health legislation rather than other more appropriate means.

e) Preventive detention
Under the 1983 Act, detention and compulsory treatment of people with a diagnosis of personality disorder was only allowed if it was judged that the condition was 'treatable'. This was to prevent long-term indefinite detention but the government viewed this as a loophole which should be closed. Detention was now to be allowed in cases where the person's problems could be 'managed' – a much less stringent criterion than 'treated'

In addition, the government wanted to find a mechanism for detaining people thought to be dangerous regardless of whether they had received a criminal conviction or, if they had received one, to continue detaining them after they had completed their sentence. Whilst this might be regarded as a breach of the Human Rights Act recent case law suggests that this actually provides relatively little protection for those regarded as being of 'unsound mind' (Bindman et al, 2003).[3]

These areas of concern meant that I saw the proposals as a missed opportunity to rethink the rights of mental health service users. I felt that it would be less discriminatory to not have separate mental health legislation at all and, instead, to look at the issue of impaired judgement across the board, incorporating mental health problems into a broader Incapacity Act (Parliamentary Office of Science and Technology, 2003). I had worked in public sector mental health services for over ten years and, having moved to an academic post I hoped to have more time and energy to influence policy. But where to put one's energies?

Weighing up how to influence the proposals

I considered working through the British Psychological Society (BPS), my professional organisation. Reasons for this approach included: the government were open to meetings with professional groups; the expert discourse was thus accorded social status and access; if critical people were not involved there was the danger that only those concerned with 'guild interests' (Hare-Mustin and Maracek, 1997) would be; there was also the possibility of encouraging the BPS to become more involved with the Mental Health Alliance – a broad grouping of sixty independent sector charities, survivor groups and professional bodies. Reasons against professional-level involvement included the dangers of achieving short-term gains without challenging the notion that professional knowledge is value-laden and provisional and that the government might seek to buy psychologists off with the seductions of apparent power and influence.

It also seemed possible to intervene through alliances and collaboration with mental health service user/psychiatric survivor groups and groups of critical professionals like the Critical Psychiatry Network. I was already involved with the Critical Mental Health Forum in London. Here there were good reasons for becoming involved. There has been a tradition of critical professionals working as 'allies' of survivor groups like the Hearing Voices Network. It seemed possible that a coalition could be built, but one which would also put the experiences and concerns of those likely to be subject to compulsory treatment at the forefront. There were no real reasons against other than a limited resource of time and energy.

I would like to say that I endeavoured to weigh up the relative merits of these different domains of intervention but the reality is more prosaic. Events were fast-moving and I ended up becoming involved with both. A large part of the reason for this was a result of the organic development of personal contacts with individuals and groups over time.

Working within professional structures

The initial part of my involvement with the BPS consisted largely of lots of discussions with colleagues in the BPS Division of Clinical Psychology (DCP) in order to formulate a response. The BPS has a total membership of approximately 30,000 and there are about 6,000 clinical psychologists in the UK of whom just over 4,000 are members of the division. We were keen that the society should present a consensus statement since we felt a united front would have more influence than a position where the government could divide and rule. However, as a result of our consultations with other BPS members, it became clear that a consensus statement rejecting compulsory treatment and its extension into the community and which rejected notions of personality disorder *per se* was not possible. One reason for this was that the notion of personality disorder was in common use by many forensic clinical psychologists. Moreover, many currently worked with people under 'section' but felt they had little influence over the sectioning process even when they were the main profession involved. As a result, some were attracted to the possibility of acquiring clinical supervisor powers. I was disappointed but not that surprised by this but judged that we could make progress on other areas so instead we focused on areas of agreement, especially the need for stringent criteria (e.g. relating to capacity to consent) limiting the use of compulsory treatment.

For me, the experience of negotiating compromises in order to maintain a united front was problematic. Critical psychology does not and cannot provide a blueprint for action in situations like this. I worried that, at the first hurdle we were prepared to concede on important points of principle and wondered whether others would be critical of these decisions. On the other hand, it seemed to me that there was more prospect of getting the government to concede on the issue of criteria. Maybe it would not be possible at this point in history to achieve the wholesale review of mental health legislation I thought was necessary. The main thing I learnt from this experience was that it was important to treat such decisions as provisional and to continually keep them under review. There were three main areas of action which I will briefly summarise.

a) Engaging directly with the government
BPS representatives arranged to meet with senior civil servants. The rationale here was to use our socially-sanctioned expert position and the institutional structures of the Society to add weight to our comments. However, the effects were hard to determine. For example, from our first meeting in March 2001, it was clear that whilst these officials were open to refining certain details (e.g. which psychologists might become clinical supervisors) there were other areas where policy was more settled. Officials wanted to have the powers to detain people before they went on to commit offences. However, we argued that predictions of dangerousness for people without a history of violence were notoriously unreliable. Moreover, the society had repeatedly suggested that it would be better to address the risk to the public from people considered to be dangerous through criminal justice legislation. We felt that issues of risk applied across the board and not just to those who had acquired psychiatric diagnoses. We were concerned that, once again, people with mental health problems were being discriminated against and that the government was attempting to address public protection through the back-door via mental health legislation. However, this was a major policy decision which would have required decisions by ministers rather than civil servants and ministers were reluctant to move on this point. I began to realise that officials would only make significant changes if Ministers were persuaded to change their views. This would only happen if political pressure was brought to bear outside of those meetings and, after a few months, I disengaged from this area of activity for a period.

b) Working with the Mental Health Alliance
The Mental Health Alliance was set up to respond to the Mental Health Act reforms and it put considerable work into maintaining a united front on the reform proposals. One danger, however, was of a lowest common denominator approach where more radical critique was constrained. Policy became what the organisations could agree on which often revolved around basic rights (e.g. the right to have an

assessment) and so the Alliance's slogan was 'rights not compulsion'.

It was clear that many Alliance members did not know how to respond to the DSPD provisions and there appeared to be a conceptual vacuum about the issue of dangerousness and DSPD. As a result, psychological expertise in developing non-medical conceptualisations of mental health (e.g. British Psychological Society, 2000) and risk was important and one of my colleagues took a lead on this. Work with the Alliance involved attending a lot of meetings, reading and commenting on many drafts of documents. Several policy sub-groups were formed and I joined one relating to the compulsory use of physical treatments like Electro-convulsive therapy (ECT). We agreed on some very useful principles to govern such use. Currently, legislation allows the use of treatments like ECT without consent, particularly as an 'urgent' or 'life-saving' treatment and I wanted the group to agree that this should stop since there is little evidence for its efficacy (Johnstone, 2003). Some of the Alliance's member organisations said that ECT should never be given to a person without their consent if they had the capacity to consent but that if they lacked the capacity to consent, it could be given in limited circumstances (e.g. as an 'urgent' treatment).

Once again, I was disappointed by this and found compromises like this difficult – I felt guilty and impotent. It is easy to criticise politicians for selling out but harder to reconcile this when you are the person making the compromises. Again, I consoled myself by acknowledging that we had made a small step forward on this issue: we had a higher threshold for ECT than currently and had developed much more stringent criteria which provided a mechanism for reviewing the efficacy and safety of ECT under stringent conditions in the future. However, these principles kept on disappearing off later drafts of the policy, supposedly for reasons of space.

c) Intervening with the BPS membership

I and my colleagues threw ourselves into writing articles which would reach different sections of the membership, encouraging people to write the Department of Health and their Members of Parliament about the proposals. We travelled to meetings around the country speaking to groups of clinical psychologists and a public debate was held.

It is a feature of many professional organisations that they are relatively undemocratic and the BPS is no different. I was surprised by how easily a small group of people could influence policy. The society as an institution seems happy to allow people to devise policy provided they can avoid attracting too much active criticism. The difficulty is that the sheer amount of work involved (reading documents, going to meetings, resolving disputes between different parties, taking telephone calls, responding to emails) becomes extremely wearing – an issue I discuss in more detail below. However, it raised an important question for us: did we need a mandate from the membership in order give more weight to our comments? Reasons for this included the strength that popular support would give to DCP policy. We also felt that it was important to evaluate what we were doing and how representative we were of members' views – we did not want to get to a position where consensus was threatened at a later stage which could then present the government with an opportunity for exploiting divisions. The major reason against was the danger of them not sharing our view and some of our colleagues suggested that it was a mistake to ask the membership what they thought for precisely this reason. We decided to take the chance and sent out a survey with *Clinical Psychology*, the monthly DCP newsletter, in the summer of 2001 to all 4,160 members.

Six hundred and eighty-one members responded – a response rate of just over 16 per cent. Although this was low, it was hard to judge if this was an unusually low response rate since this was the first time this kind of survey had been conducted and we were aware that the percentage of members who voted in BPS elections was often very low. The survey (Cooke et al, 2002a) focused on three key areas where the society already had a developed policy and we sought to see how many members would agree with that position. Only twenty-nine per cent felt we should resist the development of proposals for clinical psychologists to become clinical supervisors, compared with seventy-one per cent who thought we should be 'open to this development'. Fifty-two per cent were willing to become clinical supervisors if offered appropriate training with thirty two per cent unwilling to volunteer if given the choice and only sixteen per cent willing to refuse 'even if put under pressure'. However, ninety-nine per cent agreed that 'access to psychological interventions for people who have exhibited violent behaviour should not be dependent on the person being assessed as "personality disordered"' and eighty-four per cent agreed that mental health legislation was an inappropriate vehicle for public protection. Furthermore, ninety-one per cent agreed that compulsory treatment should not be based on unreliable predictions of dangerousness.

Overall, the responses were in line with the position we had adopted and thus gave us a mandate. However, I was disappointed and angry that there was only a small number prepared to reject the clinical supervisor role. It seemed to me that clinical psychologists were either being too fatalistic or too open-minded. A generous interpretation might be that many members had not felt informed enough to definitively reject a concept about which they had only been informed a few months before. However, a glance through some of the comments written on the survey about this role suggested a variety of reasons: that it might help weaken psychiatry's grip on power; and that psychologists would use the powers more humanely than psychiatrists. Other, even more depressing, comments suggested that we should ensure that pay was commensurate with the new powers.

This experience showed me that certain resources are required in order to sustain oneself in working for social change. I realised that I needed to see some sign that battles could be won and that there was a constituency of support. I eventually became a less active member of the society's working party towards the end of 2001. Whilst there was some disappointment and tiredness on my part it would be all too easy to view this as just another example of activist burnout. However, my withdrawal was also based on a pragmatic evaluation of where I was directing my energies. The BPS work was taking up huge amounts of time and energy and I felt much of my time was spent like a diplomat trying to help develop consensus and my own views were being squeezed out in the process. I also felt that the impact of the Society was quite limited at this point. Clearly, the policy was being driven politically and ministers did not seem to be open to rethinking fundamental aspects of their policy. I felt that my time would be better spent trying to increase political pressure on them.

Working with the Critical Mental Health Forum and other groups

The Forum was set up at the beginning of 2001. Together with the Critical Psychiatry Network and Mad Pride, we had organised a picket of the headquarters of the Association of British Pharmaceutical Industries and of the first day of the Royal College of Psychiatrists' annual conference in July of that year. These had been modestly successful in getting media coverage which was an important part of our strategy.

Attendees at the forum included current and ex-service users and survivors, critical mental health professionals (some of whom had also used psychiatric services themselves) and academics and researchers. Whilst all shared broad critiques of the mental health system, there were differing views about priorities and solutions. For example we had a number of discussions about compulsory treatment and its extension into the community. Strong arguments were made against it, both by professionals and by people who had been subject to it: it was an abuse of the human right to self-determination and was dehumanising; it obscured the fact that people often didn't comply with 'treatment' as this solely consisted of psychiatric drugs with unpleasant side effects. Similarly, strong arguments were made for it by members including people who had been subject to it: that, whilst unpleasant and distressing at the time, it did mean that people in crisis and who had not been fully aware of what they were doing had been contained and not gone on to harm themselves. Similarly, some worried that the use of compulsory treatment would increase especially in a context of loose criteria and increasingly defensive practice. Others felt that, if some element of compulsion was necessary, people should not be forced to go into in-patient wards which were often poorly-resourced and frightening places to be. It was hard to come to a consensus statement against compulsory treatment *per se* and discussions like this led to the decision to call ourselves a 'forum' for debate rather than a group which might imply a unified position. Although consensus was not possible on this issue, there were plenty of other concerns on which we could agree – for example that service users should have a choice of what treatment they would prefer, that it should be a last and not a first resort and so on (see Critical Mental Health Forum, 2002, for more detail).

In August 2002 we organised a demonstration, which about fifty people attended, outside the Department of Health headquarters and released a statement on the reforms (Critical Mental Health Forum, 2002) which was included with a petition which we handed into the prime minister's office in Downing Street.

As with our previous actions, we felt a media strategy was important and a survivor-run film company, Listen to the Voices, recorded the demonstration and it was covered in professional magazines like the Nursing Times and the Health Service Journal whilst Community Care used the demonstration to lead a feature on the reforms (Leason, 2002). The Morning Star invited me to write a feature on the reforms and it was also covered in Disability News. However, although we had sent out fifty media releases (aided by the BPS press office and the independent survivor-run Mental Health Media) we got no coverage in the mainstream media. This is not an unusual experience for activists. To popular tabloid newspapers, whose sales are seemingly fuelled by an endless diet of celebrity stories we were, no doubt, an irrelevance. However, broadsheet journalists were, on the whole, more receptive. Unfortunately, many said that they did not cover demonstrations *per se* and that, anyway, they were waiting to cover the Mental Health Alliance's planned rally in London in September. Unfortunately, this rally was cancelled at short notice because of extensive press coverage of the murder of two children. The man then suspected (and now convicted) of killing them had been briefly sectioned (though he was later judged fit to stand trial) and some Alliance members were worried about the public reaction to a rally against the Mental Health Act proposals.

Incensed by the rally's cancellation, a number of survivors set up a new group, *No Force* and took over the organisation of the rally, largely via email. It went ahead with 300-400 people attending with placards and a samba band. Another petition was handed into Downing Street as the rally made its way down Whitehall past the Department of Health and then onto the old Bethlem asylum. It was tremendously inspiring to see the rally organised so well at such short notice and without the involvement of professionals' organisations.

I saw these demonstrations and lobbies as helping to provide a focus for, and increasing political pressure on, the government at particular moments, especially during periods of consultation. By September 2002 the Department of Health received 1,900 largely negative responses to their consultation. The bill was delayed for two years whilst the Department of Health worked to redraft it to allay concerns. As this paper was being completed a new draft bill was published (Department of Health, 2004) and early indications are that there have been some changes to the legislation. Campaigners remain hopeful that further changes may follow the scrutiny committee's report in 2005.

Reflecting on the interventions

Engagement at a professional level is fraught with difficulties. On the one hand it appears to offer some short-term gains, notably access to government. On the other, as Parker (2003) has argued, 'the idea that nicer people might influence those in power and ameliorate the worst aspects of the Mental Health Bill is also a warrant for institutional recuperation of the opposition; with pernicious consequences well beyond the "engagement"'.

There is a danger of exaggerating how much influence one can have over the government (see for example a fascinating debate about this in Kinderman and May, 2003) but there is an equal danger of not taking official opportunities to influence policy, especially at a time when the government has a massive parliamentary majority. I think we should engage with government but also continually evaluate our actions and remain constantly vigilant about whether we are falling into a position of collusion or making a compromise too far.

Decisions about how and when to engage need to be debated. We also need to keep these decisions under review as what is appropriate and helpful at one moment may not be at another. For example, engagement at a professional level was only useful at those times when the government was forced to listen to the views of professionals, psychiatric survivor organisations and other groups. Early indications are that the new draft bill has made some concessions which suggests that change is possible when governments are faced with united opposition from professionals and service users, both groups also exerting political pressure through their Members of Parliament. Even sections of the media were supportive.[4] Mobilising popular protest has at least made the government think again and pressure will need to be kept up as the legislative process goes forward.

Peter Campbell (1999) has discussed some of the politics involved when survivors collaborate with professionals. Of course, in their training, professionals are socialised in practices of contributing to and organising meetings and this creates the danger that professionals can take over in these situations. Unfortunately, effective collaboration takes time and resources and, particularly when legislative reforms are moving at a fast pace, I felt there was not enough time to do this issue justice – another thing to bear in mind if one is spreading one's activities too thinly. I was never sure whether my time in collaborative groups was best spent providing administrative or theoretical support, to ally with survivors or just to get out of their way. Indeed, many survivor groups are forced into alliances because their funding is uncertain (Campbell, 1999). Moreover, whilst professional organisations like the BPS may appear to side with survivors there are likely to be conflicts with their own interests. Indeed, many organisations continue to see psychiatric survivors as 'other' rather than recognise that many of its members are or have been users of mental health services (May et al, 2003). In this respect it has been heartening to see well-established survivor-run groups like Mad Pride and new ones like No Force and Outcry set up because of a growing dissatisfaction with the lead taken by the Alliance and the lack of authentic voices representing survivors (Main, 2003).

The late Pete Shaughnessy, one of the founders of Mad Pride, argued strongly that debates needed to occur outside of what he saw as the ghetto of mental health conferences and magazines and he was involved in a range of actions which did just that (Shaughnessy, 2003). My experience of the media has been that it is possible to do this in a modest way providing both that the journalist is open to this and one is flexible (e.g. BBC News online, 2004; Leason, 2002; Radcliffe, 2003). I think critical psychologists need to become more skilled at intervening in the mainstream arena of the media, learning from other successful campaigns. Organisations like Mental Health Media and the BPS run useful media training days. For those who do not feel appropriately skilled it is perhaps important to reflect on what particular contributions you can make and, at the least, put journalists in touch with survivors.

The final theme I want to discuss is how to cope personally in campaigns like these. In the first eighteen months I took on far too much in relation to this campaign and was trying to work at a level which was personally unsustainable. Things were made more difficult by the fact that I was juggling different kinds of activities in both the BPS/Alliance and the forum in a manner reminiscent of Ussher's (2000) attempt to balance both mainstream and more critical research. Time was swallowed up in a sea of activity. Eventually, I decided that I needed to focus on a smaller range of activities and to do only those things which I felt accorded most with my values. I also decided to work harder at breaking tasks down so they could be easily shared and the forum set up a demonstration-planning sub-group in 2002 to do this. Similarly, now that a new draft bill has been published, I will be resuming some activity within the BPS where we will be attempting to adopt a 'workstream' approach where different groups of people take a lead on activities about which they feel more competent and committed. I will be focusing my energy in the workstream which will be lobbying for changes in the new bill.

However, such innovations do not get away from the fact that these activities are personally wearing. What has been most difficult has been the unpredictability of the amount of time involved. One can sustain a burst of energy on a number of fronts only for a short time but changing social policy takes years. My first involvement in this campaign began in 2000 and now, four years later, the process is still ongoing and is likely to continue for another two years. I have found that it is important to set clear limits on what one personally can do.

I hope that this account is useful in helping others develop and elaborate working models to weigh up the kind of interventions in which they wish to become involved. This kind of action, especially where it cuts across different roles, means that it is not possible to give clear map-like directions to others. However, although complex, inspiring, fun and occasionally tiring and disappointing, direct interventions into social policy are important and necessary if we are to move towards a better world.

Notes

1. Descriptions of people receiving psychiatric interventions are highly contested (Campbell, 1999). In this article I will use the term 'psychiatric survivor' to refer to groups who would self-identify in this way, 'in-patient' if I am referring only to those in hospitals and 'service user' elsewhere – the latter term is the one currently most used in UK policy documents..
2. In the UK legislation goes through a number of stages. First, a green paper is published for consultation summarising a variety of policy options. Second, a white paper is published in which the government outlines its preferred policy option. Increasingly, at this point, the government now publishes draft bills for 'pre-legislative scrutiny' especially where they are more contentious. This is then followed by a bill which is first presented in one of the houses of parliament where it goes through different stages of scrutiny and where amendments are proposed and voted on. Following this it is passed onto the other house to go through the same stages. Finally it receives Royal Assent and a time is set for its implementation.
3. The 1998 Human Rights Act incorporated the European Convention on Human Rights (1950) into British law. Article 5 states that 'everyone has the right to liberty and security of person. No one shall be deprived of his liberty save in the following cases and in accordance with a procedure prescribed by law ... the lawful detention of persons for the prevention of the spreading of infectious diseases, *of persons of unsound mind*, alcoholics or drug addicts, or vagrants' (European Convention on Human Rights 1950, emphasis added). This text, written in 1950, was clearly a product of its time and its inclusion in British law without revision thus enshrines discrimination against a number of marginalised groups including people with mental health problems.
4. The Independent on Sunday, for example, ran an excellent campaign against the proposals whilst the health editor of the Independent, who had attended several Critical Mental Health Forum meetings as an observer, published a book critical of many of the reforms (Laurance, 2003).

Acknowledgements

Thanks to Pippa Dell, Jane Selby and two anonymous reviewers for commenting on an earlier version of this paper. In addition, I'm grateful to Bipasha Ahmed, Irina Anderson and Mary Boyle of the Critical Psychology Group at the University of East London for their comments and support. Thanks also to members of the Critical Mental Health Forum and the BPS mental health legislation working party.

References

Ahmed, B. (2003). *'So you're here to slag us off then': problems and challenges in conducting critical psychological research*. Paper presented at International Conference on Critical Psychology, Bath, August.

BBC News online (2004). 'Who is to blame for tube murder?'. BBC News online 24 February [http://news.bbc.co.uk/1/hi/england/3516945.stm] [accessed 29 February 2004].

Bindman, J., S. Maingay and G. Szmukler (2003). 'The Human Rights Act and mental health legislation'. *British Journal of Psychiatry* 182: 91-94.

British Psychological Society (2000). *Recent advances in understanding mental illness and psychotic experiences*. Leicester: British Psychological Society, [Available: www.understandingpsychosis.com] [accessed 22 February 2004].

Burton, M. and C. Kagan (2005). 'Liberation social psychology: learning from Latin America'. *Journal of Community and Applied Social Psychology* 15: 63-78.

Campbell, P. (1999). 'The service user/survivor movement'. Newnes, C., G. Holmes and C. Dunn (eds). *This is madness: a critical look at psychiatry and the future of mental health services*. 195-209. Ross-on-Wye: PCCS Books.

Cooke, A., D. Harper and P. Kinderman (2001). 'DCP update. Reform of the mental health act: implications for clinical psychologists'. *Clinical Psychology* 1: 48-52.

Cooke, A., D. Harper and P. Kinderman (2002a). 'DCP Update. Criticisms and concerns'. *Clinical Psychology* 13: 43-47.

Cooke, A., D. Harper and P. Kinderman (2002b). 'An invitation to debate: do clinical psychologists care about the Mental Health Act reforms?'. *Clinical Psychology* 15: 40-46.

Critical Mental Health Forum (2002). 'Critical mental health's response to the draft mental health bill: "Choice not compulsion". *Asylum: The Magazine for Democratic Psychiatry* 13: 7-8 [Available: http://www.critpsynet.freeuk.com/criticalmentalhealth.htm] [accessed 26 February 2004].

Dell, P. and I. Anderson (2005). 'Practising critical psychology: Politics, power and psychology departments'. *International Journal of Critical Psychology* 13. 14-31.

Department of Health (1999a). *Review of the mental health act 1983: report of the expert committee*. London: The Stationery Office.

Department of Health (1999b). *Reform of the mental health act: proposals for consultation*. London: The Stationery Office.

Department of Health/Home Office (1999c). *Managing dangerous people with severe personality disorder*. London: The Stationery Office.

Department of Health (2000). *Reforming the mental health act*. London: The Stationery Office.

Department of Health (2002). *Draft mental health bill*. London: The Stationery Office.

Department of Health (2003). *In-patients formally detained in hospitals under the Mental Health Act 1983 and other legislation*, England: 1992-93 to 2002-03. London: Department of Health.

Department of Health (2004). *Draft mental health bill*. London: The Stationery Office.

Council of Europe (1950). London: 'European Convention on Human Rights'. [http://www.hrcr.org/docs/Eur_Convention/euroconv.html] [accessed 26 February 2004].

Hare-Mustin, R.T. and J. Maracek (1997). 'Abnormal and clinical psychology: the politics of madness'. Fox, D. and I. Prilleltensky (eds). *Critical psychology: an introduction*. 104-120. London: Sage.

Harper, D. J. (2004). 'Storying policy: constructions of risk in proposals to reform UK mental health legislation'. Hurwitz, B., T. Greenhalgh and V. Skultans (eds), *Narrative research in health and illness*. 397-413. London: BMJ Books/Blackwell Publishing.

Ingleby, D. (1974). 'The job psychologists do'. N. Armistead (ed.), *Reconstructing social psychology*. 314-328. Harmondsworth: Penguin Education.

Johnstone, L. (2000). *Users and abusers of psychiatry. Second edition*. London: Routledge.

Johnstone, L. (2003). 'A shocking treatment?'. *The Psychologist: Bulletin of the British Psychological Society* 16: 236-239.

Kinderman, P. and May, R. (2003). 'Yes minister, but ...'. *Asylum: The Magazine for Democratic Psychiatry* 13: 24-30.

Kitzinger, C. (1997). 'Lesbian and gay psychology: A critical analysis'. Fox, D. and I. Prilleltensky (eds). *Critical psychology: An introduction*. 202-216. London: Sage.

Laurance, J. (2003). *Pure madness: how fear drives the mental health system*. London: Routledge.

Leason, K. (2002). 'News analysis of opposition to mental health bill'. *Community Care* 22-28. August: 20-21.

Main, L. (2003). *Hue and outcry. Mental Health Today*. September: 10-11.

May, R., J. Hartley and T. Knight (2003). 'Making the personal political'. *The Psychologist: Bulletin of the British Psychological Society* 16: 182-183.

Paré, D.A. and G. Larner (eds). (2004). *Collaborative practice in psychology and therapy*. Binghampton, NY: Haworth Press.

Parker, I. (2003). 'Psychology is so critical, only Marxism can save us now'. Submitted to Historical Materialism.

Parliamentary Office of Science and Technology (2003). 'Postnote: Reform of mental health legislation'. London: Parliamentary Office of Science and

Technology [Available: http://www.parliament.uk/post/pn204.pdf] [accessed 21 August 2004.]

Philo G. (ed.). (1996). *Media and mental distress*. London: Longman.

Prilleltensky, I. and G. Nelson (2002). *Doing psychology critically: making a difference in diverse settings*. 158-166. Basingstoke, Hampshire: Palgrave Macmillan.

Prilleltensky, I. and G. Nelson (2002a). 'Psychologists and the process of change: making a difference in diverse settings'. Prilleltensky, I. and G. Nelson. *Doing psychology critically: making a difference in diverse settings 158-166*. Basingstoke, Hampshire: Palgrave Macmillan.

Prilleltensky, I. and G. Nelson (2002b). 'Psychologists and the object of social change: transforming social policy'. Prilleltensky, I., and G. Nelson. *Doing psychology critically: making a difference in diverse settings 167-176*. Basingstoke, Hampshire: Palgrave Macmillan.

Radcliffe, M. (2003). 'Word power'. *Guardian* 16 July.

Reicher, S. (1996). 'The reactionary practice of radical psychology: revoking the Faustian contract'. Parker, I. and R. Spears (eds). *Psychology and Society: radical theory and practice 230-240*. London: Pluto Press.

Rose, N. (1985). *The psychological complex: psychology, politics and society in England 1869-1939*. London: Routledge and Kegan Paul

Salize, H. J. and H. Dressing (2004). 'Epidemiology of involuntary placement of mentally ill people across the European Union'. *British Journal of Psychiatry* 184: 163-168.

Sayce, L. (1998). 'Stigma, discrimination and social exclusion: what's in a word?' *Journal of Mental Health* 7: 331-343.

Shaughnessy, P. (2003). 'Stigma: from personal experience'. *Asylum: The Magazine for Democratic Psychiatry* 13: 6-9.

Ussher, J. (2000). 'Critical psychology in the mainstream: a struggle for survival'. Sloan, T. (ed.). *Critical psychology: voices for change*. 6-20. Basingstoke, Hampshire: Macmillan Press.

Willig, C. (1998). 'Social constructionism and revolutionary socialism: a contradiction in terms?' Parker, I. (ed.). *Social constructionism, discourse and realism*. 91-104. London: Sage.

Willig, C. (2003). 'Professional critical psychology: a contradiction in terms?' *Symposium* discussant at International Conference on Critical Psychology, Bath, August.

Willig, C. and J. Drury (2004). '"Acting-with": partisan participant observation as a social-practice basis for shared knowing'. Paré, D. A. and G. Larner (eds). *Collaborative practice in psychology and therapy*. 229-241. Binghampton, NY: Haworth Press.

Negotiating identity within the politics of HIV/AIDS
Developing interventions for young South Africans

Kerry Frizelle

> Many HIV interventions aimed at youth in South Africa have been criticised for not acknowledging the complex context in which identities and sexual behaviour are constantly negotiated. This paper shares the thoughts of a psychologist attempting to develop meaningful and effective HIV interventions amongst youth. The paper argues that prevention programmes need to move away from deficit models of youth development towards a view that youth are capable of engaging meaningfully in decisions regarding their well being. Youth should be encouraged to view their identities as projects in the making and to be positive about the uncertainty of life so that they are in a better position to negotiate their way through challenging life situations. The paper suggests that youth need to be given more opportunities to debate HIV/AIDS as a fascinating reflection of their times and to enable them to become critically aware of the way in which contextual factors impact on their sexual identities. The paper proposes that interventions include more open and honest debate about sexual desire and experiences that move beyond narrow heteronormative constructs of sexuality. It argues that discussion groups run by well-trained facilitators can provide a safe context in which young people can begin to understand and negotiate their location within the context of HIV/AIDS.

Introduction

I am a registered psychologist working within the context of HIV/AIDS in South Africa. In this country we all have reason for much concern. The first systematically sampled, nationwide, community-based survey of the prevalence of HIV in South Africa estimates a figure of 11.4 per cent. This estimate is very similar to the 11.2 per cent (4.84 million) provided though modelling by the Department of Health (Shisana, 2002).

Eighteen million (44 per cent) of South Africa's population is under the age of twenty (Walker, Reid and Cornell, 2004). In the recent past there has been increasing concern about the effectiveness (and appropriateness) of HIV intervention programmes targeted at the youth of South Africa. These programmes locate the cause of sexual behaviour at the individual level and assume that information about the dangers of HIV and how to prevent it will enable and motivate individuals to safeguard their behaviour (Campbell, 2003). HIV infection rates are rife amongst young people *despite* an increase in HIV intervention programmes. A report by the Medical Research Council (Dorrington, Bourne, Bradshaw, Laubscher and Timaeus, 2001) presents comprehensive data on adult mortality rates and suggests that it is reasonable to interpret the rise in the mortality of young and middle-aged adults in South Africa since the late 1980s as being largely, if not entirely, a consequence of HIV/AIDS. The report estimated that about forty per cent of deaths amongst adults aged fifteen to forty nine in South Africa in the year 2000 were due to HIV/AIDS.

For the last five years I have been involved in training HIV/AIDS counsellors and more recently become interested in the development of appropriate and effective HIV prevention interventions amongst youth. It has been a difficult area of interest. At times I feel desperately hopeless and wonder whether it will ever be possible to design an intervention that will positively impact on the risky behaviour of youth. There are so many factors that contribute to the explosive statistics in our country and increase the risk of infection amongst our youth that I sometimes find myself questioning whether or not it will *ever* be possible to curb the epidemic. For example, despite South Africa's progressive constitution, which places emphasis on the need for gender equity, South Africa remains a fairly patriarchal society. In 1998, South Africa had the highest per capita rate of reported rape in the world. It was estimated that there were 115.6 rapes for every 100,000 of the population. With only one in twenty cases reported it is likely that there are close to one million rapes a year in South Africa (Dorrington and Johnson, 2002). The often violent and 'forced' nature of rape increases the chances of infection (tearing provides a direct entry point for the virus). In addition to sexual behaviour factors that increase the risk of South Africans to infection, Dorrington and Johnson (2002) identify a number of other factors including bio-medical factors, social risk factors, and economic and political factors that have contributed to the rise of HIV prevalence in the country. Working in such a context is difficult and demanding. Many argue that the only solution is affordable and accessible treatment. While I agree that treatment is essential I see the need for a continued commitment to HIV-prevention.

This paper presents some thinking and ideas around designing HIV interventions for youth. At one stage I was convinced that it was possible to change the risky behaviour of youth if only we could approach them in the *right* way. Over time I have had to come to terms with the very pessimistic nature of the epidemic. I have had to acknowledge that sexual behaviour (the primary way in which HIV is spread in South Africa) is complex and full of contradictions and nuances. Even the most well conceptualised and well planned interventions cannot always control the sexual behaviour of a young couple in the heat of the moment. For a long time I hid this paper, too afraid to develop it because I questioned its value. My work, however, with young school learners has forced me to reconsider. In my experience youth in South Africa are *desperate* for open and honest discussion about sexuality. Recently over seventy local high school learners from one grade *volunteered* to attend an after school sexuality workshop over three weeks. It has been suggested that one HIV person is capable of infecting five other people in their life-time (Whiteside and Sunter, 2000). I have therefore come to believe that even if an intervention prevents only one more infection it was well worth the energy invested.

Background

There have been a number of suggestions as to why youth seem particularly vulnerable to infection. One cannot, for example, ignore the fact that as drugs become an increasingly popular form of recreation amongst young adults alcohol brands are stepping up on the advertisement of their products. For example if we consider advertisements and the packaging for alcoholic beverages such as Bacardi Breezer it becomes apparent that the target population are the younger generation who have perhaps not been exposed to drugs or simply do not have the money to purchase them. Any increase in the use of drugs and alcohol undoubtedly increases the chances of engaging in unsafe sex. Young adulthood is also often characterised by sexual exploration and a start to a lifetime of negotiation through the complex world of intimate relationships. Psychology attempts to provide a developmental explanation for the risky behaviour of youth by categorising youth as a vulnerable period of development (Wyn and White, 1997). This view of youth is often (re)produced by the media which positions young people as likely to engage in risky behaviour unless they are closely monitored and supervised by 'more experienced' adults. As a critical psychologist I consider these representations and constructions of youth to be problematic, resulting in limited and narrow responses to the challenges of youth.

These understandings and representations of youth have lead to the implementation of numerous HIV/AIDS interventions amongst the youth. Many of these interventions are based on the findings of knowledge, attitudes, practices and behaviour (KAPB) surveys. While Macphail (1998) recognises the value of these types of surveys, she is critical of their positivist underpinnings and particularly concerned with the way in which they pay little attention to the societal, normative or cultural contexts within which such knowledge and attitudes are *negotiated* or *constructed*. Campbell (2003, p.7) argues that many interventions have assumed that sexual behaviour is shaped by the conscious decisions of rational individuals. Locating the cause of sexual behaviour at the individual level has led to individual behaviour interventions that largely ignore the way in which sexual identities are 'collectively negotiated' (Campbell, 2001) in particular contexts. Wilbraham (2002, p.7) is critical of the way in which representations of youth as a time of upheaval in which youngsters are more prone to the influence of peers and risk-taking has produced 'research, and health education materials, that are obsessed with premature, promiscuous and irresponsible teen sex'. Mugabe (2001) voices concern about interventions that are designed and implemented without prior consultation with youth themselves.

A literature review conducted by Macphail (1998) suggests that although extensive research has been done on HIV and adolescents, little of this research has paid attention to the influence complex social negotiations around sexual identity may have on HIV incidence rates. She argues that there is an urgent need for more attention to be paid to these social dimensions of adolescent sexuality so that more effective intervention programmes can be implemented among the youth of South Africa. In addition, it is argued that more emphasis needs to be placed on the way in which the social and political context contributes to the subjective experiences of young people and how these contextual factors often make it difficult and problematic (but not necessarily always impossible) for young people to translate information into behaviour change. Further, it is suggested that too many HIV interventions fail to grapple with the embodied experiences of youth and, more importantly, the way in which desire impacts on their ability to engage in safe sex.

The following is a discussion of some of my thinking around youth and HIV interventions in South Africa. The context of HIV defines it as a 'work-in-progress' as it is likely to change and develop in reaction to new research and insights from personal experience.

Ongoing constructions of the self

Negotiating the self

HIV/AIDS is primarily a *relational* disease because it is primarily a *sexually* transmitted disease. Decisions to engage in sexual behaviour are often (although not always) premised on some form (and differing degrees) of social negotiation. This challenges the idea that sexual behaviour is primarily a rational decision determined by existing knowledge, attitudes and perceptions. Calhoun (1996, p.223) argues that 'to see identities only as reflections of "objective" social positions or circumstances is to see them always retrospectively. It does not make sense of the dynamic potential implicit – for better or worse – in the tensions within persons and among the contending cultural discourses that locate persons'.

Impacting on any aspect of a young person's life is a variety of discourses, offering complementary and contradictory versions of what it is to be young. People's identities are achieved by 'a subtle interweaving of many different threads' (Burr, 1996, p.51). There is a thread (or a discourse) of age, gender, and sexual orientation in addition to political, cultural and economic threads. As Burr (1996) argues, these 'threads' are woven together to produce the fabric of a person's identity. Young people (like all people) are constantly engaged in a process of negotiation with these multiple and sometimes (if not often) contradictory versions of the world.

In addition, young peoples' bodies come to assume increasing significance as they develop physically and sexually. By placing so much emphasis on the way in which youth are socialised, many HIV/AIDS interventions fail to take seriously the biological and physical dimensions of the body. Shilling (1993, p.199) argues that as the body develops 'it is taken up and transformed, within limits by social factors' and that 'the body is not only affected by social relations but forms a basis for and enters into the construction of social relations'. This is certainly the case when we consider the nature of sexual interactions, which require a number of direct and indirect social interactions that engage the body. As Calhoun (1996, p.283) puts it 'just as we are not radically isolable individual creatures whose beings end at our skins, so our humanness is not sharply separable from the broader biological world or from the technologies we have created'. From this perspective, the design of interventions needs to be premised on an understanding of the way in which young peoples' bodies are influenced by and influence social relations. It also points to an acceptance that certain dimensions of our embodiment might be more open to social intervention than others (Shilling, 1993).

The preceding discussion suggests that we cannot simply discover *the* 'youth psyche' from which we can 'extract' wrong attitudes or incorrect knowledge that can be easily changed or replaced with the 'right' knowledge with the hope that it will somehow 'stick' and keep individuals out of 'trouble' in the future. This does not work; simply because interventions of this nature fail to recognise that youth are almost constantly negotiating with themselves *and* others their attitudes, beliefs, knowledge and bodies. This complex process of negotiation is not limited to the experiences of youth; adulthood is as tenuous as youth and offers little reprieve from the complex process of identity construction. Youth, however, does mark an exploratory start to the lifetime process of negotiating one's identity and positioning in a web of social relations and meanings. As Wyn and White (1997, p.9) suggest, 'the period of youth is significant because it is the threshold to adulthood, and it is problematic largely because *adult status itself is problematic*'. Understanding identity as a constantly negotiated construct problematises the assumption that youth can be moulded in a particular direction or simply guided away from trouble through the transmission of accepted social values or 'rules'. In addition it highlights the importance of engaging youth in more critical and conscious ways in the process of identity construction. This, however, requires a shift away from deficit models of youth development towards a view that youth are capable (albeit in varying ways) to engage actively and consciously in decisions regarding their own well-being.

The unitary and internally homogenous individual
Many psychological discourses suggest that the process of identity constitution *should result* in a normally stable and minimally changing identity. One example is the way in which socialisation theory views identity formation as a prior condition of adult participation in social life (Calhoun, 1996). These theories are informed by and inform wider, more prevalent discourses of youth that are reproduced by empirical research and/or psychological theory (Wilbraham, 2002). These discourses characterise youth as a troubled and crisis-driven period of development, which precedes an adult identity that is more fixed and stable. From this perspective, the development of a settled or fixed identity is considered to be an indication of psychological health. Calhoun (1996, p.221) argues that this view of people erases the capacity for an 'internal dialogicality'. He therefore argues against investing any category of identity with any definitive meaning or viewing individuals with a unitary or fixed identity. Rather, identity should *always* be viewed as a project in the making and not a settled accomplishment, pointing to 'the fact that in living we invest ourselves in identities not statically but with an orientation to the future and to action'. Identities are therefore not discovered but continuously created. From this point of view people do not have a single, unified or fixed self but are rather fragmented, having a multiplicity of potential selves (Burr, 1995). Individuals are constantly faced with the challenge of knitting together the different phases of their existence, social relationships and roles (Calhoun, 1996). From this perspective it is healthy to assist young people to expect and cope with change and uncertainty. Samuels (2001, p.3) argues that one of the most beneficial things we can do for people is to help them to 'face up to the inevitability of disappointment'.

This view of identity appears (and potentially *is*) liberating. If we view identity as a social construction and argue that it is human beings who build these constructions, then in principle it is possible to reconstruct our identities in ways that are more facilitating for us (Burr, 1998). This is, however, not the case – primarily because people do not experience themselves in this way. People in general are constructed in a complex set of social relations and tend to continue constructing themselves in a way that will give them a sense of stability and self-coherence and will therefore resist competing discourses because they contradict their *sense* of self. Samuels (1989, p.2) suggests that we are faced with a pluralistic task 'of reconciling our many internal voices and images of ourselves with our wish and need to feel integrated and speak with one voice'. The discourse of psychology has historically emphasised (and constructed) the latter wish with its widespread approach of essentialism. Some schools of psychoanalysis, for example, argue that individuals must pursue a project of integral identity (Calhoun, 1996). In sum, people do not see themselves as 'projects in the making', but rather as individuals with a particular personality or certain unchanging attributes.

Another reason why people are unable to simply reconstruct themselves is because contextual factors like the economy, the state and other very large-scale institutions that often reinforce our sense of self appear to be alien forces:

> bewildering, and powerful beings rather than the abstractions critical thinkers may see them to be. They are reified, and the baffling way in which they confront us makes this reification not an easily escapable form of self-consciousness but an almost unavoidable condition of practical thought in the modern world. Their functioning can be grasped well only through statistics, theories, cybernetic concepts, and other intellectual tools which are both poorly distributed among the population, and also at odds with the direct understanding which people gain of their immediate surroundings (Calhoun, 1996, pp.209-210).

Calhoun (1996) argues that people talk about these large-scale systems as though they are autonomously functioning entities (like the weather) rather than creations of human social action. The effect of these institutions on human subjectivity and identity are therefore maintained in a very powerful way because social practice and discourse sustain each other; practice is the realm in which discourse has real effects upon people. Social practices, structures and material conditions are therefore inseparable from our concepts of self (Burr, 1998), and our experience (and control) of our bodies.

From this perspective we cannot deny the power of social practices and structures that place young people at risk of HIV infection. For example, we have only to consider the way in which prevalent discourses around masculinity and femininity place men and many women at risk of HIV infection. The use of a condom is another example of a highly politicised practice. In a country known for its forced sterilisation practices during the era of apartheid it is hardly surprising that many youth are sceptical of the 'white' condom, arguing that condom campaigns may be another effort at an indirect form of social control.

We need to do more than just acknowledge the presence of the biological, socio-political and economic in sexual behaviour. We need to spend more time discussing with youth the *way* in which their sexual experiences are embodied and socialised and how these experiences are integrated into their ongoing constructions of self.

In addition, we need to think of ways in which youth may begin to *understand* the way in which socially created systems have an impact on their behaviour. This critical insight into the processes of formal politics may not always enable complete agency on the part of youth, but will certainly contribute to an increased awareness of the way in which their lives are constrained by those processes that 'seem increasingly irrelevant to the lives of ordinary people (and especially young people)' (Wyn and White, 1997, p.150).

Risking suggestions

If we take seriously the argument that young people's sexual behaviour is constrained by a number of contextual factors and bodily dimensions, the possibility of an effective intervention diminishes rapidly. This is the paradox; we continue to work at changing behaviour in a context where contextual factors make this a difficult (and some would argue even impossible) task. While it is important to recognise that certain contextual factors and social practices constrain the behaviour of youth, it is crucial that the influence of such factors is not mistaken as an inherent inadequacy on the part of all youth. In recognising the way in which contextual factors constrains their behaviour, young people are in a better position to resist and challenge (albeit with differing degrees of success) the influence of these factors on their behaviour. For example Campbell's (2003) research identified a number of contextual factors including gender inequalities, economic constraints and limited access to condoms that undermined the ability of a group of South African youth to engage in safe sex. However, she also provides examples of youth (although in the minority) who are able to behave in counter-normative ways. She describes a few young women who were able to gain control over their sexuality through condom-use and HIV-testing. While the majority of young women found it hard to negotiate condom use with their male partners because of powerful constructs of masculinity this particular group of women had somehow managed to successfully challenge the resistance of their boyfriends to use condoms. Holland, Ramazangolu, Sharpe and Thompson (1992) suggest that women's empowerment is a *varied* experience depending on the particular context and relationship a women finds herself in. In one relationship she may find herself able to assert herself or negotiate safer sex, but this may not be easily transferred on to her next relationship. Agency and the ability to resist the influence of contextual factors is *varied* and we should be encouraging our youth to anticipate and capitalise on such occasions when they do arise, even in contexts where such opportunities are sporadic.

Campbell (2001) argues that providing people with information about the risk of HIV/AIDS only changes the behaviour of one in four people, and that those who do tend to change their behaviour are likely to be more educated and wealthier than those who do not. People invested in HIV/AIDS interventions should be asking how they could maximise the number of people who change their behaviour after receiving information about HIV/AIDS. Two general comments can be made: 1) *large-scale* behaviour change will not be a reality until major social change occurs: for example until constructs of masculinity begin to shift, until education is a reality for the majority and until employment is made more accessible many young people *will* continue be locked into problematic sets of interpersonal relations that place them at risk of HIV infections; and 2) interventions need to be premised on a more thorough understanding of young people and their complex set of daily interactions and negotiations with prevalent discourses and their own and others' bodies.

Burr (1998) suggests that perhaps all we can do is make recommendations for those practices or perspectives, which appear to create *possibilities* for increasing freedom, choice and quality of life for those who need it. The following suggestions/recommendations are put forward tentatively and it is hoped that others may engage with them creatively in an attempt to come up with more appropriate and effective intervention programmes for youth of South Africa. There is the possibility that they, like other interventions, may prove to be ineffective suggestions that need to be reconstructed or abandoned.

Disrupting the self

We need to risk 'disrupting' the way youths experience themselves. Samuels (1989, p.5) proposes that 'the tendency towards multiplicity and diversity is as strong – and creative – as the search for unity or a striving for hegemony' and that through the process of bargaining between conflicting interests, creative rather than destructive results can be produced. Burr (1995) suggests a process of 'discursive positioning' which involves recognising the discourses and positions that are currently shaping our subjectivity and then working towards occupying a 'healthier' position for oneself. Theories of fixed identities have led us to underestimate both the struggle involved in constructing our identities and the tension inherent in the fact that we all have multiple and *incomplete* identities (Calhoun, 1996).

This suggests that providing youths with the opportunity to see themselves in less coherent ways may not be as 'disturbing' or problematic as psychological theories of identity may suggest. By encouraging them to see themselves as a project in the making, youths are prepared for (and may even come to expect) the possibility of changes in identity and are likely to be more oriented towards future action. In this way youths will be more prepared for situations that challenge their previously held views, beliefs or sense of self. If we encourage youths to see their identity as an *ongoing* project they are more likely to reflect on their past experiences and make more carefully considered decisions for *future* action. For example, youths who have already become sexually active may be more likely to consider the option of secondary abstinence if identity is understood as less fixed and stable. Decisions become oriented towards the future rather than being locked into past experiences or understandings of the self.

The work of Gelatt (1989) comes to mind and may help to clarify the preceding point further. Gelatt (1989, p.252) explains that in the modern world rational, objective decision-making is not possible because 'Today the past is not always what it was thought to be, the future is no longer predictable, and the present is changing as never before'. He therefore proposes a new decision-making strategy called 'positive uncertainty' that helps individuals deal with change and ambiguity and accept uncertainty and inconsistency. He agrees that to be positive (comfortable and confident) in the face of uncertainty (ambiguity and doubt) is paradoxical, but is exactly what individuals need for effective decision-making. From this perspective individuals are encouraged to 'know what you want and believe but do not be sure' (Gelatt, 1989, p.254). In other words, individuals are encouraged to expect their wants and beliefs to be challenged or changed as they engage actively with the world around them. In addition, the ability to imagine or create the future is encouraged as a useful tool for projecting oneself into future scenarios. It is suggested that we need to teach youths to develop an attitude of positive uncertainty so that they are able to reflect on (or deconstruct) past actions, and construct tentative future actions rather than repeating past behaviour that may be potentially damaging, like unsafe sex. Again, this points to the importance of shifting pervasive understandings of youth. In order for young people to develop positive uncertainty, pervasive representations of youths as incapable of coping with the confusions and contradictions of youth will need to be challenged. It also requires being confident that such confusions and contradictions can bring about creative (as opposed to destructive) solutions.

Constructing a political identity
The idea that the majority of large-scale institutions are experienced as alien to the majority of people rather than as a result of social actions suggests that we must provide some 'organisation of analysis and discourse that enables people to understand and exert some control over the systems they have created' (Calhoun 1996, p.211).

Calhoun (1996) proposes that 'social movements' are often powerfully meaningful and emotionally significant and therefore present opportunities for individuals to change salient identity constructions, but because we have come to view ourselves as asocial and apolitical we have missed these significant opportunities. The implication is that if we can create a discourse that enables youths to understand the ways in which they construct and are constructed by wider social and political systems we will also provide them with an opportunity to exert *some* control over these systems. The political (and highly emotionally charged) context of HIV/AIDS in South Africa, for example, provides an excellent opportunity to engage youth with the discourse of HIV/AIDS in a meaningful way that is more likely to lead to identity reconstruction and behaviour change than one-off information delivery sessions or talks on the risk of HIV infection.

The preceding point is highlighted by Crewe (2001) who argues that from her experience there have, to date, been three primary responses to the topic of HIV/AIDS. The first is 'resigned boredom', the second 'prejudice and hostility' and the third 'bleeding heart desperation'. These responses lead to a number of hazardous outcomes like disinterest, fear and denial. She, however, argues that there is the potential to create a fourth response, one of 'fascination and engagement'. In her discussion Crewe (2001) highlights problematic discourses around the experience of youth. She suggests that adults find pride in young people conforming rather than when they challenge, 'and herein lies the crisis around AIDS. We do not engage them in the fascination of the subject. We do not use AIDS to lay bare the social prejudices and narrow-mindedness that drive the epidemic and we do not give them the confidence that they can live through and beyond this epidemic' (Crewe, 2001, p.3).

Rather than using the context of HIV/AIDS as an opportunity for youths to engage critically with the world around them we end up adding

> HIV/AIDS as another reason to fear their sexuality, to delay it, to be ashamed of it and worst to be covert about it, trapped into a world view that condemns rather than one that celebrates difference and identity, rather than one that debates and challenges, rather than one that openly and honestly looks at this epidemic and how it is our construction of it as much as how we behave that is creating the crisis. (Crewe, 2001, p.4)

Crewe (2001, p.7) concludes by arguing that only when we get young people to debate AIDS as a socially, culturally, economically, politically fascinating reflection of our times will we be able to unlock the fascination of identity construction and construct 'new patterns of understanding and new possibilities for a creative and dynamic future in which HIV/AIDS is an integral part, but a part that carries hope and not despair'. We need to engage youth in current debates around HIV/AIDS, as this process will enable youths to reflect on the way in which wider social systems, like cultural and economic systems, are impacting on their sexual identities.

Embodying sexual identity

The work of Crewe (2001) also points to the fact that we need to talk more openly and honestly with youths about their sexual experiences. This requires more than telling them information and providing them with facts; it involves providing young people with a forum in which they can speak openly, honestly and directly about their bodies' biological development and their sexual experiences. This should include an exploration of the way in which young peoples' identities are constructed and would involve discussing with youths the different sources of information that inform their sexual identity and have important implications for their potential negotiation of safe sex. This would include opening up discussions about the messages they receive from home, from their peer groups and popular culture and how this matches up to or contradicts their actual experiences.

Holland et al (1992) highlight that it is important to explore the influence of personal pressures, social pressures and gendered pressures on one's sexual behaviour. Personal pressures are incorporated into the way in which an individual conceives, organises and understands their own sexual pleasure. Social pressure emanates from the cultural and institutional contexts within which young people are located: family, peer, mass media, and culture, for example. Gendered pressures refer to those pressures that are experienced in terms of young peoples' expectations and understandings of what it is to be a sexually active male or female. The work of Holland et al focuses on pressures coming directly from men, but it is argued that it is important (if not essential) to explore the gendered expectations young men and women have of themselves and each other around sexual behaviour.

Burns (2002, p.6), in her commentary on a conference focussed on gender equity in African schools in the context of HIV/AIDS, summarises the keynote addresses by Dr Kirumura and Dr Welbourn as a call to recognise that for interventions to be more successful, young women and men need to be allowed to be 'protagonists on the path to pleasure, pain and personhood'. She goes on to argue that despite these urgings the discourses around sexuality during the conference risked reducing sexuality to 'a model of heterosexual interpenetrative missionary-style rapid coupling' (2002, p.8). This concern is followed with a bold set of questions: 'Why, many asked, was there not more talk of the range of sexual pleasures? Of the historical and ethnographic knowledge of sexuality across time and space? Of inter-cultural sex pleasures (*ukusoma*)? Of sucking and licking and masturbation? Of same-sex pleasure and pitfalls, as well as heterosexual challenges and pleasures? Of dreams and dramas of the self?' (Burns, 2002, p.8). This commentary by Burns (2002) highlights the way in which HIV interventions tend to (re)produce and reinforce very narrow constructs of sexual behaviour. Despite talking about sex, many interventions fail to move beyond the boundaries of heterosexual intercourse. Many fail to talk about the sets of complex interpersonal negotiations that take place around sexual interactions. Many fail to talk about bodily pleasures and sexual desire. Almost all fail to acknowledge the possibility of homosexual practices, or sexual practices that fall outside of socially accepted practices. Why? Perhaps out of an unfounded fear that if adults talk so openly with youths they will be encouraging them to become sexually active. Such a view is informed by beliefs that the adolescent's body is 'awash with hormones and physical changes that outstrip psychological maturity (e.g. moral and intellectual reasoning capacities, emotional stability, etc.)' (Wilbraham, 2002, p.6). In this way youths are rarely prepared for the intricacies and variations of sexual relations and are often forced to learn through trial and error. This suggests that the work of sex researchers and psychologists of human sexual development need to be drawn into the HIV/AIDS debate more fully.

Spaces for dialogue and discussion

The question that remains to be answered is how do we go about creating safe opportunities to 'disrupt' young adults' sense of self as fixed and stable? How do we promote moments in which they can engage with fascination with HIV/AIDS? How can we encourage open and comfortable opportunities for young people to reflect on their sexual development and identity? My own experience of supervising HIV/AIDS research using focus groups provides a possible answer. I have supervised two sets of research that involved students running focus groups with school learners and undergraduate university students. In addition I have trained undergraduate students to run discussion groups with school learners as a community outreach project. My experience of these groups is that they provided excellent opportunities for young people to engage in a process of deconstruction, reconstruction and construction of their understanding of their location within the HIV/AIDS epidemic. The relational nature of sexual identity construction became apparent as these youths engaged in discussion with each other and a facilitator (of a similar age and background). Green and Hart (1999, p.24) argue that focus groups provide opportunities for participants to 'obtain immediate feedback on their own views and constructions of reality, as their stories are challenged, corroborated or marginalised by their peers. Peers provide an appropriate audience for the "stories" which are told about accidental occurrences, and which are less likely to be told in individual interviews'. Through this process young people gain more insight into how they perceive themselves as sexual and social beings and are given a forum in which their voices and stories are validated and taken seriously.

It is suggested that while engaging in the focus groups the learners became more aware of the way in which systems, like cultural and economic systems, were impacting on their sexual behaviour. The Indian learners, for example, became more aware of the way in which religious institutions (or beliefs) were likely to impact on HIV infection rates. They highlighted the way in which religious ways of understanding have prevented religious leaders and parents from talking about sexual behaviour (Frizelle and King, 2002). This was confirmed recently when a group of honours students in psychology approached numerous Indian university students and invited them to be part of a focus group on campus that aimed to understand youths' sexual behaviour. The honours students were perplexed as to why none of the students they had approached would agree to be part of the groups until one of them asked an Indian student why he did not want to join. His response was that 'you just don't talk about those things'. This experience serves to confirm just how effective the focus group is in creating opportunities for young people to engage in a process of critical reflection and social construction. While the university students would not *volunteer* to talk about sex in a focus group scenario, those youths at the predominately Indian school who had been given *permission* by their principal to join a focus group exploring the same issue, engaged in the process enthusiastically and expressed gratitude for the opportunity to do so (Frizelle and King, 2002).

It is therefore suggested that an effective intervention with youth would be to comprehensively train young facilitators to run discussion groups with young people. These facilitators should be of a similar age and background to youths they are working with. They should have comprehensive knowledge and information about HIV/AIDS and other sexually transmitted diseases, but the primary aim of the discussion groups should *not* be about giving youths facts. The groups should be about facilitating a process in which young people are given the opportunity to engage meaningfully and critically with issues like sexual behaviour and the social epidemic of HIV/AIDS. The facilitators need to be trained to encourage youths, during these discussions, to reconstruct the way they perceive themselves, to develop positive uncertainty and to open up for exploration, the way in which the wider social systems around them impact on their lives and decisions. They should be given the opportunity to ask questions and to talk about often avoided topics like sexual desire and pleasure.

In order to create such spaces for dialogue and discussion, facilitators will need to be trained in participatory learning approaches. Campbell (2003) points out that despite changing educational approaches in South Africa, many youths are still largely exposed to (and used to) didactic teaching methods, which undermine autonomy or critical thinking by the youths.

Many may ask how this idea is different to the idea of peer educators. Peer education groups are modelled around well-informed peers of the *same age* and from the same community or school talking among themselves in an unstructured way about sexual behaviour and HIV/AIDS. This is becoming an increasing popular form of intervention within the South African context. However, recent research by Campbell (2003) has highlighted a number of concerns with the peer education model. In her evaluation of a peer education programme Campbell (2003) found that although youths had been taught participatory methods of learning they did not have enough previous experience with the approach and therefore tended to drift to the more familiar method of didactic methods. In addition, youths had not been given enough time to develop critical thinking skills and therefore were often not able to use participatory methods to initiate critical discussion. Most peer educators tended to rely on passing on facts as this was easier and more in line with their own experiences.

In contrast, discussion groups aim to provide a semi-structured environment, within which young people can be given the space to talk openly and spontaneously about the issues that concern them. This will require using slightly older facilitators who have been more thoroughly trained in the area of participatory methods and who have therefore had experience in creating opportunities for generating critical discussion. The difficulty with HIV/AIDS interventions is that the facilitators will need to balance fact-giving with the desire to create a space for unstructured discussion that is directed by the issues raised by the participants. Achieving this balance is crucial to the success of these groups. While it is of utmost importance that myths and inaccurate knowledge about the disease be disrupted, it is also crucial that the participants do not feel lectured by the facilitators. In this way the task of the facilitator is a complex and difficult one that requires thorough training. It is therefore suggested that the groups be run by someone a few years older, more experienced and well-trained than the participants while still providing the opportunity for addressing certain issues with someone of a similar age (Frizelle and King, 2002).

The significance of this difference lies in the warnings by social scientists that suggest that peer education runs the risk of reproducing unequal gender relations. Campbell (2001) warns that males tend to dominate many peer education scenarios while women feel reluctant or unable to assert themselves. In her recent evaluation of a peer education programme Campbell (2003) found that the relationships between the peer educators served as a microcosm of the same gender relations that often contribute to unsafe sex. So while it is important to acknowledge the ability of youth to engage critically with these ideas, it is also important not to assume that all young people will necessarily have the level of skills or insights that are required to engage other youths in critical thinking. In addition, they may not yet have the ability to critically reflect on their own gendered positions and therefore be unable to challenge ideas around gender relations that may arise during the discussions.

Conclusion

There is a need to pay closer attention to social interactions in the context of HIV/AIDS (Leclerc-Madlala, 2002). We need to explore in more detail the social negotiations that occur at the individual level, but we also need to explore more closely the way in which wider contextual factors may or may not inform people's responses to the epidemic. As Leclerc-Madlala (2002) suggests, a false security is currently being generated by the media-hyped prospect of mass-scale, anti-AIDS treatments and hope for a vaccine. It is crucial to consider how political and social changes like these will impact on the way in which people choose to behave during the HIV/AIDS epidemic. For example, do young people take seriously the risk of HIV infection when they are being given a false sense of security of anti-AIDS treatments? How does the way in which President Mbeki's questioning of the link between HIV and AIDS (Walker, Reid and Cornell, 2004) influence young peoples' understanding of their risk of infection?

These are issues that are often not discussed or debated with the person on the street; in particular they are seen as 'above' the mental capacities of our youths. It is argued that these issues are interesting and can initiate opportunities for exciting debate amongst the youth of South Africa. As Crewe (2001) has argued, it is only when we open up these social interactions and processes for exploration and debate that we are likely to bring about substantial and meaningful behaviour change. This paper has consistently argued that before effective interventions for youths can be developed, prevalent and pervasive ideas about youth need to be challenged. It is argued that youths *are* capable of being engaged in meaningful discussion and debate about their perceived risk of HIV infection and their location within the epidemic.

It is crucial that those involved in the design of interventions move away from frameworks that construct youths as always vulnerable and in need of constant and close monitoring, supervision and direction, towards a model that accepts that youths are capable of developing a greater sense of personal agency. Interventions that help youths accept and anticipate change and ambiguity will be helpful in preparing them to deal with the multiple and diverse situations they are likely to find themselves in. Rather than seeing the need to be consistent, youths should be encouraged to anticipate the contextually driven nature of human behaviour and in this way become less afraid of the struggle and tensions that characterise the process of identity construction.

In sum, we need to explore ways in which we can use HIV/AIDS to create a platform 'for more thoughtful, less pompous, and less self-righteous discourses and examinations of sexual personalities, avoiding the false pieties warned about in the work of scholars from Freud and his late twentieth-century re-interpreters, to scholars of Foucault' (Burns, 2002, p.8).

References

Burns, C. (2002). 'A commentary on the colloquium: Instituting gender equality in schools: Working in an HIV/AIDS environment'. *Agenda* 53: 6-10.
Burr, V. (1995). *An introduction to social constructionism*. London: Routledge.
Campbell, C. (2001). 'HIV/AIDS research in South Africa: developing theory through action for action'. Key note address at the AIDS in context conference, University of Witwatersrand, Johannesburg.
Campbell, C. (2003). *Letting them die: Why HIV/AIDS prevention programmes fail*. Cape Town: Double Storey Books.
Calhoun, C. (1995). *Critical social theory: Culture, history and the challenge of difference*. Oxford: Blackwell.
Crewe, M. (2001). *Mythologies and crisis*. Paper presented at the National Union of Educators Conference, Cape Town.
Dorrington, R., D. Bourne, D. Bradshaw, R. Laubscher and I. M. Timaeus (2001). *The Impact of HIV/AIDS on adult mortality in South Africa*. Pretoria: Burden of Disease Research Unit, South African Medical Research Council.
Dorrington, R. and L. Johnson (2002). 'Epidemiological and demographic'. Gow, J. and C. Desmond (eds). *Impacts and interventions: The HIV/AIDS epidemic and the children of South Africa*. Pietermaritzburg: University of Natal Press. Pp 13-57.
Frizelle, K. and J. King (2002). 'Learning through action: University students input into HIV interventions'. *AIDS Bulletin* (December): 10-12.
Gelatt, H. B. (1989). 'Positive uncertainty. A new decision making framework for counselling'. *Journal of Counselling Psychology*. 36: 252-256.

Green, J. and L. Hart (1999). 'The impact of context on data'. Barbour, R. S. and J. Kitzinger (eds). *Developing focus group research. Politics, theory and practice*. London: Sage. Pp 22-35.

Holland, J., C. Ramazanoglu, S. Sharpe and R. Thompson (1992). *Pressured pleasure: Young women and the negotiation of sexual boundaries*. Women Risk AIDS Project: Paper 7. London: Tufnell Press.

Leclerc-Madlala, S. (in press). 'On the virgin cleansing myth: Gendered bodies, AIDS and ethno-medicine'. *African Journal of AIDS Research*. Vol.1.

MacPhail, C. (1998). 'Adolescents and HIV in developing countries: New research directions'. *Psychology in Society*. 24: 69-87.

Mugabe, M. (2001). *Social, cultural and historical factors that should inform HIV/AIDS interventions and policy in South Africa: The role of social science research*. Paper presented at the 'AIDS in context' conference, University of Witwatersrand, Johannesburg.

Samuels, A. (1989). *The Plural Psyche: personality, morality and the father*. London: Routledge.

Samuels, A. (2001). *Politics on the couch: Citizenship and the internal life*. New York: Other Press.

Shilling, C. (1993). *The body and social theory*. London: Sage Publications.

Shisana, O. (Principal Investigator). (2002). 'Nelson Mandela/HSRC study of HIV/AIDS'. Cape Town: Human Sciences Research Council.

Walker, L., G. Reid, M. Cornell (2004). *Waiting to happen: HIV/AIDS in South Africa*. Cape Town: Double Storey Books.

Whitside, A. and C. Sunter (2000). *AIDS: The challenge for South Africa*. Tafelberg: Human and Rousseau.

Wilbraham, L. (2002). 'Parents talking to youth about sex and AIDS: Some problems with health and education materials'. *AIDS Bulletin* (December). 6-9.

Wyn, J. and R. White (1997). *Rethinking youth*. London: Sage Publications.

Professionals becoming researchers
Collective engagement and difficulties of transformation

Lise Bird, Sue Cornforth, Duane Duncan, and Shirley Roberson[1]

his paper canvasses some of the dilemmas faced by a cross-disciplinary group of researchers influenced by post-structural, feminist, and queer studies questions. Our research centred on our professional practice in the areas of youth violence, educational psychology, counselling ethics, and geography teaching. Each of us was committed to exploring possibilities for 'transformative' research relevant for our practice, but questions about its purposes and possible transgressions contributed in different ways to a collective sense of unease. We reached some consensus about transformative research as being attuned to political sensitivities, often including a Foucauldian critique of disciplinary knowledges, and leading to a reflexive engagement with ethics as well as a commitment to collaborative process. The paper indicates aspects of this collegial work in our quest for new insights into the complexities of research that purports to be transformative while at the same time sensitive both to its specific location and to wider ethical implications.

'Transformative' is no longer a dirty word in psychological research. Research that might consider its own political implications, even in seeking some 'catalytic' validity (Lather, 1986), is achieving greater acceptability in social research. The quasi-canonical *Handbook of Qualitative Research* (Denzin and Lincoln, 2000) makes over thirty references to transformation, albeit from a disparate array of methodological traditions. Research with 'transformative' aims has become a central concern in critical psychology, in contrast to traditional psychological research methods through most of the twentieth century (cf. Coolican, 1994). 'Transformative' research has had a longer period of acceptance in education (e.g. Connell, 1980).

Difficulties in defining transformative research were a major concern of our cross- disciplinary 'discourse group'. This group, inspired by the Manchester (UK) Discourse Unit, grew from a Foucauldian reading group of current and former thesis students of the first author to a more collegial grouping as we lived together through various life-altering events, such as redundancy, bereavement, leaving the discipline of psychology for education, leaving the discipline of education for sociology (N.B. not the same person), or returning to primary school teaching. The group, initially a larger collective of ten, met fortnightly over three years. We encompassed thirty years' difference in age, and a range of sexual orientations, backgrounds, genders, workplaces, and countries of origin, though all of us could claim membership of the dominant (European) cultural group in Aotearoa New Zealand.

Over time the group's explorations led each of us to question previously unproblematic transformative goals in our own research. We found the group an important source of support in dealing with ethically sensitive issues that arose in particular settings, e.g. in research about counselling and therapeutic practice that claims expertise in both transformation and responsiveness. We also wanted to be more spontaneously open to transformative opportunities that could arise during a research project.

Transformation and political sensitivity are, after all, respectively founded on influence and a flexible relationship with confidentiality. Who, if anyone, has the right to cause change for another person? When, and for what purpose, should privately collected material be made public? We struggled with defining our ethical obligations in the research encounter, preferring not to discharge our responsibilities simply through adherence to a set of code-based rules. Such a view of ethical rules as formulaic and finite has been termed 'deontological' (see Schwandt, 2000); that is, based on abstracted, universal moral principles. In our view, any human encounter becomes a new ethical engagement.

As events arose that threatened to derail research through litigation or despairing self-doubt, our view of ethics/practice became more intertwined. As Neiman (2002) notes, wherever the 'is' and 'ought' (the research encounter and its transformative possibilities) come together in the judgement that 'this ought not to have happened', we are at the point 'at which ethics, and metaphysics, epistemology and aesthetics meet, collide and throw up their hands' (p.4). This is uncharted ground.

The creation of this written text was a long process only partly reflected in the chorus of voices here marshalled into a coherent narrative. The reflections we offer may be helpful for others involved in research by and with professionals, since new possibilities emerged from our sharing of hopes and difficulties. We present some key dilemmas we faced, territorialised (Deleuze and Guattari, 1987) into sites such as 'ethics' and 'sensitivity' that map onto major uses of the word 'transformation' in qualitative research. Before we present our separate dilemmas, however, we start with some of the big questions with which we began.

'Transformative' research

There are various definitions of transformative research. Such research often questions taken-for-granted social structures. According to Kincheloe and McLaren (2000, p.291), 'Inquiry that aspires to the name critical must be connected to an attempt to confront the injustice of a particular society or public sphere within the society. Research thus becomes a transformative endeavour unembarrassed by the label political and unafraid to consummate a relationship with emancipatory consciousness'. Many in our group liked this approach, with its language both clear-headed and virile. Transformation is unproblematic in this view, since there is an assumed consensus about oppressive social structures and some guide to the right steps needed to overcome them. There were times when we were prepared to follow such a standpoint, for example in support of therapists who advocate for children in sexual abuse cases.

Though each of us drew on different theoretical genealogies, the work of Foucault was a common thread. Foucault argued that critique 'should be an instrument for those who fight, those who resist and refuse what is' (Foucault, 2000, p.236). His early writings gave us heart in both opposing postmodern relativism and questioning foundational truth claims. We all concurred with Foucault's often-described aim 'to generate doubt and discomfort, and to help stimulate a wider process of reflection and action leading to other and more tolerable ways of thinking and acting' (Gordon, 2000, p.xvii). A central transformative task for several of us was the goal of challenging the mainstream disciplinary practices of psychology and geography. Such approaches have a long genealogy in feminist work (e.g. Oleson, 2000), and in critiques of 'positivist psychology' that no longer require continual justification (e.g. Fox and Prilleltensky, 1997). There are also extensive feminist and cultural critiques in geography (e.g. Bondi et al, 2002). On the other hand, we recognised a tendency to create something of a straw person in this interpellation of a misogynist ogre into traditional disciplines. Once we began to discuss specific research problems, the supposed certainties of our cross-disciplinary standpoints began to blur.

Foucault's writings describe transformative action as a likely consequence of critique. At the same time the writings indicate scepticism about ultimate solutions, leaning towards multiple possibilities. Questions of action moved us even further, as we goaded ourselves to move beyond the moral high ground of a marginal disciplinary position to consider future possibilities for change. We saw change as more than opposition to the status quo, or the relativism of the endless new; transformative change also seemed to us to imply change in a 'positive' direction, towards betterment of conditions for a group of people. We were mindful that poststructural sceptics (e.g. Lyotard, 1984) might argue for multiple viewpoints on transformation, since positive change, like good mental health and social justice, may have various, contested meanings. Defining an action as positive might be contingent upon a particular local/socio-historical setting (Foucault, 1980). Our mental health professionals brought things back to earth by arguing that a more encompassing view of transformation would include its own contradictions. Change might not always be positive, but it could still create movement to make a difference; even discomfort and disturbance could be transformative. There might then be no ultimate arbiter of the effect of this change, though there might be a series of people and institutions that pronounce on its success (e.g. outcomes-based research, or participants' views a decade later).

While acknowledging the pleasures of critique, alluded to above, we also recognised the dangers involved in labelling research 'transformative'. In traditional experimental study in psychology that adheres to a particular vision of 'scientific method', the researcher attempts to control the 'subject's' experience, while the world outside the laboratory is assumed to be a neutral void. One of us recalls suggesting at an Australian conference that children's performances in cognitive studies were made possible by many wider socio-cultural, historical, political and practical factors, such as electrical workers' provision of light and heat for the experimental setting (Bird, 1988). These comments were described as 'new-age' by a sceptical member of the audience. To speak of research as having 'transformative' goals in such a setting and at such a time was risky professionally. More recently, another of us (SR) was troubled by feedback from the university's human ethics committee that suggested that her strategies for attending to the needs of research participants were a form of therapy, and therefore inappropriate to the research setting. Indeed the strategies were seen by the committee (but not by our group) as potentially unethical because they risked confusing therapy and research for participants.

These discussions brought us to the crux of our desire for and fear of transformation. We were confronted with the idea that, just as it is not possible to know in advance the causal sequence that might follow an action of transformative research, it would never be possible to predetermine an outcome. A researcher may be caught between, first, the intellectual rigours of questioning different standards of evaluation (thus re-presenting Lyotard's urgent ethical concern that to 'enforce a rule in a *différend* is to enforce the rule of one discourse or the other, resulting in a wrong suffered by the party whose rule of discourse is ignored'[Nuyen, 1998, p.175]) and, second, deciding to take steps to make something different.

Despite postmodern sensibilities that made us squeamish about action for change as potentially arrogant or deluded, we stuck to a standpoint of sorts, a consensus about wanting to forego the pleasures of certainty tied to a deontological position (i.e. based on an abstract moral code). We did not want simply to decry the narrow positivism of traditional empirical research in our various disciplines, or assert a monothetic programme for change that hides its own foundational claims, and hence is inevitably exclusive to its other. For an object or practice to be 'transformed' implies an originary object, which must become separated (excluded) from its future existence (as an improved object). This creates a dualism of the object and its surplus or 'other'. Derrida (1994) has pointed to the inevitable contamination each member of such a pair has with its other half. If it is a person that is being 'transformed', such labelling invites a rational, objectivist, cause-effect view that considers people as unified and coherent agents that can be 'improved'. This suggests that such a person (or social institution) was faulty or unacceptable in his or her pre-change form. This raises another danger of transformative research, an issue of momentous concern in Foucault's work: hidden normative assumptions. Only by disrupting norms might it become possible to consider meanings previously unseen or unheard in everyday conversation and social practice. We did not want to seek a single alternative possibility for transformation that might produce another oppressive – though alternative – norm.

For some members of the group a sense of helplessness and despair was felt after so much discussion of transformation. More than one person wondered if we had deconstructed the term 'transformative' into meaninglessness. An end result of continual deconstruction has often been a criticism of the perceived relativism of postmodernism (Lather, 1991). Yet, despite the potential difficulties of a normative concept of transformation, useful change may be possible.

Our different approaches to 'transformation'

Research has implications, material effects: research matters. Questioning normative conceptions of the term 'transformation' led the group to turn a critical lens back on itself towards the assumptions underpinning our respective research projects. We had disparate hopes of the (r)evolutionary potential of research. For most of us, the very notion of transformation was problematic; too embedded in narrow disciplinary paradigms to offer any possibility of change. We had key divisions from the start; while some were interested in changing disciplinary norms and practices, others were more interested in the here-and-now research setting, e.g. facilitating positive change for participants.

One particularly cogent and recognisable trope in the language of research objectives is the 'contribution to a project of disciplinary change'. For some members of the group, rather than attempting change for others through research, the act of research can contribute to a deconstruction and diversification of dominant conceptions, understandings, and practices. Such research tends to be cross-disciplinary, involving multiple researchers, theories, and methodologies. The exact parameters of such a project cannot be defined, and thus the authority of any particular research endeavour is subject to a wider cross-disciplinary form of ethical regulation. For many of us, the aim was to shift the goalposts of acceptable knowledge. For example, the psychologist/social worker (SR) wanted to challenge the traditional, scientific approach to 'youth violence' through a consideration of wider cultural practices that reinscribe violence in the performance of normative New Zealand masculinity. The geographer (DD) wanted to challenge the same disciplinary protocols that maintain 'earth sciences' as a hard, objective field. The counsellor/psychotherapist (SC) wanted to interrogate the philosophical foundations of her profession and territorial assumptions about the nature of praxis. The educational psychologist (LB) wanted to problematise that field's lingering hopes for psychological acceptability and its stereotyping as atavistic scientism within education.

We often discussed the loud voice of the dominant disciplinary perspective, at its least an internal whisper that challenged any 'thinking otherwise'. This metaphoric disturbance created resistances in our attempts to position our work outside dominant frameworks, to become 'other' to the discourses under scrutiny. Instead, participants felt invited into a space where a valorising of deontological ethics made culpable individual selves, as if we had failed to perform our ethical duty. In this sense, ethical consideration could be employed as a self-surveillance to prevent the troubling of taken-for-granted knowledges.

Some of us experienced an alienating and intimidating engagement with institutional ethics committees. In New Zealand, most universities rely on somewhat obscure, medically benchmarked binary codes (e.g. research participation must be described as 'anonymous'/'not anonymous', a challenging feat in a country of four million people). The regulation of our research through these processes necessitated the assimilation of our respective voices into the disciplinary fold, remapping us into 'legitimate' constructions of knowledge with expected paradigms. According to these regulatory processes, alternative, critical methods produce illegitimate knowledge. For example, one member's expertise in counselling/therapy was a criterion for ethical approval of the research, yet that person was required to ensure that such expertise would not be used in any research interview. Instead, the interviewer was expected to maintain an objective, scientific (neutral) manner in order to elicit objective (normative) responses from participants. The ethical requirement implied that the counsellor/therapist doing research might be tempted to winkle unconscious secrets from unsuspecting interviewees. Such a passive view of participants leaves little room for an engaged, responsive interaction with the interviewer, surely limiting possibilities of transformation for either researcher or participant. The ethical requirement also suggested that possibilities for change are acceptable only at the analysis stage of research, i.e.

removed from any possible taint of involvement by participants. This dominant deontological perspective seems at odds with more post-structural accounts of ethics as an encounter with the face of the other, which requires a response and a relationship of respectful communication (e.g. Peperzak, 1993). We continue to 'walk the line' on such ethical issues in several projects.

Within the group there was a desire to resist the impetus in dominant, positivist research practices to define problems and impose solutions on individuals and communities. Yet, simultaneously, we hoped that our own research practices would not devolve into a relativistic 'do-nothing-for-fear-of-doing-wrong' position. We were especially wary of the possibility of being co-opted back into reproducing and validating the status quo, thereby silencing emerging uncertainties. From this location we tried to create new possibilities for engaging in research with transformative aims, though the group had contradictory views about ways to achieve this. For example, the youth violence researcher (SR) did not consider the critical feminist research aim of 'empowering' participants to be ethically sound, or particularly transformative, when applied to interviews with young men about their criminal violence. A project to increase the self-esteem of a young rapist would raise inevitable questions about its potential for cultural transformation, e.g. for reducing societal violence. She considered that change for others might be possible through disciplinary change influenced by considering the power/knowledge nexus within relevant discourses.

The notion of contributing to a wider 'project' of disciplinary change sent chills down the spines of many of us, as if what was once unspeakable would now shout in the light shone over it by 'the disciplinary change project'. In some cases, for instance regarding 'child abuse', 'exposure' of disciplinary collusion was viewed as having encouraging transformative possibilities, e.g. protecting a child's right to privacy and confidentiality. Though, as we discovered in our reflecting on our own professional regulation, what might seem to be positive in one sense might also close down opportunities for alternative positive experiences: e.g. the right to privacy can be used to protect a perpetrator of abuse, thus enabling the abuse to continue. Speaking this 'unspeakability' could lead to professional suicide.

Rather than trying to avoid the discomfort of experiences of regulation, we used the group to explore the ways in which our researcher selves were being conditioned to produce ethically limited research outcomes. The result of this was an identification of what we considered ethics to be, and part of that definition included the possibility that the dominant voice regulating our research practice might not be 'right'. The provision of a space for discussing that dilemma with colleagues facilitated a much more profound sense of ethical care than the ethics code, with its focus on individual researcher responsibility, had allowed.

We all concurred with the view that when researcher and participant meet face to face, ethics become a crucial part of the encounter.

> The other's face (i.e., any other's facing me) or the other's speech (i.e., any other's speaking to me) interrupts and disturbs the order of my, ego's, world; it makes a hole in it by disarraying my arrangements without ever permitting me to restore the previous order. For even if I kill the other or chase the other away in order to be safe from the intrusion, nothing will ever be the same as before. (Peperzak, 1993, p.20)

The face of the other, when no longer an object, demands a response and an ethical responsibility. In this way, Seurich (1997) notes, the recognition of the other is both ontological and epistemological in constituting 'both who the problem group is and how the group is seen or known as a problem' (p.107). As Lowenthal and Snell (2001, p.23) write, 'if ethics is defined as putting the other first, as Levinas, the French phenomenological philosopher, defines it, then this is what all relationships should strive towards'. The group concurred that the loud voice of the dominant disciplinary perspective could sometimes appear as an internal voice challenging any 'thinking otherwise'. This metaphoric disturbance created resistances in our attempts to position our work outside dominant frameworks, to become other to the discourse under scrutiny. Ethical relationship was a key element of our research. Yet our research was sometimes criticised as unethical from the dominant perspective. This demand for consistency, neutrality, and objectivity had a disempowering effect on our research and required constant monitoring, if we were to foreground the other.

We were mindful of Seurich's (1997) suggestion that taking a position of individual responsibility, that is, responding to internal governmentality rather than to the face of the Other, may have the effect of lessening the social impact of the work we do. He suggests that a focus on individual ethical practices may allow institutions to go unchallenged. Thus ethical codes may become the technology for controlling the professional subject within a less obvious operation of power. He also argues that the focus on individual ethical performance may act to keep public documents away from scrutiny. The place of ethics in institutional practices can thus be seen, as it was experienced by us, as ambivalent. We struggled to resist an ethical self-monitoring in favour of re-cognition, re-spect and re-thinking. Each contributor to this paper sought solutions that were both potentially transformative and sensitive to possibilities of harm in the research situation.

The ideal researcher

The group attempted to visualise our various goals and dilemmas as a way to clarify our different views of transformative research. We shared a common vision of the 'ideal' Foucauldian-influenced researcher as both politically aware/committed and poststructurally savvy, but the ethical issues referred to above affected our projects in different ways. We used a drawing exercise to allow each person to articulate a vision of the ideal(ly sensitive, transformative) researcher. Our geographer (DD) had used this method to encourage research participants (secondary school teachers) to reflect on the ways in which their bodies – their dress, appearance (e.g. hair, piercings), and behaviour (expressive or 'closeted') – might be in conflict or tension with their stated professional identities. Such an exercise can prompt discussion of sensitive and sometimes taboo issues. For example, Duncan's (2002) research with drawings led teachers to wider discussion of the ways in which their bodies, identities, and selves are regulated by unspoken or unacknowledged power relations. Drawings allow the interplay of a multitude of tensions, contradictions, positionings, and perspectives. In a picture it is possible for a body to 'be' in two places at once.

After the drawing exercise, we analysed our differing drawings, creating a shared space to embrace the polyvocality of our contradictions. One person (SC) drew the ideal researcher as a moving entity of six heads on rubbery necks, each looking in a different direction with a different facial expression, grounded to the earth with sturdy boots, indicating the importance of steady grounding in (or despite) muddy, everyday realities. Elongated arms reached out from the researcher to make connections with other arms and hands reaching in from off the page –literally reaching out in all directions to connect with diverse others. At the centre of the picture, between heads and boots, was a big, red, beating heart, showing the counsellor-as-researcher putting care (love) and emotion at the centre of enquiry. This pointed to the complexities involved in research deconstructively reflecting on professional ethics (e.g. NZAC, 2004), a task requiring sensitivity towards all the people connected through these codes, and reminding the researcher not to get overly enamoured with deconstructive theoretical analyses.

A second drawing (by DD) also put a stylised red heart at the centre, this time in the middle of a recognisable body with a question mark above its head. As in the first drawing, the feet were firmly on the ground, though one foot was slightly raised on a box inscribed with the words 'doing it carefully, meaning not to offend anyone'. This was a reference to some of the difficulties involved in finding research participants who felt 'safe' enough to discuss appearance/presentation/sexuality issues in a school setting (Duncan, 2002). This researcher was able to find participants only after approaching teachers' union contacts, since there were hardly any responses to requests via posters and a science education newsletter. Apparently the topic was one few teachers were prepared to discuss, perhaps not surprising given the sort of surveillance teachers are currently under regarding covert sexual expression and touching in the classroom (Jones, 2001). The drawing also held more text, with questions posed directly for the viewer at either side; one of these queried just who was to be transformed by the research: '… outcome/change? empowerment? Me? Them? us?'

Another researcher's drawing reflected not so much an ideal as the difficulty of finding one. In a drawing entitled, 'the student as researcher', this therapist portrayed the thesis-researcher as a cross-eyed clown with open mouth, like one of a row of wooden clown-heads in a circus sideshow, where people attempt to win a prize by throwing balls into the mouths moving from side to side. Underneath the clown's head were different possible theoretical stances for the research including 'Foucault', 'psychoanalysis', and 'feminism', with a line of 'clinical practice' supporting all the different possibilities. This drawing showed the contradictions involved in choosing one theoretical standpoint that might exclude important issues of practice, and perhaps showed some feeling of nihilistic relativism that can face the researcher unsure how to juggle the demands of the academy and potentially opposing community concerns, while acknowledging respect for clinical experience.

The head of the researcher featured in another drawing (by SR), which had small smiling faces of participants nearby. A large eye gazed at a thick line behind which could be seen a colourful melee of faces of the research audience displaying mixed reactions, including pleasure, disturbance, concern, perplexity, and anger. This drawing explored the difficulty of producing alternative understandings of an issue such as 'youth violence' (Roberson, 2002) and highlighted the expectation that disturbance/discomfort arises out of critique. Various wiggling lines suggested that ideas and truths generated from research are not linear but move in a variety of directions, whether expected and known or unexpected and unknown. Transformations that might be elicited/provoked were depicted as enabled as well as constrained for the researcher, participants, and the research audience, as boundaries between different discourses blur.

A final drawing (by LB) showed a multi-coloured collection of bodies of researchers, depicted as overlapping body parts in different pastel colours and shapes. One arm at the front held a Maori *kete* (an indigenous woven basket) from which emerged an explosion of flying fragments. The assembled researchers faced towards the 'topic' of the research, issues of human biodiversity, depicted as a large yellow chick next to an egg (chicken/egg) under the erasure of a crossed circle. The *kete* traditionally refers metaphorically to a container for knowledge; here it was meant as a citation of the cover of Chris Weedon's (1987) book showing the exploding handbag of feminist postmodern fragmentation. This researcher's drawing held onto the ontological realism of the integral, contained (knowable) body of the individual researcher, despite the assemblage of heads and arms, because individual bodies in the group depicted were separately identifiable by colour. After viewing the drawings of others – that eschewed individual bodies of researchers – this researcher reflected (with some dismay) on her contradictory desire to reproduce the enlightenment ideal of the (recognisably embodied) 'scientist' producing knowledge through engagement with an 'object' of study.

The drawing exercise helped us to identify the ways in which our imaginations were constrained by disciplinary research practices, encouraging us to reflect on the ways our researcher-selves were regulated to produce intelligible and marketable research-products. We did not end with a consensual, monolithic collage of the ideal transformative researcher. Rather, our contradictory desires became clearer as we questioned the 'project of transformation' and explored the cultural meanings of research that aims to be both post-structurally informed and committed to change.

In reflecting on these drawings, the group considered that the ideal researcher might be in both a fixed and movable position, reaching out, changing, evolving, and transforming through the connections made with other people. The ideal researcher may attempt to achieve shared understandings by seeking out a diverse community of researchers, rather than seeking the position of the independent, isolated explorer. Difficulties may be encountered by the researcher who attempts to be immersed in the viewpoints of others if the researcher's unitary positioning is fragmented in a juxtaposition of multiple subjectivities. While these difficulties may seem desirable in postmodern terms, there may still be disciplinary expectations on the part of the researcher that enable as well as constrain the transformations that might be elicited/provoked. This may be particularly difficult for a researcher positioned between the positivist tradition of a 'home' discipline, a critical, feminist focus on 'empowerment', and poststructural reflexivity.

The articulation of ideals led us to a discussion of dilemmas in respective research projects – opening up moments when what we might desire to achieve gets sucked back into the jet engine of the normal. Transformative research began to seem more of a becoming – in the midst of all the sensitivities – rather than an end-point. Such an emphasis is not on what is ethical and what is not, but on finding ways to hold discussions in those moments when what is ethical is contradictory, before what is difficult becomes lost or denied, and any power for something really exciting and new is reclaimed and colonised by the dominant logic. Creative possibilities were born out of negotiating our research practices in the wake of our ideals, though this process raised dilemmas for all of us.

Dilemmas in conducting 'transformative' research

In our attempts to position our research in a transformative space, we found ourselves facing numerous ethical dilemmas that contradicted our wish to challenge or create change. In discussion, the group claimed those moments when externally imposed definitions of right or wrong created confusion and dejection: when what was rhetorical or unquestioned felt centrally important and 'real' to us. In the interest of the multiple, we highlight several particular dilemmas here.

How ethical, for example, is it for a member of the dominant group to make use of, or interpret, indigenous (Maori) voices? Is it possible to name the excluded without also speaking for the group? Although one researcher did not wish to engage 'the colonising gaze of the heroic other', she wanted the freedom to claim her own position and not allow a silencing through fear of being inappropriate, especially in sensitive areas such as obesity, abuse, and gender.

As the geographer (DD) approached the transgressive territory of desire, emotion, bodies, and sexuality in education, he found himself caught in power relations that invited positioning as banal or perverse. On more than one occasion he had to defend the value and worth of raising questions about what appeared to some in his discipline as immaterial or unnecessary. Defence of his work left the geographer feeling exposed, as if he embodied the 'deviance' he was attempting to question in his work. These tensions raised doubts in the geographer as to his own validity as a researcher, but also strengthened his belief in the merits of trying to transform the ways we speak in the classroom.

The youth violence researcher (SR) experienced a paradigm clash in which institutional ethics committees were caught in a contradictory dualism, using both 'vulnerable' and 'violent' to describe participants. This refused a place to any thinking otherwise. Resisting invitations to join in either objectification, she instead chose to focus on the power relationships that place youth as other to the researcher. Her (Roberson, 2002) critique of such a dualism allowed for the acknowledgement and incorporation of the complexities and contradictions, the uniqueness and fluidity, of real people: a better fit with her professional experience of working with young offenders and survivors of violence.

The developmental/educational psychologist (LB) sought to de-naturalise normative assumptions of educational psychology, which has disciplinary and regulatory powers over students' lives. In order to retain both her own and her participants' presence as subjects and sceptics, she chose to engage a 'double vision', dividing herself in two through the creation of a mock documentary in which her voice is heard both as narrator and as embodied but elusive educational psychologist. Participants then had the chance to question the narrator of the documentary in a group discussion. This performance used recognisable, popular cultural forms to unsettle the normal/ab-normal dualism; it also displayed the powers of psychological knowledge while simultaneously troubling their authority, opening a space to invite new constructions of ethical selves.

There were occasions when researchers experienced a challenge to their own safety or well-being. All of us experienced levels of distress in the planning and conduct of research, suggesting the dangers involved. We used phrases such as 'caused me a great deal of anxiety', being 'buffeted around', 'I was scared', and 'quite a challenge'. For example, in communicating his work to colleagues, staff, the ethics committee, and participants, the geographer went to great lengths to avoid positioning his work with the loaded terms 'sex' and 'sexuality'. At times this strategy left him questioning his own ethics, yet simultaneously laid bare the discomforting effects that the language of bodies and Eros can produce. Our emails to each other wrote of the 'danger of exclusion', 'charges of psychosis or insanity', 'it is a major turn-off to others', e.g. when raising questions of postmodern subjectivities in discussing 'empathy' or 'transference' with counselling colleagues. The statement, 'I was directly experiencing the power of the discourse', describes the position of speaking 'other' to a dominant discourse (in the required responses to an institutional ethics committee) that positioned young people who had been violent as abnormal, dangerous, and troubled.

Interestingly, many of us felt that, insofar as we managed to resist being positioned as other, we became transformed ourselves. This transformation was not as unethical other, but in identification with a different set of power relationships that spoke 'otherwise'. People in the group have changed jobs, countries, professions, and disciplinary homes. Transformed by her struggle, as one person put it, 'Ultimately the dilemma was transformative for me'.

Group process and transformation

We do not mean to present too rosy a view of the group's work here. Over time we have worked on ways to deal creatively and supportively with our differences, though this has not always been easy or successful. We have tried to create a space in which differences are heard and acknowledged, and ways are found to move on together, without creating camps or a false consensus. For example, it was not easy when someone decided to leave the group. We had varying degrees of comfort with post-structural notions of subjectivity, and some contention around the view that such notions might entail loss of authorial voice for people only recently being given room to speak as political beings (e.g. Hartsock, 1987). We were aware of the influence of certain challenging professional debates. For example, Hood's (2001) controversial book, *A City Possessed*, dealing with allegations of sexual abuse in Christchurch, New Zealand, put professional competence under negative scrutiny in the public domain. This offered strong invitations to form different political allegiances. Our failure to reach a consensus, even after attrition of dissident voices, left feelings of uncertainty. The writers continue to reflect on and debate these issues from the diversity of our perspectives.

As one of our members wrote before she left to take up a psychotherapy practice in another part of the country:

> We were all dealing with difficult and often culturally taboo subjects and the expression of our work in a supportive environment helped impart courage and the conviction that 'the unspeakable' could be spoken about without risk to the speaker. Utilising Foucault's unique way of analysing issues to question where we come from, how we make sense of things, or what we can say at any given time, Certeau uses the analogy of cartoon characters walking on thin air: as long as they don't notice that there is nothing beneath them they are fine, but as soon as they notice that they are not on firm ground, they fall into a void. I am indebted to the group for providing the firm ground underneath, as the void at times seemed imminent, and for being there through difficult professional periods and the inevitable periods of isolation involved in thesis writing. (Bird et al, 2002)

Another comment gives further flavour of our group process. One member likes to remind the group of their first meeting, when they mentioned an interest in the topic of childhood masturbation. This person waited with some trepidation for others to respond, and remembers that 'there was a respectful silence, and then a few thoughtful questions. I thought, these are my kind of people! Where else would you get this kind of reaction?'.

The counselling and therapy expertise of several members helped us to maintain sensitivity towards members of the group, especially in times of personal trauma. As was perhaps not surprising, given the group's composition, there was considerable expertise in group facilitation. After our group's presentation to a national education conference (Bird et al, 2002), audience members remarked on the usefulness of the group's critical approach in its potential application to their own work. Several people thanked us for describing difficulties with research that attempts to be transformative, rather than giving a tidy summary of findings with the messy parts edited out.

We began over time to hold and to expand on those moments when possibilities emerged and the ordinary appeared transformed. At the same time there were institutional constraints on us, not least of which was the national regime of tabulating outputs for research by, for example, determining the 'worth' of a publication by dividing it by the number of authors. Another constraint appeared in the guidelines communicated by the university's ethics committee to one researcher in the group (mentioned above), indicating that therapy and research must be separated. In our experience the therapist's expertise strengthened the relationships in the group and in our ethical commitments. Work by one of us (SC) on a deconstructive theoretical analysis of the New Zealand Association of Counsellors (2004) Code of Ethics was greatly influenced by our discussions, particularly of the complex ethical considerations faced by practitioners struggling to meet deontological guidelines while being 'true' to their own understandings of the sensitivities involved in working with participants. Those of us doing field research were also correspondingly challenged and extended by this person's philosophical considerations.

A difficulty that can emerge in a group where much trust has been built up over time is that it becomes more difficult to bring in new members. The group has changed from one open to changed memberships, followed by a period in which there was a majority decision to keep the group closed (i.e. not have new members), and eventually a renewed sense of openness. As members follow jobs and scholarships elsewhere, there has been sadness at change, but also a happier recognition that the intense group-work reflected an important sharing that served its time and will not be forgotten as we all move into new becomings.

The becoming researcher

One aspect of our group process often remarked upon was its capacity to be energising (even if 'energised towards irony', as one member put it), no matter how tired we might have felt before our evening meetings. Knowing that others were happy to share the burden/understandings/responsibilities of being a critical researcher on a similar journey was a great pleasure, as signalled below by our geographer.

> Much of my own work has focused on finding ways to acknowledge and celebrate the pleasure we experience in our professional and working lives. So often that pleasure is deemed inappropriate, even banal, or considered contrary to 'getting the job done'. Within the group, it has

been possible to express the pleasures, the sensations, the passion aroused through the research. The group has facilitated a space for me to acknowledge the excitement that this kind of work produces in, through, and beyond 'me', while the similar passions of others have let me know that I am not alone. Though our discussions have perhaps perpetuated the idea that transformation occurs external to us, at the wave of a hand, or inside us, as a progression or emotional growth, we have tried to avoid the all-knowing, all-seeing researcher of traditional positivist research practice. If we are to counter the political imperative that keeps masculinism in its place of privilege within the academy and beyond, then we must acknowledge that transformation moves through us in ways we cannot fathom or control. For me, the strength and possibility of research communities are in providing a space to acknowledge the pleasures of transformation. The dirty notion of producing change for others is challenged when we engage our 'selves' in group and community practices that deconstruct the certainty of our own singular vision.
(Bird et al, 2002)

As this collaborative research group alters shape, there are a number of positive directions of becoming that we hope may emerge from our collaboration. Many of us experienced resonance with the view of our youth violence researcher:

I can now see that the root of my early dissatisfaction with mainstream psychology was actually with its philosophical foundation. So my dissatisfaction was not something that could be simply fixed by producing more of the same kind of knowledge, as I had originally intended. After much struggle it became clear to me that I could not complete my research within mainstream psychology. Consequently, my research audience has shifted more firmly towards/with other professionals who have an impact on young people who have been violent, whether teachers, police, or residential workers. I also believe that embracing a different paradigm in my research enables me to develop more options in my professional practice than I ever had before. Through my journey so far, particularly with this group, I have a deeper appreciation of diversity and multiple truths and I'm excited by the acceptance of contradictions in myself and in others. My own thinking and development are richer from being exposed to the ideas and questions of others. I believe I am becoming a more critical and aware researcher as a result.
(Bird et al, 2002)

Reflections such as these indicate some of the reflexive work we all did during group meetings, by email, separately and together, both on our research and on the process of creating the research group itself.

This paper has given an 'insider' view of a group of researchers working intensively together over some years to create a space for responsive, reciprocal, and emergent research support. Our focus on finding a way to carry out 'transformative' research led us to engage with ethical issues on a number of planes. We struggled to ensure that we worked with 'safe' collaborative practices, especially when differences among us threatened to send us in opposing directions. Given our commitment to reflexivity and care in our ethical responsibilities, we tried not to smooth our differences over but to recognise our diversity, even when this was uncomfortable, divisive, or unresolved. Though some aspects of similarity (e.g. being critical researchers) may make a group like this easier to come together, it continued to surprise us that we found commonality despite our considerable divergence. We have all, at one time or another, found a sense of belonging in our experience of the multiple (see Peters, 1998).

Note

1. Order of authors is alphabetical. Authorship reflects the commitment of people able to put time into this writing project. We would like to thank everyone in the wider group, including Fiona Beals, Francesca Costa, Deborah Dentice, Carol O'Connor, and Jill Young, for their wisdom and support on the journey.

References

Bird, L. (1988, August). 'Achievement motivation: a feminist critique'. Paper presented to the Australian Developmental Conference, Sydney, Australia.

Bird, L., F. Beals, S. Cornforth, D. Duncan, C. O'Connor and S. M. Roberson (2002, December). *Transformative possibilities for critical and sensitive discourse research*. Paper presented at the New Zealand Association for Research in Education, Massey University, Palmerston North, New Zealand.

Bondi, L. et al (2002). *Subjectivities, knowledges, and feminist geographies: the subjects and ethics of social research*. Lanham, MD: Rowan and Littlefield.

Coolican, H. (1994). *Research methods and statistics in psychology* 2. London: Hodder and Stoughton.

Connell, W. F. (1980). *A history of education in the twentieth-century world*. Canberra, Australia: Curriculum Development Centre.

Deleuze, G. and F. Guattari (1987). *A thousand plateaus: capitalism and schizophrenia*. (Trans. B. Massumi). London: Athlone.

Denzin, N. K. and Y. S. Lincoln (eds). (2000). *Handbook of qualitative research* 2. Thousand Oaks, California: Sage.

Derrida, J. (1994). *Specters of Marx: the state of the debt, the work of the mourning and the new international* (Trans. P. Kamuf). New York: Routledge.

Duncan, D. (2002). *The 'teaching body': a queer geography of New Zealand secondary school teachers' embodiment*. Unpublished Masters of Arts in Geography thesis, Victoria University of Wellington, New Zealand.

Foucault, M. (1980). *The history of sexuality* 1. (Trans. R. Hurley) New York: Vintage Books.

Foucault, M. (2000). 'Questions of method'. Faubian, J. D. (ed.). *Michel Foucault: Power* 3: 223-238. New York: The New Press.

Fox, D. and I. Prilleltensky (eds). (1997). *Critical psychology: an introduction*. London: Sage.

Gordon, C. (2000). 'Introduction'. Faubian, J. D. (ed.). *Michel Foucault: Power* 3: xi – xli. New York: The New Press.

Hartsock, N. (1987). 'Rethinking modernism: minority vs. majority theories'. *Cultural Critique* 7: 187-206.

Hood, L. (2001). *A city possessed: the Christchurch Civic Creche case: child abuse, gender politics and the law*. Dunedin, New Zealand: Longacre Press.

Jones, A. (ed.) (2001). *Touchy subject: teachers touching children*. Dunedin, New Zealand: University of Otago.

Kincheloe, J.L. and P. McLaren (2000). 'Rethinking critical theory and qualitative research'. Denzin, N. K. and Y.S. Lincoln (eds), *Handbook of qualitative research* 2. Thousand Oaks, California: Sage. Pp.279-314.

Lather, P. (1986). 'Issues of validity in openly ideological research: Between a rock and a soft place'. *Interchange* 17(4): 63-84.

Lather, P. (1991). *Getting smart: feminist research and pedagogy with/in the postmodern*. New York: Routledge.

Lowenthal, D. and R. Snell (2001). 'Psychotherapy as the practice of ethics'. Palmer Barnes, F. and L. Murdin (eds). *Values and ethics in the practice of psychotherapy and counselling*. London: Open University. Pp 22-31

Lyotard, J. F. (1984). 'The postmodern condition: a report on knowledge'. (Trans. G. Bennington and B. Massumi). Minneapolis: University of Minnesota.

Neiman, S. (2002). *Evil in modern thought: an alternative history of philosophy*. Woodstock, Oxfordshire: Princeton University Press.

New Zealand Association of Counsellors (2004). 'Code of ethics'. [Available: http://www.nzac.org.nz/ (Date accessed: 26 February)].

Nuyen, A.T. (1998). 'Jean-Francois Lyotard: education for imaginative knowledge'. M. Peters (ed.). *Naming the multiple: poststructuralism and education*. London: Bergin and Garvey.

Oleson, V. L. (2000). 'Feminisms and qualitative research at and into the millennium'. Denzin, N. K. and Y.S. Lincoln (eds), *Handbook of qualitative research* 2: pp.215-256. Thousand Oaks, California: Sage.

Peperzak, A. (1993). *To the other: an introduction to the philosophy of Emmanuel Levinas*. West Lafayette, Indiana: Purdue University.

Peters, M. (1998). *Naming the multiple: poststructuralism and education*. London: Bergin and Garvey.

Roberson, S. M. (2002, May). 'The challenges and implications of researching youth violence using a critical approach'. Paper presented at the 'Health Policy, Practice and Research in the 21st Century: Making a Difference' conference, Auckland, New Zealand.

Schwandt, T. A. (2000). 'Three epistemological stances for qualitative inquiry: interpretivism, hermeneutics, and social constructionism'. Denzin, N. K. and Y. S. Lincoln (eds). *Handbook of qualitative research* 2: 189-214. Thousand Oaks, California: Sage.

Seurich, J. (1997). *Research methods in the postmodern*. London: Falmer.

Weedon, C. (1987). *Feminist practice and poststructuralist theory*. Oxford, UK: Basil Blackwell.

Playing the game
Professionalisation and depoliticisation

Jane Callaghan

his paper analyses extracts from a series of interviews with senior South African women students, exploring accounts of training in psychology. It is part of a larger project, challenging the appropriateness of professionalisation and western models of psychology in the South African context. Using resources from discursive, postcolonial and feminist approaches, and the sociology of the professions, this paper analyses the operation of a discourse of professionalisation. It unpacks the way in which this discourse constructs a linguistic polarisation that renders some aspects of subjectivity as 'professional' and others (the political, the personal) as 'non-professional'. In adopting the identity of 'professional' it becomes necessary to relinquish a range of other subject positions which are regarded as incompatible with the requirements of professionalism. This includes a disavowal of both personal and political affiliations. It is argued that, within professional psychology, political ideas can only be expressed on the periphery (for example, from the ghettoised position of 'community psychologist'). The political and professional psychologist cannot co-exist. The paper articulates some of the discursive cracks in the framework of professionalisation, and makes some suggestions for training practice in South Africa.

Key words: South Africa, applied psychology, political psychology, professional training, professionalisation, depoliticisation.

South African psychology (as expressed through bodies like PsySSA – the Psychological Society of South Africa) has become increasingly preoccupied with professional issues in the period of transformation following the first democratic elections in South Africa. Although lip service is paid to the need to develop an appropriate psychology for South Africa, this organisation has done little to further political engagement between psychology and its context, preferring to focus on organisational restructuring and developing new professional training and categorisation. In this paper, I consider the discourse of professionalisation in psychology training, particularly exploring the ways in which this discourse obscures and militates against social and political engagement.

Psychology in South Africa – A brief history[1]

South African psychology has been in the process of restructuring over the past eleven years. With the demise of the old professional body, The Psychological Association of South Africa (PASA), and of the South African Medical and Dental Council (under whose remit the psychological association functions), it was hoped that psychology would shake off its involvement with the oppressive regime of the past and forge itself anew. PsySSA was created in an environment of optimism as left-wing psychologists, in particular, hoped it would bring a more socially engaged and appropriate form of psychology. This paper, in contrast, starts from the critical position of seeing as central the political engagement of psychologists in South African social life, and the development of psychological theory and practice that enables psychologists to work critically and appropriately in the South African context.

Psychology in South Africa has had a mixed history. It has been argued that psychology's silence on the issue of political oppression during the apartheid years (Dawes, 1985), and its involvement in the pathologisation of black people and culture (Parekh and Jackson, 1998) rendered it complicit with the government. Biesheuwel's (1987) keynote address to the PASA conference epitomises the dominant position of psychology at the time: that political engagement would compromise psychology's objective neutrality and undermine its scientific basis, and was consequently inappropriate. When examining the training and practice of psychologists in South Africa, it is important to examine the philosophical and ideological underpinnings and political effects of the type of psychology that we import or create. The psychology that we teach in departments throughout South Africa is one that has its origins in the north, and which takes as its basic unit of analysis the 'individual'. This concept is not politically unproblematic.

There has been a flurry of significant publications focusing on psychology in and for South African contexts, including books (e.g. de la Rey, 1997, Seedat et al, 2001, Swartz and Gibson, 2002) and special issues of the *South African Journal of Psychology* (*SAJP*, 2001) and *Psychology in Society* (*PINS*, 2003). Despite such initiatives, I would argue that there has been only minimal change in the way in which psychology students are trained, particularly at postgraduate level in applied fields, and the ways in which psychologists in this country practice. The re-curricularisation of psychology training to allow a D Psych and B Psych qualification is being implemented with little apparent consideration (from those driving the changes) of the ways in which these new qualifications might be used in South African public and NGO sectors, or of the kinds of structural changes needed to make them work (for example, the creation of jobs within the public and NGO sectors in which B Psych students might work). A new professional exam (which students must take at the end of their training) has been introduced by the professional board to provide external validation of the qualifications in an attempt to standardise postgraduate applied psychology training. Looking at what is required to pass this exam, with its heavy focus on diagnostic criteria, it becomes clear that the attempts of some academics to refocus South African psychology on its context have not really filtered through to the professional board. While there are examples throughout South Africa of modules within psychology courses that do attempt to address critical and political issues in relation to both theoretical and applied psychology, nonetheless this appears to have little impact on the training and practice of professional psychologists.

Much of the optimism around the construction of a new professional body, PsySSA, was that it promised to provide an organising structure within which psychologists could tackle the difficulties they faced in constructing a more appropriate and socially engaged psychology for South Africa. The increasing preoccupation of this body with 'guild' issues, concerns about parallel qualifications with international organisations, and a focus on questions of professionalisation, has therefore been disappointing to many psychologists committed to the development of socially responsible ways of working.

Professionalisation
The sociology of the professions locates the rise of the idea of professionalism in protectionism and 'guild' concerns (concerns with the

promotion, maintenance, and smooth running of the profession). Johnson (1972) suggested that professional groups create a market and control it to gain status, privilege and legal protection. Typically, professions offer a particular form of esoteric knowledge. The transmission of such knowledge requires lengthy training and close supervision (Etzioni, 1969).

This literature suggests that professionalisation is the process whereby organisations or individuals lay claim to a particular form of recognition (that of expert knower) within a particular social and ideological context (Erant, 2000). The status of a profession depends on its capacity to sustain its position as 'expert'. Variance in the competencies and qualities of individual practitioners presents a challenge to the professional claim of 'expert status'. Licensing and other structures of professional control stabilise this interpersonal variation, bolstering the individual claim to expert knowledge with institutional authority (Friedson, 1983). The legitimacy of 'professionals' is established through their claim to technical and moral superiority. Licensing guarantees the technical superiority, while codes of ethics and the emphasis on a 'service ethic' bolster claims to moral superiority (Carr-Saunders, 1928; Parsons, 1951; Goode, 1960; Millerson, 1964; Friedson, 1968; Etzioni, 1969; Gouldner, 1979).

The character of professions shifts with changing configurations of political and institutional forces, and within a framework of professional dynamics (Abbott, 1988; Light, 1993). In South Africa it is necessary to frame the process of professionalisation within the context of rapid social and political transformation, and against a backdrop of increasing globalisation. These factors present a dual pressure for professional psychology in this country.

The practices of licensing and legislation of a profession are typically determined by the profession itself, regulation being conducted internally by its own members. Typically, professionals operate with a degree of 'legitimate' autonomy, and the quality of their work is guaranteed by regulatory and disciplinary processes of professional bodies. Professional bodies guard their capacity to self-regulate quite jealously. However, with the patterns of globalisation, and the shift to viewing professionals as a commodity for exchange on global markets, these forms of self-regulation are increasingly being challenged, making way for greater standardisation, external monitoring and assessment. The response by many professional bodies to this pressure has been to introduce further layers of internal monitoring and regulation (Evett,

1999). In post-apartheid South African psychology, we see this trend clearly, with the introduction of board exams at the end of professional training, the increasing importance placed on standardisation of the curriculum, and the monitoring of continuing professional development. It is clear that psychology in South Africa must reconcile paradoxical demands. Local structures demand appropriateness, contextualisation and radicalisation of the profession. Global structures demand increased accountability and standardisation of training and accreditation.

Rapid political change in South Africa has thrown psychology into disarray as it seeks to respond to these changes while maintaining its professional status. In today's South Africa the demand for social transformation, social responsibility, and political accountability pressures professional bodies to produce training and services that are appropriate to the needs of society. The chief pressures are to produce an 'African' psychology, appropriate to the people of South Africa, and to produce a socially relevant psychology, able to respond to pressing socio-political problems (like poverty, violence, HIV/AIDS, and contribution to national reconstruction). It has had to undergo radical overhaul from being a profession that colluded with apartheid structures to being one that is appropriate and responsive to its new context. So psychology faces a conundrum. To survive as a profession, it must respond to the shifting political context. To do this, however, it needs to relinquish the authoritative and authoritarian structures that have made it a 'profession' in the first place.

Startlingly absent from most theorisation of professionalisation is reflection on the discursive construction of 'the professional', and the induction of the student into the web of practices that constitute 'professionalism'. Erant (2000) suggests that there is a need to differentiate the ideological practice of 'professionalisation' from the process of 'professionalism' (a set of skills). This differentiation hints at a key construct within the discourses of professionalisation: the polarisation of 'the personal' and 'the professional'. 'The professional' is a neutral figure, reified and depoliticised, who *has* professional skills (and through such 'ownership' is implicitly individualised). As my analysis will suggest, student accounts of training experiences are constructed within this disingenuous polarisation. Their professional identity is constituted as separate from the personal/political, the latter being marginalised in practice.

In a series of interviews, groups of women trainees portray how they position themselves in relation to tensions between subject and object, professional and personal, professional and political. In analysing their accounts, I unpack and highlight the implications of these tensions for a consideration of 'professionalisation' and 'appropriateness' in the development of South African psychology. I argue that the preoccupation with professionalisation, together with a focus on the 'individual', produces psychology as an essentially conservative institution.

Method

The extracts analysed here are taken from interviews conducted with women students[2] in psychological training programmes at South African universities over three years. They span the period from the beginning of their masters training, through to just before, or just after, their registration with the professional board.

Most of the interviews were conducted as focus groups (the first round of interviews involved only focus groups; but by the third round, these groups had dispersed and some students were either unavailable and untraceable, and in those cases individuals were interviewed). Students were interviewed within groups with other members of their masters class. Focus groups were the preferred methodology because they encourage participants to be active and engaged in the research process. Thus focus groups were hoped to enable participants to have significant influence on the interview agenda, allowing them to talk to each other, as well as to the interviewer (Kitzinger, 1994; MacDougall and Fudge, 2001). As a generative method, focus groups facilitate the expression of a broader range of reflections than those which might have been laid down by the researcher in a less dynamic format (Kitzinger, 1994).

Participants came from four South African universities (three historically white and one historically black), where they were being trained as clinical, counselling or educational psychologists. (One industrial psychology student was also included.) Students were approached in their classes. All volunteers were interviewed. In most institutions, most women (twenty-four of the twenty-six) were interviewed at M1 level. Eight groups were interviewed at M1 level and three groups (eight participants in total) at M2 (internship) and M3 level (post internship students, who were either completing research or beginning professional practice). Several individual staff interviews and six focus groups with honours students were also conducted (not discussed here).

The analysis of this material draws on resources from discursive practice (e.g. Burman, Kottler, Levett and Parker, 1997), informed by feminist and postcolonial theory (e.g. Fanon, 1967; Mama 1995). My analysis is guided by the approach to discourse analysis suggested by Parker (1994). This method is informed by a Foucauldian understanding of discourse and power, which facilitates an exploration of the ways in which individual identities are produced within a web of discursive practices.

In order to change the way in which psychology is taught and practised, it is necessary to look closely at the way in which the training of psychologists takes place. As a lecturer at an historically disadvantaged university (1996-1999) and as a masters student myself (1993-1995) I was acutely aware of masters training as an uncomfortable, often painful or even brutalising experience (this will be detailed further in the discussion). In this analysis I seek to explicate some of the ways in which power is performed within training institutions, and the ways in which the identity of 'The Professional Psychologist' is constructed. A politically informed discourse analysis (Burman, 1991) is well positioned to allow this kind of analysis, through its attention to the ways in which power relationships are constructed within language.

Analysis

Relationships between staff and students

The status of 'professional' offers certainty, power, knowledge and competence (Rose, 1989). Being a professional is set up as the 'end product' of masters training, guaranteeing students' ascension to the elevated rank of 'psychologist'. Throughout their training, students are also expected to take on the characteristics of the professional, whilst, at the same time, never forgetting their position as students. In the literature of professionalisation, students are typically cast as 'individuals'[3] with plastic behaviour and moral values who await the socialising drive of professionalisation. For example, Becker et al (1961), in their study of medical students, suggested that students' behaviours did not reflect strongly-held values (e.g. political views, religious beliefs, ethical values, and a sense of affiliation), if these were deemed unacceptable to the medical setting. Students are seen as 'modelling' professional socialisation (through mentoring and supervision: Howe, 2002). In this literature, we can see clearly the conceptual uncoupling of the 'person' (as a social and political being) from the 'professional'.

In the medical setting, much of this is seen to be achieved through a 'hidden curriculum': the 'processes, pressures and constraints which fall outside ... the formal curriculum and which are often unarticulated or unexplored' (Cribb et al, 1999) – for example, an understanding of power relationships and hierarchies within the medical establishment, 'appropriate' ways of relating to patients and other professionals, and expected ways of behaving both at work and in other social settings. In psychology, I suggest, the content of this 'hidden curriculum' involves a presumption that psychologists should embody the qualities of the idealised subject of psychology – the independent, adult 'individual'.

Within academic institutions, the lecturer maintains a sense of distance from the student, and entrenches their position as 'not equals'. This ensures the expert position of the lecturer, framing him/her as 'knower', while the student must take up the position of 'learner'. In the quote below, we begin to see the action of psychology's 'hidden curriculum', operating to position student G in a way that makes her receptive to 'professionalisation', while at the same time trivialising her other needs and affiliations as inappropriate to a trainee.

> G: Ja. I mean I know certainly where I am now, in comparison, I mean there is a sense of distance. (...) Even now, I feel I really am at the bottom of the food chain. And sometimes, if there are things I might want to say that are critical about the way things are done, or I might want to raise certain issues, I am so very careful, of how I do it and who I say it to. And there are some people who I *know*, it is safe to raise some issues with, and others who are just not safe. And part of it is because they are your supervisors, or they are the head of your department, or they have some kind of say in your, whether you get registered as a professional. And there's part of me that doesn't want to get known as a *betoger* [political agitator, troublemaker], (laughs a little) you know, or one of those ... (...) You know. So you find yourself just *holding* that, or not saying something that you might feel quite strongly about.

G describes an overt set of power relations in which her position 'at the bottom of the food chain' is clear to her. Being at the 'bottom of the food chain' is the most dangerous and vulnerable place to be. In a world full of predators, she is a harmless herbivore, with no teeth or claws of her own. She presents herself as helpless in relation to more senior staff. Relationships between staff and student are set up in such a way as to necessarily strip students of their radicalising potential within training institutions, and by extension, within the profession more broadly. Her ability to speak, to raise 'issues' (presumably issues of race, class, gender, language), to challenge the institution, is curtailed by three factors – her knowledge of her position within the institution, her understanding that it is not safe to speak to certain members of staff (those who have power over her and are in a position to make decisions about her future – supervisors, heads of department), and her own concern not to be identified as a 'betoger'.

The deployment of this term 'betoger' is particularly interesting here, because of its political connotations in South Africa. 'Betoger' was a term the apartheid government and other conservative power structures often used to describe political agitators – for example, people who were identified as trade union leaders. G's use of the term does seem to denote her identification with the 'betogers' of the past, a sense of her own political activity and her aspiration to be critical and subversive, but at the same time, recognising the dangers of doing that to her own career and advancement. The literal meaning of 'betoger' is 'bewitcher'. The connotations of magic are important as they help tie the political to the mystical and hence 'non-scientific': something inappropriate to professional psychology.

G articulates clearly a sense (articulated by most students) that 'career' is constructed as an individual project – one of 'self-management'. In his Foucauldian analysis of accountancy, Grey (1994) explores the ways in which professionalism becomes a project of self management. Rose (1989) demonstrated that, through webs of knowledge and expertise, the subject is identified and produced as autonomous; not only free to choose, but required to choose, and to be responsible for those choices. Thus students construct themselves as individual professionals, with associated rights and responsibilities as constructed by professional codes of practice.

G presents herself as navigating the dangerous waters of the training institution, and while she recognises the role of the institution in laying out the choices available to her, nonetheless she constructs herself as making personal choices, of choosing to abandon, or, at least, decentre her political commitments in favour of career advancement. She has located herself as actively choosing the limitations the institution lays out for her, abandoning – even undermining through the choice of the term 'betoger' – the identity of political activist.

For other students, the construction of professionalisation as a project of the self is even more evident. Becoming a psychologist involves an internalisation of the core values of the profession, being 'therapeutised' into a role that is simultaneously one of colleague and student, adult and child, powerful but socially and politically powerless, active but docile. The difficulties of being positioned as psychology's subject and object, professional and student, are further amplified by students:

> **NM:** Ja, I think that, I remember last year, I got a report. (...) That said I was not co-operative, because I *disagreed* with my supervisor. So that was part of the, the record. That I was not co-operative. And *most* of the time, you're scared to stand up for what you *think* is right, or what you *think* is suitable for that context. And you just back down and do *whatever* the thing is. One of these days, I was saying to S, (...) the internship is supposed to make us *professional, assertive,* erm *empowered*. But instead, when you're there, you're like a *little* baby, you're supposed to say yes mummy, [yes mummy.
> **SM:** [It's just the opposite of what an internship as a psychologist is supposed to be about.
> **PG:** [Yes, yes
> **NM:** And you find that you just bottle all that anger, and all that disappointment, and when someone speaks to you, you just say 'oh, ja, ja, ja'. 'oh, ja, ja, ja'. (dismissively)
> **PG:** and then you get labelled passive aggressive (laughter)

This construction of the professional implies a responsible, adult role, in which the ability to stand up for one's self, and to challenge inequities, would be a necessary feature. However, the students rapidly learn that this is only a partial story. Their lecturers and supervisors have fuller access to the professional bag of tricks, and the very status of 'professional-in-training' which authorises certain forms of speech can be used to undermine them. Of particular note here is the use of psychological skills of diagnosis and pathologisation. The discourses of psychology bestow upon its professionals that capacity to *describe* individuals, and in so doing can *prescribe/proscribe* who they are and what they *can* be. So the qualified psychologists have the capacity to label students as 'unco-operative', as 'passive aggressive' and in so doing, they infantilise and pathologise the students' resistant behaviour, repositioning the resistant or politicised student as unco-operative, unhealthy children. They are, in that moment, separated from the position of 'empowered, assertive professional', and relegated to the position of 'student/patient'. Students quickly learn that to get ahead, to *become* professional psychologists, they must assume an appearance of co-operation, of agreement with professional norms, while their sense of outrage or disagreement is squashed, or expressed in 'non-professional' spaces. This is articulated by N, below, when she says 'Being an intern means you should just keep quiet and do whatever they say'.

> **NM:** I think that's the main thing about the internship. Being an *intern* means you (...) a *doormat* or (...) don't know, that you're a *tea girl*, that you're everything (...) belittling.
> **SM:** No rights.
> **NM:** You don't have rights, you don't have *anything*. You just do whatever anyone says. That's how I felt. And what I was just saying to S, I read this book which was an inspiring book. And I sat and thought (makes sound through teeth) why should I (...) let my whole year be *uncomfortable* because I feel that my, my (...) my *talents* or (...) my *abilities* are not fully shown in the department. And I'm *afraid* to show them, because I think maybe they'll, they will say, she's too (...) greedy, she's ... You always think of something they will *say*, because, even if you do something *good*, there must be something *negative*. Being an intern means you should just keep quiet and do whatever they say.

I was interested in two other images within this extract: that the position of being an intern is understood as a 'doormat' or a 'tea girl' and that students feel that they have 'no space to grow' in the internship. Within a South African context, the concept of a 'tea girl' is both heavily gendered and heavily racialised, In the use of this term, the student expresses the degree to which she has been created as psychology's *other*, its object. Like the 'tea girl' in the department, she is relatively powerless, almost invisible. Similarly, in reflecting that they have 'no space to grow' students signal their *acceptance* of the infantilised and 'therapeutised' position within the training institution – they accept that they are children in relation to their supervisor's adult, that their growth needs to be facilitated by the more knowledgeable professional.

It is important to note that, in contrast to the accounts presented here, many students report the experience of training as relatively unproblematic. While the masters training is portrayed as uncomfortable, these students view it as a necessary to their professionalisation. They accept relatively straightforwardly their positionings as students, falling into the role of 'acolyte' or 'apprentice' (Callaghan, 2003a) relatively seamlessly, before taking up their position as professional psychologist. More politicised students, women who saw themselves as feminist or as left-wing, students with a history of involvement in student struggle, and black students were more likely to find the process of professionalisation problematic (in the ways identified in the extracts quoted in this article). Reading through the transcripts, conducting my analysis, and hearing the comments of other academics and professional psychologists, I note how difficult it is to imagine an alternative psychology and pedagogy, in which paradoxical positionings of subject and object, professional and student might be dissolved. This is the case, I think, both for students and for educators/trainers. Dichotomous positionings are inscribed in psychological theory and embedded in institutional (professional and academic) structures, and these positionings produce *us* as psychologists. The tensions articulated in students' accounts reveal fissures in the system of professionalisation which can be explored further. Such analysis might provide a basis for resisting the politically conservative pressures of professionalisation, and might facilitate the emergence of more explicitly politicised applied psychologies.

Playing the game

As students take on the role of psychologist, they learn to 'play the game' that enables them to be recognised as a 'professional'. The 'game' involves learning to suspend other aspects of self:

> **PG:** I wasn't being treated like how I *should be* (...) and er, it frustrated me, because I couldn't do *anything* about it, because they are people who can determine my future and I had to just go along with it (...) Be *nice*, you know, be *false*. You know? Smile (...) at their silly *jokes*. Complement them on their stupid clothing, which I didn't even *like* (laughter). I was told, this is the *only* way to get through your internship. And the thing is, it *worked*.
> **NM:** It *does* work.
> **PG:** It works (...) But the sad thing there was it *wasn't* a professional thing.

In P's account, 'the game' involves relating to people in a way that is in keeping with their view of professional behaviour. This excerpt demonstrates the ways in which 'playing the game' constructs the process of professionalisation as a project of self-management. Becoming a 'professional' is not 'a professional thing', but a personal one. It involves conformity to an image of professionalism that involves the entire range of self-presentation. Stronach et al (2002) similarly describe the way in which surveillance and governmentality serve to construct an image of 'the authentic' teacher or nurse. They suggest that by universalising the definition of the professional and inflating its importance a 'collective individual' emerges: no longer 'a psychologist', but 'The Psychologist': someone who does not just *act* professionally, but *is* a professional.

To become 'The Psychologist', training programmes require that students relinquish the subject position that *resists* in favour of a more passive, unchallenging identity. This is policed through professional performances (case study presentations, supervision, quarterly progress reports), through interpersonal interactions with members of staff, through the incitement to students to take on the role of professional by simultaneously offering and withholding that status, and through labelling behaviour as pathological or immature that is not in keeping with the hegemonic image of 'The Psychologist'.

NM: Ja, ja. I think that's (...) the *main* issue. Erm, erm, I *used* to be this, this *assertive* person, who like, liked to quote their views when different. I remember in our honours class [

PG: [I *knew* you then (laughter)

NM: [I used to argue. I used to *stand up* for what I thought. But *now* if anyone says anything, I say (ironically, in a little girl voice) *'oh, (...) ok\'*. Even if I *don't* go along with *that* (...) I wouldn't *argue* (...) with a *senior*. I'd just keep quiet. And *tell*, maybe, my, erm, erm, my other interns that 'oh, I didn't think that, or that was right, I don't think that should go *on'*. But you wouldn't, I *will* say you do lose *part* of yourself.

Professionalisation, playing the game, is about being silent, when you *feel* you should be speaking, about *pretending* to agree with things that in fact you think are rubbish. It also involves carving out a space in which it *is* possible to articulate the subaltern voice, but this space is always a marginal one – in G's case, discussion with other interns.

In her talk about playing the game, G alternates between a critique of the power structures of psychology, in the form of the counselling centre in which she works as an intern, the department, and adopting its language herself. Many of the students suggest that the relationship between them and their supervisory group (the department) is structured to encourage conformity. The training institution's response to G's attempt to 'raise certain issues' of race and language are seen as an attempt to suppress those concerns, to depoliticise her: 'the lesson I learned was not to raise, what could be considered more *social* issues, that are perhaps critical of (...) of the role psychology is playing'. She frames this as a kind of game, which she becomes increasingly adept at playing. While her supervisors undoubtedly know that she has not changed her mind, nonetheless, as long as she 'plays the game', mutters on the sidelines, and keeps real critique out of the public domain, everything is fine.

It matters that the student learns to 'play the game' primarily in case and quasi-therapeutic supervisory settings. Case presentations are set up to assist students in performing the role of 'The Professional': it is theatre. Pomerantz, Ende and Erikson (1995, p.45) suggest that the case study is a discursive exchange in which 'educators get novices to discover for themselves precisely what the professionals hold should be discovered'. It is not a straightforward exercise in socialisation: rather, through the process of presentation, students are encouraged to acquire the patterns of professional thought and behaviour. In the interview quoted above, G learns that there is no space, when presenting a case, for an account of social context beyond the most anodyne version of the 'bio-psycho-social' model. Social context can, apparently, just be talked away, if G can only sufficiently embody the qualities of 'The Psychologist'.

G hints at severe consequences if she doesn't 'play the game'. The psychologists she can talk to also play the game, and induct her into it. For example, she refers to a psychologist taking her to one side and suggesting that she not challenge authority directly: 'for your own good'. The case study setting teaches her psychology's 'official language' (Bourdieu, 1991; Lingard et al , 2003, p.605) suggest that the case presentation is one of the means whereby 'professional membership is regulated and evaluated by reference to an established set of community standards and values that are reflected in the presentation genre'. The genre involves mastering what can and cannot be said by 'Psychologists', and guarantees entrance to the profession, and continued success within it.

While it might be argued that these professional performances are a necessary aspect of training, we need to question whether they need to be used in such conservatising ways. As academics, supervisors, trainers, our professional identities have also been constituted through these kinds of performances, and it requires considerable deconstruction of our own positionings as psychologist, supervisor, 'betoger', to enable an interaction with students that does not reproduce these constructions of either the apolitical 'professional individual' or the marginalised and largely ineffectual political psychologist.

G does not know how to make the links between the theoretical grounding of critical psychology she learnt in her undergraduate and honours courses, and this new, applied work of being a psychologist in South Africa. When she asks her supervisors and lecturers about these links, she poses difficult questions, questions to which lecturers and supervisors probably also lack answers. However, it is important that we construct spaces within supervisory relationships for an articulation of these questions. Present regulatory systems and supervisory relations often require that students provide *answers* to psychological and social problems, that they present their knowledge with certainty, that they embody 'the professional psychologist' by being assertive. We require of our students a command of psychology, and they fear that if they are hesitant and unsure they will not make the grade (many students, for example, referred to the spectre of 'termination' of their internships in their accounts of supervision and quarterly reports). Students described the ways in which they neatened up the rough (often socio-economically driven) edges of their work, in order that they could present a more seamless presentation of their case material. In doing this, they sanitise their formulations of the *context* of their work, they remove the social and political from the supervision relationship. Is it possible that this sanitisation is a response to a knowledge that we, like them, do not have the answers to the difficult questions that our political context presents? The student who asks questions that we cannot answer risks being labelled as 'difficult'. These questions are intimidating for left-leaning psychologists. They are perhaps even more threatening to psychologists whose political orientations are conservative, and whose interests lie with the maintenance of 'professional' psychology.

These paragraphs indicate how psychology maintains its conservative stance in the face of immense social needs in South Africa. By making students 'play the game', by encouraging conformity through the deployment of both pathologising terminology and a therapeutic style of relating with students who do try to tackle these issues, the status quo is maintained. This is not just because those who educate students are cruel, but for a variety of reasons: the profession's need to safeguard its own tenuous position in the rapidly changing context of post-apartheid South Africa, resulting in a need for consolidation rather than self questioning; the reality that some of the questions students ask are just too hard; the reality that psychology is often peopled by conservative individuals who are not open to political questions.

By allowing the student some (peripheralised) place to discuss her feelings about these social issues, psychology diffuses her objections to its asocial nature – it allows her space to ventilate, without ever having to acknowledge or deal with her challenges. Challenges to the status quo, including attempts to develop more appropriate psychologies that engage better with their context, remain ghettoised. Although contained in other students' accounts, this process of ghettoisation is most clearly demonstrated in G's conversation with a colleague/mentor, who indicates clearly that the 'appropriate' place for social and political critique of the profession is in a less public space (private conversation – not in the mainstream setting of the case conference). A further dynamic in students' accounts (discussed later) is the way in which applied psychology in South Africa has constructed the enclave of 'community psychology' and 'critical psychology' as peripheries where the theorisation of a more socially relevant psychology might be articulated, without ever seriously impacting or changing the nature of mainstream psychological practice.

The interplay of subject and object within psychology is clearly laid out. Students attempt to take their 'rightful position' as subject of psychology – as psychologist. However, the rug is swiftly pulled from under them by the more powerful subjects, and they are turned into the object of the professional gaze. Racial and linguistic concerns are swiftly turned back on the student, converted into her 'issues' and seen as a slur on her professional abilities. They become 'symptoms' of her own inadequacies, her own inability to cope, deflecting critique from the social and political, back onto the individual.

Although G at times is placed in the position of object of the therapeutic gaze, and thus slips into position of the other of psychology, the absence of the 'other Others' is striking in her description of this process. When she talks about race, racism and language, it is clear (to a South African) that she is talking about the difficulties psychologists encounter in working with black African people, and vice versa. (These might include language difference, power differentials, cultural misunderstandings, unfamiliarity with psychological work, inappropriateness of the mode and philosophical basis of the psychological model, unresponsiveness of the psychological model to social and economic difficulty, etc). However within this interview, G is forced into the position of 'speaking for' the Other.

G's image of what constitutes a professional psychologist is clearly one of a politically neutral, objective figure. This is contrary to her own vision of the kind of psychologist she would be when she entered training (she had envisioned herself as working in NGOs, in a relatively politicised role, as an agent of social change). G suggests that those who 'slip through the net', and make it through professional training with strong political beliefs are increasingly ghettoised as 'just community psychologists' – not real psychologists. Within this discourse, real professional psychologists are seen as those who maintain an objective and neutral stance. There is no space for strong political, religious or other beliefs within this model. This view of professional psychology is maintained by a refusal to engage in critique on the basic assumptions of psychology.

Psychology is in the business of describing and prescribing what it means to be an 'individual'. The way in which psychology constructs the individual through its activities of surveillance, and controls those individuals through regulatory and bureaucratic practices has been well documented (e.g. Henriques et al, 1998; Rose, 1992). Psychology's construction of the 'normal individual' prevents us, as psychologists, from understanding the ways in which human experience is constituted socially. It severs the individual subject of psychology from the social contexts within which they live, and blocks an engagement with the political. The way in which psychology's 'proper work' is laid out for professionals pressures us to work with and as 'individuals'. This is achieved both theoretically, and institutionally: although as individual clinicians we might wish to take a more social and political view, the lack of appropriate theory, and of institutional links to social and political organisations and more socially oriented professions, makes this difficult to achieve. Within South Africa, psychology has largely served the interests of mostly white and middle class client groups. While students are often taught the theory and practice of 'community psychology' at university, and encouraged to think socially about the problems their clients might face, this rarely translates itself into post-qualification practice. Most psychologists in South Africa still work in private practice.

When psychology constructs a universal, acontextual, apolitical individual as its unit of analysis, it does not only prescribe that for its patients or research subjects: it normalises that view of humanity for all people – including the psychologist. As I have already noted, in the training of psychology students, the consequence of this theorisation of human experience as individual experience is the production of the 'individual professional' – a professional psychologist stripped of personal and political affiliation. In the face of this potent production of self as 'The Psychologist' students who do not comply, who are uncomfortable with the form and practice of psychology into which they are inducted, articulate some sense of self operating beneath or parallel to this performance. For example, P disparagingly mutters that she would 'smile at their silly *jokes*. Complement them on their stupid clothing, which I didn't even *like*', G talks to another, understanding professional, and expresses her scorn towards the training institution, and N talks to other interns. In this way they signal that the image of the 'Collective Individual', 'The Professional Psychologist', is a *construct*, that obscures a wide range of practices and positionings.

However, by presenting these alternatives as an 'essential self', something that must be kept separate from their professional persona, the students inadvertently contribute to the maintenance of the idea of 'The Professional', peripheralising and marginalising all that does not conform to it as the realm of 'the personal' or 'the political'. They warrant the discourses of the profession, by using its own language to define themselves *as* individuals, playing different roles in different contexts. In their sense of splitting their professional self from their 'true' self, students simultaneously challenge the production, and play into it through the deployment of psychological language. Fanon (1967) suggested that by adopting the language of the oppressor, the oppressed are forced to participate in their own 'closing off'. All challenges to the construct of 'The Professional' are thereby neatly partitioned off in a 'part' of the self that has no apparent place in the performance of 'The Psychologist'.

The process of professionalisation is therefore an ambiguous one for students. Although the position of professional psychologists confers a status, it is a status of a particular sort, and it authorises only a very specific type of speech, and a particular platform from which to speak. With the status necessarily comes loss, the sacrifice of aspects of self that might want to speak differently. Political ideas can only be expressed on the periphery, in private or from the ghettoised position of 'community psychologist'. The political and professional psychologist cannot co-exist within this framework.

It is notable that 'The Psychologist' remains an imperfect construct in students' accounts. The personal may have been relegated to a peripheral position, but it is not silenced entirely. Students do articulate the marginalised 'personal/political', they speak them in jokes, in mutterings, in safe spaces. In one university in particular, students had a clear 'underground network', where knowledges of survival were passed on from one cohort of students to the next. These utterances provide a fruitful base to begin to theorise how the deadening weight of the depoliticised professional might be resisted, and training of students reformulated.

The description of becoming a professional as learning to 'play the game' signals the performative aspect of this identification (Butler, 1990). Although the professional discourse requires that students *become* 'The Professional', they are, in fact *doing* 'The Professional'. In her analysis of accounts of the self-construction of Indo-Dutch women, Pattynama (2000) suggests that one strategy for negotiating the tension between identifications that are assigned and those which are self-ascribed is to 'strategically and consciously play with all the different images of femininity'. Extending this analysis to the psychology students interviewed here, we can see that the 'assimilation' of students into the profession is inevitably partial: they play the roles of the professional, but they do not *become* the professional. This is not to suggest that the action of professionalisation is not 'real' for students. Rather I suggest that there are cracks in the apparently monolithic structure of the profession, and that resources for resistance are present within its discursive patterns.

Conclusions

Psychology's focus on professional issues is seen as a de-politicising and/or politically conservative force within the discipline. Students' accounts of professional training suggest the project of 'becoming a psychologist' is an identity project, a project of self-management, which produces them as 'The Psychologist'. 'The Psychologist' embodies the qualities of psychology's 'individual' – universalising, neutral and ahistorical. This construct of 'professional psychology' obscures its own politically conservative effects, as well as blocking any radical potential psychologists might have. Students refer to the process of professionalisation as 'learning to play the game' – a representation that signals a potential disjuncture in the apparent deadlock of professionalisation. Because professionalism is constituted as a set of qualities and skills that can be learned, and the professional is constructed as a being separate from the personal/political, these affiliations continue to be articulated alongside the discourse of professionalism, and provide a commentary on the construct of professionalism and the identity of the individual professional.

Training towards a more radicalised and politicised psychology in South Africa might begin by working with these marginalised and peripheralised mutterings. In talking to psychologists about this project, it became clear that students and staff were aware that supervision had become a reified process in psychology training, one in which students were producing idealised accounts of what was really going on in their work with clients – accounts that were consistent with the 'individual professional'. Enabling the articulation of the more dissenting voices in supervision might be a first step in allowing a more radical version of psychology to be expressed. A theorisation of a politicised psychology, that goes beyond the idealised 'professional practice' needs to be taken out of the ghetto of community psychology, and articulated within the mainstream spaces of case conference and supervision.

Acknowledgements

I'd like to express my gratitude to Erica Burman for her considerable help and support in the preparation of this article, and to Rebecca Lawthom for her helpful comments on an early draft. Thank you also to the two anonymous reviewers, whose insightful remarks were greatly appreciated, and to Jane Selby, for her extensive comments on a draft of this article. Finally, thank you to the women who participated in the interviews reported on here, who gave so unstintingly of their time.

Notes

1. The scope of this paper does not permit a full consideration of the history of psychology in South Africa. For a more detailed account, please see Hook et al (in press), the special issue of *Psychology in Society*, 27, 2001 on Critical Psychology, or Seedat et al (2001).
2. Women students were interviewed in this study because it was felt that their position as both the subjects (as professionals in training) and objects (as psychology's other) would render their accounts of training in and for

a South African context particularly illuminating. However, gender *per se* has not been a focus in this article, and a closer gender analysis can be found in Callaghan (2003a and b) and in future publication.
3. In this paper, I use the term 'persons' to refer to a politicised view of self that is embedded within a social framework. The 'individual' is used to denote the reified psychological construct, psychology's apolitical and asocial subject.

References

Abbott, A. (1988). *The System of Professions. An Essay on the Division of Expert Labor.* Chicago and London: University of Chicago Press.

Becker, H.S., B. Geer, E. Hughes, A. Strauss (1961). *Boys in White: Student Culture in Medical School.* Chicago: University of Chicago Press; 1961.

Biesheuwel, S. (1987). 'Psychology: science and politics. Theoretical developments and applications in a plural society'. *South African Journal of Psychology* 17 (1): 1-8.

Bourdieu, P. (1991). 'Case presentations'. Thompson, J. B. (ed.) (1991). *Language and symbolic power.* Cambridge, MA: HUP.

Burman, E. (1991). 'What Discourse is Not'. *Philosophical Psychology* 4 (3): 325-342.

Burman, E., A. Kottler, A. Levett and I. Parker (eds). (1997). *Culture, Power and Difference: Discourse Analysis in South Africa.* London: Zed Books/Cape Town: UCT Press.

Butler, J. (1990). *Gender Trouble: Feminism and the Subversion of Identity.* New York and London: Routledge.

Cribb, A. and S. Bignold (1999). 'Towards the reflexive medical school: the hidden curriculum and medical education research'. *Studies Higher Education* 36:195-209.

Dawes, A.R.L. (1985). 'Politics and Mental Health: The Position of Clinical Psychology in South Africa'. *South African Journal of Psychology* 15: 55-61.

de la Rey, C., N. Duncan, T. Shefer and A. Van Niekerk (1998). *Contemporary Issues in Human Development: A South African Focus.* Johannesburg: ITP.

Etzioni, A. (ed.), (1969). *The Semi-Professions and their Organisation.* New York: Free Press.

Eraut, M. (1994). *Developing professional knowledge and competence.* London: Falmer Press.

Fanon, F. (1967). *Black Skin, White Masks: The Experiences of a Black Man in a White World.* New York: Grove Press.

Friedson, E. (1983). *Professional dominance.* Chicago: Aldine.

Friedson, E. (1970). *Profession of Medicine, a Study of the Sociology of Applied Knowledge.* New York: Harper and Row.

Grey, C. (1994.). 'Career as a project of the self and labour process discipline'. *Sociology.* 28 (2): 479-497.

Henriques, J., with W. Hollway, C. Urwin, C. Venn and V. Walkerdine (1998). *Changing the Subject: Psychology, Social Regulation and Subjectivity* (2nd ed). London: Routledge.

Johnson, T. J. (1972). *Professions and Power*. London: Macmillan.
Kitzinger, J. (1994). 'The methodology of focus groups: the importance of interaction between research participants'. *Sociology of Health* 16: 103-121.
Light, D. (2000). 'The medical profession and organizational change: From professional dominance to countervailing power'. Bird, C. E., P. Conrad and A. M. Fremont (eds). *Handbook of Medical Sociology*. Upper Saddle River, NJ: Prentice Hall. pp.201-216.
Lingard, L., K. Garwood, C. F. Shryer and M. M. Spafford (2003). 'A certain art of uncertainty: case presentation and the development of professional identity'. *Social Science and Medicine*, 56: 603-616.
MacDougall, C. and E. Fudge (2001). 'Planning and recruiting the sample for focus groups and in-depth interviews'. *Qualitative Health Research*. 11: 117-126.
Mama, A. (1995). *Beyond the Masks: Race, Gender and Subjectivity*, London: Routledge.
Parekh, A. and C.-A. Jackson (1998). 'Families of Children with a Mental Handicap'. de la Rey, C., N. Duncan, T. Shefer and A. Van Niekerk (1998). *Contemporary Issues in Human Development: A South African Focus*. Johannesburg: ITP.
Parker, I. (1994). 'Discourse Analysis'. Banister, P., E. Burman, I. Parker, M. Taylor and C. Tindall (eds). *Qualitative Methods in Psychology: A Research Guide*. Buckingham: Open University Press.
Pattynama, P. (2000). 'Assimilation and Masquerade: Self-Constructions of Indo-Dutch Women'. *The European Journal of Women's Studies* 7: 281-299. GAP.
Pomerantz, A., J. Ende and F. Erickson (1995). *Precepting conversations in a general medical clinic. The talk of the clinic. Explorations in the analysis of medical and therapeutic discourse*. Hillsdale: Lawrence Erlbaum Associates
Rose, N. (1999). *Governing the Soul: The Shaping of the Private Self* (Second Edition). London: Free Associations Books.
Seedat, M., N. Duncan and S. Lazarus (2001). *Community Psychology: Theory, Method and Practice – South African and other Perspectives*. Oxford: Oxford University Press.
Stronach, I., B. Corbin, O. McNamara, S. Stark and T. Warne (2002). 'Towards and uncertain politics of professionalism: teacher and nurse identities in flux'. *Journal of Education Policy* 17(1): 109-138.
Swartz, L., K. Gibson and T. Gelman (eds). (2002). *Reflective practice: Psychodynamic ideas in the community*. Pretoria: HSRC.

Distinguishing myself in hysteria

Paula M. Smith

This article demonstrates how syncope moments, unexpected voids or break points in personal storylines, like syncopation in music, when exposed to feminist poststructural analysis and written against the accepted authority and patterns of meaning-making, expose other ways of interpreting and knowing that can be transformative and productive of social change. It shows the author unexpectedly challenged to examine the effects of patriarchal interpretations of storylines from a place of hysteria, embodied resistance and seeming powerlessness. It attempts to bring the reader into the process of change itself, to share ways of analysis and reading/writing. It suggests that such an approach has liberatory potential for professionals experiencing contradictions and for innovators whose creativity seems to be undermined through managerial regulation.

At the heart of things, as with the poststructuralist movement overall (if one can speak of it in such terms), is the need to analyse analysis, understand understanding, interpret interpretation. And once such a task is undertaken, one of the consequences is a self-reflexivity that must challenge the very discursive practices in operation (Fuery, 1995:10).

Introduction
The particular interaction I examine in this writing holds within it conflicts and dilemmas, that, as a young woman religious in the midtwentieth century, I could not have been trained to meet. I was experienced as an educator. I identified with the questioning of many

cultural and political practices that world movements of the 1960s and 1970s brought to my life. Formed in patterns of religious life based on many centuries of unquestioning acceptance of male authority in the Catholic church, I found myself in an unusual resistance – an hysteric, intuitive and emotional resistance – that became a turning point in understandings of patriarchal interpretations of storylines, and that offered insights for future reflection and agency.

I invite you the reader into glimpses of my attempts to give new meaning to some aspects of my story(ies) presented through a number of layers of writing in a feminist poststructural framework. I invite you into three different levels of writing, spaced at different times in my professional development:

1978 – firstly into a meeting between the young woman religious I was (whom I now call Emma – in 1978 Education Consultant in a Catholic Education Office in a rural Australian diocese, recently returned from an exposure trip to the Philippines) and the bishop of the diocese. I give imaginative reconstruction to the scene I evoke. Richardson gives me incentive to use such techniques – 'they do penetrate more when the voices become "characters" in dramas, but most deeply when the voices become embodied, take form, as legitimated co-authors, writing different meanings in differing styles, rupturing "our" text'. (Richardson 1997:73)

The reconstruction of this memory required highly disciplined use of information known at the time of the event re-membered, rejection of later insights and careful use of associative techniques. It was made with full knowledge of the research data that warned of memory as being variable and vulnerable (McConky 1995) and attentiveness to alerts from memory researchers (Haug 1992:48). The value of the reconstructed material for analysis far outweighed these limitations.

1998 – secondly into reflection of the remembered event twenty years later. The writing of this second level analysis held not only the challenge to glimpse the storylines that were earlier invisible to the subject, but to tell them in a new way. Writers like Cixous, Derrida, Foucault, Barthes and Lacan, in whose writings I had been immersed in my doctoral work, revealed possibilities that were intuitive, questioning of the power of the sentence, evocative, and aware of the need for the reader to be fully involved in the reading/writing process. I found myself having to unlearn many aspects of rational, logical forms of writing in order to be open to the possibilities of the new.

The writing that emerged showed up some of the cracks in the earlier storylines. Risks of loss of earlier identities acknowledged. A pathway revealed. Surprises. Raptus. Hysteria – that had earlier been embarrassingly acknowledged as weakness, a way of responding that involved tears and high emotion and was associated with a way of acting out when other means were not available. Now discovered as a way of resistance through the body available prior to the capacity to think. Accessible again and again if needed. Writing, an entry into new discourses, varying the positioning, new spaces opening.

Cixous and other feminist writers and theorists gave a mandate and an invitation, not only to consider hysteria differently, but to use their phrases, evocations and symbols as my own. Their sentences and meanings become part of the interpretation of the writing. In this analysis quotations are not indented, but flow in the explanation as part of the overall meaning making of the text. Cixous's words become mine.

The power of what has been called 'syncope' in this work begins to be explicated also. Seeing the hysteria as a change time, a break time, a syncope moment, a moment of possible imbalance, an interruption of the usual storyline, pushing the subject into the void of not knowing, touching deepest desire, opens mythic universes, bringing impossible ordeals, intoxication and ecstasy. Chaos and new order evolving, playing with accidents of time, carried out both consciously and unconsciously, taking the subject/writer to the edge of disorder, out of sync, against the grain, into productive discord. Clement (1994), defining 'Syncope' as little deaths, linking syncope and rapture/ecstasy, indicated the way through. Syncope bringing precarious balance and the shaking of identity, 'deprives the body of its obedience to the mind'(Clement, 1994:7) while enabling the subject to get outside of earlier identifications.

2004/5 – thirdly into an acknowledgement of some significance and further reflection of the event for this time. Like Richardson: 'I welcome metaphor, imagery, evocative prose ...' (Richardson 1997:206). Other insights and metaphors and possible storylines reveal themselves. The tiger image that becomes part of this writing is one such. Insights enabling me to welcome what was previously seen to be undermining. Continuing scholarship enabling contestation of earlier knowledge and displacement of essentialist approaches to subjectivity. The potential of this process of reading/writing and analysis for enabling and assisting social and political change becoming increasingly evident.

November, 1978

The Bishop clenches his fist, bangs it three times on the table as he speaks. He is a big, florid man, his face becoming redder, puffed with the wrath he is experiencing. His voice lifts with anger as he stands, faces Emma. 'You will not introduce MACOS[1] in the schools of my Diocese. There will be no more experimenting with this dangerous learning. What has happened to you since your visit to the Philippines? You must stop this MACOS immediately Sister!'.

Emma, summoned a few minutes ago, came to the Bishop's office unconcerned. She has had very little personal dealing with him, only meets him at Diocesan Board Meetings, official functions. (They all call him Fred behind his back.) He seems to like being thought of as knowledgeable, but appears to Emma to be gullible, easily swayed by public opinion. He has invited her to sit with him at the round table just inside the door. Has questioned her about the Bruner material she is trialling. 'Is this MACOS being used in the schools in this Diocese?' Emma, at first thinking he is interested, responds unhesitatingly. 'Yes, Bishop'. She has been excited about this material for most of the year. 'Man: A Course of Studies' it is called. She introduced it to the Education Team with whom she works late last year and, with their approval, has gained a grant of a few thousand dollars to buy the films, booklets, trial the process in three schools – in Mutlegar, Corola and Orawa. The teachers, two women religious from her own congregation and a layman, have attended preparatory workshops in Sydney, and are enjoying the teaching/learning process, implementing the units with distinct flair. She has visited each of them, filmed their work with their students during the past couple of weeks. All this in her mind as the Bishop speaks: 'What is it supposed to be teaching? What is it about?'.

Among the responses she gives the Bishop is her own understanding of the overall educational goal of the material. She endeavours to share with him her expectation that the children will learn how to speak from both within and from outside an ideology. The studies of the Eskimos, some of their practices, which are so contrary to Christian thinking, are enabling the children to see that all peoples do not speak from the same position, belief system. 'I see the children learning skills of critical analysis, a valuable educational outcome', Emma volunteers at one point in the conversation. She explains how the MACOS Project was introduced in the United States a couple of years ago by a group of educators, led by Jerome Bruner, who employed the foremost thinkers in many disciplines to gather the material for him. Emma tries to tell the Bishop that the material consists of a series of case studies – Salmon, Herring Gull, Baboons, Netsilik Eskimos, the children's own family history. The case studies themselves are the means of analysing some basic concepts like life cycle, tools, language, beliefs and values. It is this movement to a deeper level of thinking for the children (fifth class in primary schools), that interests Emma. She wants to investigate its power to assist the children to move to critical skills and critical thinking.

As the Bishop questions further, Emma becomes aware that his concern has been stirred by the present situation in some of the Queensland Schools. A Mrs J. has been voicing her concerns about MACOS. Media throughout Australia have picked up the issue. 'Eskimos Drinking Blood' – has recently been splashed across the national papers as hardly a fit topic for primary school children. Now the Bishop has discovered that this same material is being used in his own schools!

Emma patiently tries to show the Bishop that this topic is certainly not a concern for Catholic school children. 'The Catholic children learn about drinking Christ's blood in the Eucharist from their earliest years. They have no problem with the concept of drinking blood. They grasp that the Eskimo group will drink the blood of the seal they have harpooned, in the same way as the Aboriginal people in Australia drink the blood of the kangaroo they catch'. 'But that reference to Christ's blood is different', maintains the Bishop. 'Not essentially. The symbol of blood is known to them. They are not frightened by the idea of drinking blood. It's part of the language they use', Emma responds. 'The children find it more difficult to understand that a grandmother in some of the Eskimo groups will willingly walk out onto the snow to die if there is insufficient food for her as well as the family. This idea the children do find difficult to grasp'.

As Emma names each example the Bishop's anger deepens; his inability to understand the educational implications of the material, or even make an effort to understand that there are educational implications, grows. His fear of something he does not understand is obvious to Emma. His only means of dealing with the dilemma now to put a stop to the experiment. He will not allow this kind of educational experiment to occur in the schools of his diocese. Emma knows this will be his decision even before he voices it.

She rises as the Bishop thumps the table; steps back from the gesture; listens to his decision and quietly walks out of the room. She knows that this is an important moment in her career but she can find no words to express the significance, even within herself. She tells the rest of the consultancy team members the Bishop's decision. She mentions it at the dinner table that evening at the convent, treating it in an understated fashion. She dismisses it from her mind over the next few days in the busyness of end-of-year activities. The Christmas party for the Office is to be held at the convent. She has a lot of preparation for that event. Before and after work over the week Emma cleans, decorates the hall for the party. She brings pots of ferns, growing plants, in from the verandahs, cloisters; satisfies herself that the hall looks better than it ever has. The evening itself proves to be an enjoyable gathering. The team bid farewell to the man who has been their leader for the past four years. It will not be the same in 1979. They will all miss Mark.

Christmas comes, goes, uneventfully. Emma packs to go on holidays as she has done over the past couple of years. The packing is an effort. She feels hot, cold, feverish. All will be well when she reaches the holiday destination. Nothing is easy. She drives on her own, as the other nuns with whom she will be holidaying have left earlier. She stops to get a drink at a couple of towns on the way. Each time she does not want to get back into the car again. It is all too hard, too laborious somehow.

The holiday cabin is a close living situation, four or five bunks in an open area. Normally Emma enjoys the company, the fun, the jokes. This year she finds it all too strenuous. She has developed a cough. Cannot cough comfortably in the night without waking everyone. One night in a fit of coughs she goes out to the car, sits there a long time. The cough becoming worse over the next days. A visit to the doctor becomes imperative. He sends her for x-rays, tells her she has pneumonia. Within the next twenty-four hours she is in hospital in Sydney. It takes a week's treatment to break the congestion on her lungs to enable her to return to Beechwood.

The two weeks back in Beechwood before she has to return to work for the new year are more restful. The first day back at the Office in late January is a hot, steamy day. Emma comes home to the convent for lunch, which she rarely does; walks to the chapel. She passes the maidenhair ferns she so carefully tends, and loves seeing so beautifully green in all their summer glory. They are massed on steps on the verandah leading to the chapel. They are her pride and joy. There is a large fern missing from the back row! Where is it? The gap is obvious. She knows who has taken it. One of the sisters, who seems to think she does not have to ask anyone for anything. Emma cannot bear to be treated so casually. Her whole being throbs with intensity of living, tautness, strain, anger she has not known how to express these past weeks.

She meets Margaret on the verandah soon afterwards, verifies that she had been responsible for taking the fern, lets forth a torrent of abusive words. 'Why could you not ask me for the fern if you needed it?' she sobs. 'Does my responsibility for these plants mean nothing to you?' She gives Margaret glowering looks, lifts her voice with each statement she makes 'Do I care for them only for people like you to give them away? Am I not to be considered at all in the things for which I am responsible?' She spits out finally 'Who do you think you bloody well are?' as she brushes past the startled Margaret who has not said a word. The wrath she is expressing making further words impossible. She has spoken harshly with a vehemence Margaret later admits frightened her.

The tears, anger she has held back for the past weeks escaping at last. She hates the Bishop. She has never admitted to herself that she hated anyone before. She has never hated like this ever. It takes hold of her this rage. It makes her furious, incensed to think this man can change her life with one command. He holds control. He can stop, with one slap on the table, all she has worked for, for two years, longer, to develop, encourage. He had not even wanted to know what she is doing in the schools until the concern about MACOS was made public.

Ten days later Emma is still crying. She can see no way out of the impasse. She disappears to her room, cries for hours. She goes to sleep exhausted, then wakes to remember the dilemma again. The tears, frustration, anger are back with her again. Each of the members of the community tries to talk with her; tells her to forget about MACOS, go back to work, show this man he does not affect her. She knows one thing for sure. She is never going back to the Office where this man holds control.

1998 reflection / analysis

This way of resistance is one of rebellion against the physical constraints that prevented the spirit from expressing deepest desires. The illness, the recurring bodily interruption like the pneumonia, that took me outside the chronological time allocations, of holidays, or work patterns; the rearrangements of my life, that refusing to return to the Catholic Education Office required; the courage to remain without direction for the next months; all built up the tension to the pitch of the extreme that expressed the refusal to continue, a turning point, a syncope moment: 'for syncope is youth. Ego orgasm testifies to the subject's capacity to escape from the world. It is a game, a child's game like those Winnicott observed, which allows itself to manipulate the jigsaw puzzle of reality by exchanging roles or sexes, moving from one heart to the next. Or rather moving from doing to being ... completely immersed in the pure female element' (Clement, 1994:229). No long discernment process: an intuitive leap to a life decision – completely immersed in the pure female element. The return, the resolution, the cure, the unburdening therapeutic. No wonder women throughout history have fainted, given in to depression in greater numbers than their male counterparts, continued to read romantic novels in which falling in love and love at first sight are credibly narrated: 'everywhere, we have run across the pebble in the road, the obstacle, the chasm that has to be leaped. And we have glimpsed weak people suddenly endowed with enough prodigious, metaphysical strength to cross over, in a single bound'(Clement, 1994:254).

The Bishop spoke his understanding of the situation, that day he called me to his office. He pointed to my trip to the Philippines, Asia impinging, and the hazards of getting involved with material like that of MACOS, which questioned the established order. He took for granted my subservient position as woman, educator in his system of schools, obedient Catholic who would do exactly as he requested. He assumed there would be no further word of the situation after he had spoken to me. From my view he missed the opportunity to speak with me of different ways of understanding, and different approaches to education.

Hélène Cixous realistically sees the complexity with which he was faced. The energy that prompted my anger to keep blazing:

> She has never 'held still'; explosion, diffusion, effervescence, abundance, she takes pleasure in being boundless, outside self, outside same, far from a 'centre', from any capital of her 'dark continent', very far from the 'hearth' to which man brings her so that she will tend his fire, which always threatens to go out. She watches for him, but he has to keep an eye on her; for she can be his storm as well: 'will I die by a storm? Or will I go out like a light that doesn't wait to be blown out by the wind, but which dies tired and self satisfied? ... or: will I extinguish my own self in order not to burn down to the end?
>
> (Cixous and Clement, 1986:91)

(That is what my companions thought I was doing – extinguishing myself in what they called a nervous breakdown – I think of it now as distinguishing myself in hysteria, resistance, voice).

> Masculine energy, with its limited oil reserves, questions itself. Whereas, the fact that feminine energy has vast resources is not without consequences – still very rarely analysed – for exchange in general, for love-life, and for the fate created for woman's desire. Exasperating: he's afraid she 'goes too far'. And the irony of her fate has her either be this 'nothing', which punctuates the Dora case – ('You know my wife is nothing to me') – or this too-much, too-much reversed into not enough, the 'not how it should be' that reminds her that her master is on the limited side.
>
> (Cixous and Clement, 1986:91).

This man had asked me to continue watching over his dark fire. He expected such service. I refused. I had wandered far from (t)his hearth. I had begun to use words differently, see different meanings. He's afraid she goes too far. I considered I had hardly begun. The vast reserves of feminine energy hardly tapped. Vast resources that resisted constraint by masculine rules (strong in patriarchal thinking) and societal structures. The bishop master of such rules. The hysteria of my response not constrained by such 'arbitrary' rules. Freedom beckoning.

This man was of course not alone responsible for the decision he made about my educational experiment. I glimpsed his tight positioning even in the midst of my turmoil. He was part of the patriarchal, clerical, hierarchical world of male domination to which I was subject. I was one of the women, not fit to govern, belonging to one of the groups of people excluded from power in the socioeconomic, political practices of the Church to which I gave allegiance (Schussler-Fiorenza 1992). I was only just glimpsing this positioning. I was also guilty of looking for advice to other authorities (lay friends, educationalists – who introduced me to the MACOS material – and academics), not to this 'properly constituted male authority' (Maitland 1983:77). In the accepted church discourse of the past centuries women were subservient, submissive, obedient (at least in the public image). I could no longer be any of these things without modification. The Bishop was not accustomed to meeting women who spoke up for themselves, struggling to be articulate. He had only one response to the situation – stop their words, shut up such women. And that is what he did (or tried to do!).

Margaret took the fern, gave it away without any word to me, unwittingly lit the fire of my anger and hysteria.

No opportunity was ever given me to demonstrate the anger, exasperation, indignation to the Bishop or his assistants, or for that matter to any in the community. I was not permitted to explain the educational orientation I had chosen to any of the authorities. Labelled dangerous, highly flammable, too forcibly enthusiastic about the project I was monitoring in the schools, my superiors negotiated with the Education Office for the termination of my contract. Kept me at a distance. Excluded me. They lamented my refusal to return to the work I had been doing. They spoke of me as ill, hysterical. So close to the symptoms Cixous gives of the hysteric – 'Anti-establishment ... revolt and shake up the public, the group, the men, the others to whom they are exhibited ... The hysteric unties familiar bonds, introduces disorder into the well-regulated unfolding of everyday life, gives rise to magic in ostensible reason' (Cixous and Clement, 1986:5).

I must have made the little world of my Mercy community a hazardous one those days.

The Mercy Superiors – Martine as Leader, Margaret her Assistant – were my companions. We had experienced the last twenty years of religious life together. I felt I was their equal, was their representative at the Catholic Education Office. They acted from within the authority structure they had inherited from nineteenth and early twentieth century understandings of hierarchical power, unquestioning obedience and submission. 'The Sisters are always to bear in mind that, by the vow of obedience, they have renounced their own wills, and resigned them to the direction of their superiors' ... (Constitutions of the Australian Union of the Sisters of Mercy, 1960). They never considered that I might not remain within the tight boundaries of that authority structure as earlier defined. They had conferred with me very little on educational matters (as opposed to the Sister of St, Joseph with whom I worked, whose leaders gave her the status of wise consultant that I was never accorded). I was moving into a position in relation to obedience that was dangerous to these women, becoming a threat to their authority. My vow of obedience, discernment of the Spirit within my life, coming to be about God's prompting, a wider discernment process, no longer just the word of these women. I refused all their suggestions of overseas study, renewal, possible leave of absence from the Congregation. It took until May of the next year, 1979, while holidaying, convalescing in Melbourne for a couple of weeks, for me to choose a direction. I sat with one of the sisters from Beechwood, my friend Pamela (then working on a Mercy National Team) at Tullamarine Airport.

I heard myself tell Pamela I thought I would work for a couple of years in another country, immersed in activity in another culture. I know now I was beginning to speak from a different place, a feminist discourse. Critiques of education systems throughout the world, deschooling issues, cultural analyses of deprived peoples in countries like Brazil by writers like Freire and Illich, had led me to believe, with many other educators of the time, that it is 'possible for human beings, through the problematising of the unity being-world (or of human beings in their relations with the world and with other human beings) to penetrate more deeply the *prise de conscience* of the reality in which they exist' (Freire, 1974:107). A challenge I took seriously to work upon in my own small milieu. MACOS like a gift, to commence in small ways to crack through into new awareness, in the schools I knew.

The trip to the Philippines in September 1978 to which the Bishop refers in the memory, funded by my Congregation: two weeks of exposure to poverty, powerlessness, oppression. I wrote to the Sisters in my Congregation on my return, telling them what it felt like to sleep on the floor in a small hut in a barrio, with the rain coming through the slats joined to make a roof, the family (there were ten members who normally lived in this small three-metre-square space), moving out of the only dry spot to give it to me. Shocked into awareness of my middle class values, of tidiness, neatness, comfort; sensing the force of materialism to sway opinion; questioning my reliance on comfort (had I not publicly vowed poverty as my way of life – this scene demonstrated that what I lived was far from the desolation and destitution of these people). Another incentive to give greater time and energy to the MACOS Project on my return to Australia.

The different positions from which each of us spoke – bishop, congregational leaders, educational colleagues and I – hardly comprehended with any sensitivity. I had learnt in the previous years, in spiritual direction talks with a priest friend who was also a Freudian counsellor, to allow some of the workings of my unconscious to surface, be expressed, be articulated. I could acknowledge my hurt, vulnerability, exposure, pain, blazing anger now in ways I would never have used in the past. No longer ashamed of such feelings, (though everyone else was certainly afraid of them). I refused to hide them, offered myself patience as the only remedy I could see from within the suffering position, to move beyond them. If I could get away I would be safe. I would not damage others with the intensity of my anger.

I held onto my anger, resistance; knew if I could walk with others of like mind I might find what I was trying to say. It was all I seemed to have left. 'This power to be errant is strength; it is also what makes her vulnerable to those who champion the Selfsame, acknowledgment, and attribution. No matter how submissive and docile she may be in relation to the masculine order, she still remains the threatening possibility of savagery, the unknown quantity in the household whole' (Cixous and Clement, 1986:91).

The power of this anger and resistance would open the world, whirl me out of Australia, expand the map to encompass frontiers and lands never dreamed possible.

2004/5 reflection

As I look to significance of this writing I am alert to Cixous' constant reminder of the multiple possible relations with a text. 'When we read a text, we are either read by the text or we are in the text. Either we tame a text, we ride on it, we roll over it or we are swallowed up by it, as by a whale'(Cixous, 1990:3). O how I know all those possibilities! 'There are thousands of possible relations to a text, and if we are in non-defensive, non-resisting relationship, we are carried off by the text ... We have to try all possible relations with a text. At some point we have to disengage ourselves from the text as a living ensemble, in order to study its construction, its techniques and its texture' (Cixous, 1990:3). I'll endeavour to extricate myself from the text, to disengage from the earlier writing, to share some reflection of its processes with you as reader here in this third section of this article.

I'll attempt to examine further some aspects of the writing process I have come to know as potentially transformative, enabling of social change:

- how the writing writes me;
- how other's writing mandates, questions, tests what I am writing/reading.

Agency, leadership capacity, or the use of power in relation to others, the provoking concept with which I began my doctoral study, took me again and again to places like this memory of Emma in 1978. The joy of discovering a way of examining the text of such memories, language and discourses – through exploration, reading, writing of surprise and unexpectedness – opened a pathway in which the previously negative could be seen as a powerful and creative resistance.

My material for exploring – the body, tears, illness, curious questionings, interruptions to what had seemed predictable professional development – aspects of my stories that had refused to go away over the years, took centre stage. Davies reminded me that: 'the landscapes we lived with/in (and our reading of them) shaped our bodies, our mode of walking and running and jumping and breathing and talking and laughing – and sneezing. They scribed us, they (in)scribed us, as much in our imagining of possibilities as in the actual physical substance of what we were' (Davies 2000:22). The challenge to follow the recommendations of writers like Davies and Cixous: 'Woman must write her body, must make up the unimpeded tongue, that bursts partitions, classes and rhetoric, orders and codes, must inundate, run through ...' (Cixous and Clement, 1986:94), as well as Derrida: '... lock oneself away with oneself in oneself, try finally to understand oneself, alone and oneself '(Cixous and Derrida 2001:21), took me immediately into new positionings, unfamiliar places and different ways of (in)scribing.

I captured the memories, events from journals, diaries and letters; restructured them in dramatic form, using Haug's (1992) research to support my method. It proved to be highly disciplined work to keep the re-enactment of the memory true to the insights and knowledge available at the time of its action. I became obsessed with issues relating to identity, subjectivity – multiple, many-faceted, language-based. Undoing as soon as creating. Crossing out. Rewriting. Giving a prominent role to the unconscious. De-scribing. Re-inscribing. Looking for a new order based on love. Letting my body write itself. Losing control of direction, carried off by the text, as Cixous (1990:3) suggests. Embodiment leading to the earth, the ground, flowers, animals, rootedness and the other. The tiger image, the strong animal that in later years became the dream image of my expression of male power and acting, manifesting itself in a number of different ways.

The co-extension of self and language is crucial in the process of this opening-out of language. The linearity and rationality of dominant discourses that had contained self and overtaken meaning are undone / become unstitched. Cixous, through her wondrous images, often indicating other ways of viewing what had earlier been burdensome for me. Hysterics, sorceresses, witches, wise women, crones, daughters, no longer excluded, displacing the (m)other in their joyful excess, stepping out of function to celebrate new storylines. Hysteria holding magic! A crossing-over point. A way of gaining voice and visibility when all other ways seemed blocked. Power gained through weakness. Passionate responses mandated and rejoiced in. Jouissance. Vistas of feminine embodied woman / women previously only available within fantasy discourses becoming accessible.

The research opened a pathway in which the previously negative could be seen as a powerful and creative resistance. No longer to be hidden. Revealed as one of the storylines only. A powerful one – recognised for its capacity to modify, change and nuance earlier self-images. A new spirituality in disobedience. This power energising, dissipating discords. I know I am more than the tears and the hysteria. I am other – creative educator, daughter, sister, fern grower, entertainer, academic historian / herstorian, poet, mystic, dreamer, delighting in the possibilities for storying anew. Time and space become intertwined in this continuing process. Time unfolding differently. I can be in the memory of 1978 and my unpacking of its depths in 1998 and at the same time in 2004/5. 'My head is spinning, I've just seen three worlds in one' (Cixous, 1998:80).

I want to use this interruptive syncope moment of insight. In this spinning moment I can leave the disengagement of this overall view of the writing and enter one of the fissures of the space of the memory once more. Come with me back into the text.

The fragment I enter is that of the ten days of tears, frustration and anger that seemed to be the living out of the consequences of Emma's hysteria. As overflowing as the tears, as new as if they happen today is the draining of all earlier understandings of relationship to the father, the male authority in family and church – the bishop its main manifestation, the leaders of the congregation other expressions. I see a young woman, beloved and loving in family and community, taking for granted her obedient, respectful and reciprocal relationship to authority and power. Cut off from this storyline in this instance with a thump on the table and a denial of creativity and innovation.

I am caught in Emma's tears and the immensity of the father's rejection. Her pain intense. Inexplicable from the discourses she knows. Rejection of the educative direction inseparable from self-identification. She is lost. I listen to her anguish surrounded by images of pain in the suffering of the Iraqi people, the women in particular; in racist violence, in loss today in the world news of tsunami and the refugee stories I hear. This pain beyond my intellect. It is in my body. Making a deep gash in my heart. I see Emma's denial of the suffering – her busyness in preparing for the Christmas party, her refuge in tears in her inability to articulate the deep hurts, her fear of the immensity of her anger if she gives it expression. I crawl into the inner spaces to see how she is protecting herself in the rain of tears and the torment. Seemingly unmanageable conflict and paradox are there. (A space I have been unable to face in so many earlier events of my life stories – the time of this writing my first courage in this regard). The rupturing of the girl-self, the disappearance of the initiative of the creative educator leaving her naked, exposed full of trembling fears.

To my amazement glimpses of flashing joyful release and surprise greet me. Unacknowledged behind the tears, keeping her tenaciously refusing to follow the dictates of her religious leaders over these ten days of anguish. What desire, beyond the law holds her so tenaciously in this site? What slippage is occurring? What transitory moment here? Desire challenging the very systems brought into play.

I see she hugs herself as she cries. Holds something in her arms. Envelopes it. Holds it close. Protectively watchful. I look closer to see what it is. It is alive, reinscribed in her loss. A small tiger cub, golden, soft, cuddly, playful. New born through the pain. Too fragile, too small, too different, to be more than welcomed. 'The tiger, like herself, is soft with ferocity' (Cixous, 1990:40): visible courage in the fear. Traces of sensation, fantasy, mythology – there in the transition.

What cost this birth of the animal figure that would become significant in later storylines. I know the unexpectedness of the tiger who bursts into the middle of the party and is easily shooed away by the child of my dreams. I know the tiger who walks on a lead with me as adult along the shores of the lake. I have not, until this writing, glimpsed its birth in those tears and anguish of 1978. I rejoice now in its visibility. What power such further investigation of memory. What taming, nurturance and control would be required over the years for the tiger's growth? What friends would be lost through the development of such instinctive power of resistance, agency, instrumentality and 'subversive excess' (Fuery, 1995:44)?

I venture back from this interruption and the text of this memory once more.

Teaching, researching and travelling in England and Europe occupied the linear time / space of the three years following Emma's confrontation with Bishop Fred. There I / Emma learn to be conscious of breaking the connectedness of this body to its main storyline. There I begin to learn to acknowledge loss and nakedness, and to be fully alive to each moment. No one in my milieu in England questioned emotive ways of responding, poetry, capacity to dance through the days as they did in Australia. I learn new courtesies, entry to new cultures (I teach International Baccalaureate students from diverse countries). Crossing borders of language, image, symbol, race, an everyday occurrence. Writers like Byatt, Turner Hospital, Jolley and many others leading me into questions of fiction / borderlines / literature – all becoming texts open to my search, recorded in my journals and letters. Travel – my privileged, constant holiday companion. Traditional cultures, knowledge, art, music, theatre, reading and dance unfolding in difference and diversity. Australia fast becoming the other.

I am there immersed in the process of unfolding.

I may not be writing this article without that journey to another country / other countries – to lands of finding my roots / dreams – 'going towards the unverifiable' (Cixous, 1993:146) to leaving home, to being displaced. I might still be caught in emotive, hysteric modes of response without the Bishop's confrontation and the possibilities of that journey. My refusal to return to the Catholic Education Office in 1978 was seen by many as rejection of professional development. My break from my career, my time in England seemingly an escape. I see it now as one of the greatest developmental times (transformation / change times) of my life. Bishop Fred has died since I first recorded this memory. Speaking of him recently to the present Bishop of Beechwood, I noted the complexity of that confrontation of 1978; my gratitude to Bishop Fred in the midst of acknowledgment of pain, loss, suffering, intuitive power and choice.

Many writers (like Cixous in this article) verify the integrity of such choices as I made – writing, working against the accepted authority and traditional linear patterns of meaning-making published stories; characters and situations echoing my own, enhancing, giving new meaning to my explorations, opening aspects of difference and possible new interpretations.

The importance of these parts of the analyses to take the spirals of meaning into new depths, heights and interruptions cannot be underestimated. Testing the writing against the other, an integral part of the process to give unfolding meaning to storylines of learners, leaders, managers, professionals holding power or considering the issue of power in / over other's lives.

If paradoxes, ambiguities, thresholds such as Emma's experience are to be fruitful, cultural contexts for training of such professionals may require many, varied programmes for immersion in difference, together with the recognition that the strongest times of potential professional growth may be the vacuum spaces, the hard places, the syncope moments or break points. In storylines like Emma's, interruptions or times of fragmentation of accepted programmes, which seem to have the capacity to problematise, may be the times of greatest acceleration of learning. Though I'm aware that not all students / professionals can risk linking the personal and the professional at this especially feminist depth.

My search for wisdom, sacred storylines, primitive origins, secret magic and mystery continues. Professional choices and choices as a woman religious remain closely allied. I have learnt I can so easily slip from one discourse to another. Gift as well as burden. I translate, endeavour to comprehend the differing positions from which I am confronted. I am learning a greater respect for difference. My searching through such diversity, fragmentation, uncertainty, alienation, for the forces / power / meanings that are culturally, racially and socially explicable, continues. I have yet to take the exploration into the deeper moral or ethical stances that confront the poststructural fragmentations themselves – though I test them in relation to four main areas: the cosmos, images and concepts of god, self-identification and group (family, community, cultural ...) responsibility. Perhaps a response from one of my readers may set me further on that trail.

I believe social change is possible through the use of such potentially liberatory processes of analysis and writing as I have endeavoured to demonstrate in this case study, noting healthy resistance as a possible response to contradiction. I believe we can assist professionals to begin to articulate their stories in a critical, powerful and enabling process of unpacking certainties, to reach beyond expected outcomes to open-ended exploration. The multiple possibilities in language and self-identification that occur can guarantee ongoing and unfolding professional and scholastic times of autonomy and agency.

Linda Brodky sums up the background to these claims:

> The poststructural narrative on human subjectivity is all the more attractive to me because of the possibilities for discursive resistance

suggested in the notion of articulation. In much the same way that theorists argue that the unity of discourse is a necessary illusion, I view resistance or interruption as a necessary illusion, if only because I need to believe that social change is possible and, further, that the possibility of shifting discursive positions and articulating positive representations of oneself is a more effective and lasting form of political resistance than either silence or violence. (1996:23)

Note
1. Jerome Bruner's *Man: a Course of Studies* (MACOS) had been introduced into NSW courses of study for Social Science Students at Tertiary Institutes in the early 1970s. The Bishop's comments and action come two years after the MACOS material had been introduced to the teachers referred to in this case study. Hence this work was already established before the mentioned trip to the Philippines.

References
Barthes, R. (1994). 'The pleasure of the text'. (Trans. R. Miller. Original work published 1973). New York: Hill and Wang.

Brodkey, L. (1996). *Writing permitted in designated areas only*. Minneapolis, Minnesota: University of Minnesota Press.

Butler, J. (1997). *Excitable Speech: A Politics of the Performative*. New York and London: Routledge.

Coakley, S. (ed.). (1997). *Religion and the body*. Cambridge: Cambridge University Press.

Cixous, H. (1991). 'Coming to writing' and other essays. (D. Jenson [Ed.]. Trans. S. Cornell). Cambridge, MA: Harvard University Press.

Cixous, H. (1993). 'Three steps on the ladder of writing'. (Trans. S. Cornell and S. Sellers). New York: Columbia University Press.

Cixous, H. (1998). 'First Days of the Year'. (Trans. and preface by C. A. F. MacGillivray). Minneapolis, Minnesota: University of Minnesota Press.

Cixous, H. and C. Clement (1986). 'The newly born woman'. (Trans. B. Wing. Original work published 1975). Manchester: Manchester University Press.

Cixous, H. and M. Calle-Gruber (1997). *Hélène Cixous rootprints: memory and life writing*. (Trans. E. Prenowitz. Original work published 1994). London: Routledge.

Cixous, H. and J. Derrida (2001). 'Veils: Cultural Memory in the Present'. (Trans. G. Bennington. Drawings by E. Pignon-Ernest). Stanford, California: Stanford University Press.

Clement, C. (1994). 'Syncope, the philosophy of rapture'. (Trans. S. O'Driscoll and D. M. Mahony). Minneapolis, Minnesota: University of Minnesota Press.

Clement, C. and J. Kristeva (2001). 'The feminine and the sacred'. (Trans. J. M. Todd). Hampshire, Palgrave.

Davies, B.(2000). *(In)scribing Body/Landscape Relations*. Walnut Creek, California: Alta Mira Press.
Deleuze, G. (1995). 'Negotiations 1972-1990'. (Trans. M. Joughin. Original published 1990), New York: Columbia University Press.
Derrida, J. (1984). *Of grammatology*. (Trans. G. C. Spivak). Baltimore: John Hopkins University Press.
Foucault, M. (1980). *Power/Knowledge: selected interviews and other writings 1972-1977*. (Trans. C. Gordon). New York: Pantheon Books.
Foucault, M. (1991). *The archeology of knowledge*. (Trans. A. M. Sheridan Smith. Original work published 1972). London: Routledge.
Freire, P. (1974). *Education for critical consciousness*. London: Sheed and Ward.
Fuery, P. (1995). *Theories of Desire*. Melbourne: Melbourne University Press.
Haug, F. (1992). *Beyond Female Masochism: Memory work and Politics*. (Trans. R. Livingston). London: Verso.
Heilbrun, C. G. (1989). *Writing a woman's life*. London: Women's Press.
Illich, I. D. (1973). *Celebration of awareness*. Great Britain: Penguin.
Irigaray, L. (1996). *I love to you: sketch of a possible felicity in history*. (Trans. A. Martin). New York: Routledge.
Isherwood, L. (2004). 'The embodiment of Feminist Liberation Theology: The Spiralling of Incarnation'. *Feminist Theology: Special edition. Embodying Feminist Liberation Theologies*, Vol. 12, No. 2, pp. 140-156.
Lacan, J. (1977). 'Ecrits: A selection'. (Trans. A. Sheridan). New York: W.W. Norton.
Maitland, S. (1983). *A map of the new country: Women and Christianity*. London: Routledge and Keegan Paul.
McConkey, K. (1995). 'Hypnosis, Memory and the Ethics of Uncertainty'. *Australian Psychologist*. Vol. 31, (1), pp 1-10.
Richardson, L. (1990). 'Narrative and Sociology'. *Journal of Contemporary Ethnography*. Vol. 19, No. 1, pp. 116-135.
Richardson, L. (1997). *Fields of play: constructing an academic life*. New Brunswick, New Jersey: Rutgers University Press.
Smith, P.M. (1998). *Giving oneself to writing: syncopations in the life of a woman religious*. Unpublished PhD Thesis. Queensland: James Cook University.
Smith, P.M. (2003). *Mapping the whirled: syncopations in the life of a woman religious*. Melbourne: Spectrum Publications.
Smith, P. M. (2004). 'Giving oneself to writing: syncopations in the life of a woman religious'. *International Journal of Qualitative Studies in Education*. Vol.17, No.1, pp.29-46.
Smith, R. (1995). *Derrida and autobiography*. Cambridge: Cambridge University Press.
St. Pierre, E.A. (1997). 'Nomadic inquiry in the smooth spaces of the field: a preface', *International Journal of Qualitative Studies in Education*. Vol.10, No. 3, pp. 365-383.

'This is a hospital, not a circus!'
Reflecting on generative metaphors for a deeper understanding of professional practice

Sally Denshire

his paper develops a matrix of literal and metaphoric descriptions of experiences in professional practice which problematises the distinction. This matrix derives from accounts of my work as an occupational therapist with young people in hospital. The lived experiences of professional practice tend to be routinely suppressed by the demand for superficial evidence in regulated contexts. I have come to understand this work as an underground practice. I deliberately take a phenomenological, hermeneutic perspective to explicating the expressive, carnivalesque and underground aspects of my practice. Reflection on a colleague's throwaway remarks revealed aspects of this occupational therapy practice as ritual magic. Metaphor, a conceptual tool that enables reflection through a combination of imagination and reason, significantly structures our experience of the complexities of professional practice, employing a kind of 'as if' knowing. Contemplating my experience of an underground practice through unpacking figurative language recalls the power of metaphor. Reflecting on generative metaphors can help us come to a deeper understanding of the subjective aspects of practice: those aspects we feel and experience rather than merely observe. Foregrounding figurative language can transcend the 'seeing is believing' vantage-point typical of narrow interpretations of evidence. Further inquiry into the lived experience of practice in contexts of regulated evidence is recommended.

Introduction

Between 1981 and 1994 I was occupational therapist with the Adolescent Medical Unit of the Children's Hospital in Sydney. In this role I initiated a series of hospital-based creative projects with young people, health workers and arts practitioners which came to be known as the Youth Arts Program. The program participants, who were 'regular customers' of the hospital aged between twelve and twenty, had experienced repeated and prolonged hospitalisation at a time of life when their struggle for autonomy was at its peak. Their developmental need for both architectural and psychic space was very real, and necessary for their service providers and researchers to comprehend.

We acknowledged participants in these peer-group activities as 'occupational beings' (Clark, Ennevor and Richardson, 1996) rather than hospital patients, that is as active, speaking subjects with the right to do personally meaningful occupations. These young people enjoyed themselves through creativity and expression, and were able to use their collective voices within the hospital walls. During their time in hospital they created masks, video art and computer-generated images, giant board games, radio documentaries, stories, poetry, sculpture and cultural events. These creative projects took place around the wards, corridors and grounds in a paediatric teaching hospital, occurring at the symbolic intersection of youth and hospital cultures.

Initially, these creative, spontaneous practices were dismissed by the hospital administrators who regarded them as peripheral to the predominantly clinical environment so did not allocate funds for staffing or resources. With hindsight, I have come to the conclusion that my involvement in these projects with young people in hospital constituted an 'underground practice', as an excerpt from my writings illustrates:

> I have always been interested in what I call 'informal work' even when I worked in a medical setting and the medical people had all these structures and forms and terminology. I felt those of us who worked in allied health really were pretty light on structures and forms and terminology – we were just called the non-medical. I've always been interested to unpack our work and to give it language and meaning; the work that was done in the corridors – that Cheryl Mattingly calls 'underground practice'. Although it sounds contradictory I would like to systematise the informal (Denshire and Ryan, 2001, p. 157).

Looking back on my own practices causes me to question assumptions about ways of knowing, construction of evidence and relations between theory and practice. I wonder how to undo the opposition of literal and metaphoric meaning in the language of the human-related professions. How might prevailing classifications of knowledge and evidence be re-worked to encompass personal and professional, and visible and invisible, so that lived experiences can be integrated into our knowledge of practice? What then are the implications for integrative ways of knowing in the case of occupational therapy, a little-known practice which has been portrayed as both underground and complex?

My Masters research into the phenomenon of reflection in occupational therapy practice involved a reinterpretation of my published writings over seventeen years. These writings are an autobiographical sequence of stories about professional practice and life pre-motherhood (Denshire, 1984, 1985a, 1985b; Denshire and Bennett, 1985) and since becoming a mother (Denshire, 1989, 1993, 1996; Denshire and Fortune, unpublished transcript, 1998; Denshire and Ryan, 2001). In the course of the research I analysed selected metaphors and terms from my writings which then informed a personal model of practice (Denshire, 2004).

The act of reflecting on what I had written also caused me to recollect things that were not recorded. Particular recollections that have stayed with me because they captured my imagination concerned a respected nursing colleague retorting, 'this is a hospital, not a circus' when I asked for access to performance space for young people in hospital, and calling me a 'Pied Piper' in my role as youth-specific occupational therapist.

So my intent in this paper is to interrogate my practice of hospital-based occupational therapy by contemplating these remarks. I will unpack the meanings embedded in particular recollections of this period of my life and work, in order to convey something of my lived experience of professional practice in an environment which has become increasingly regulated. Accordingly, this paper explicates selected aspects of a practice of occupational therapy from 'the indeterminate swampy zones' (Schön, 1988, p.3), naming and framing the artistry of practice with meaningful terms and considered understandings (Schön, 1983). The paper explores how imagination can work with reason in the construction and interpretation of evidence, and ways in which generative metaphors – that is to say those productive metaphors which enable us to reach new understandings of things

– can deepen our knowledge of practice due to their conceptual richness.

I begin by reviewing literature on privileging visual ways of knowing and suppressing lived experience in increasingly regulated climates of professional practice. I discuss the phenomenological, hermeneutic perspective I have taken when contemplating metaphors of the expressive, carnivalesque and underground aspects of practice with young people in hospital. In the first place, these recollections were attributed to my practice by someone else and I could have simply left it at that. After all, at one level, these utterances were no more than off-hand remarks made by a colleague.

However, what I recalled her saying captured my imagination. The emblematic capacity of aphorisms to convey significant meaning in few words has always interested me, and she was a nursing colleague whom I respected. It was for these reasons that I decided to use these recollections to develop a case for the power of generative metaphors to reveal the complexity of practice, in this case occupational therapy practice; indeed, to reframe aspects of professional practices as ritual magic. In closing, I discuss the scope of the paper and recommend further work on the lived experience of practice in the climates of regulated evidence in which we may find ourselves as critical professionals.

Literature review

The first part of the paper integrates literature related to current demands for superficial, visible evidence in regulated contexts, and how these prevailing expectations can routinely suppress our lived experiences of professional practice.

The rise of visual ways of knowing and the health professions

The tenets of practice currently promoted by the health professions often stem from evidence-based medicine, from theories of evidence which focus on the external and the visible, on apparent proof that is classified and hierarchical: 'real outcomes' in contemporary professional discourse (Clarke, 1999). More tenuous forms of evidence – such as circumstantial evidence within the legal profession – allude to less categorical forms of proof. Too often, the classification of evidence within the health professions is restricted to such narrow interpretations, for example, as counting bed days related to diagnosis or measuring the physical functioning of a client group before and after treatment according to clinical tests. Such superficial classifications of what is permitted as evidence will obviously hold little relevance for those seeking deeper, experiential understandings of practice (Clarke, 1999).

Of course the term 'evidence' comes from the Latin 'videre' meaning 'to see' (Simpson and Weiner, 1989). Metaphors that predominate in contemporary Western culture also privilege the visual, equating 'knowledge with illumination, knowing with seeing and truth with light', seeing in the mind's eye (Belenky, Clinchy, Goldberger and Tarule, 1986, p. 18). Such metaphors often refer to a disengaged or microscopic standpoint in order to see one prescribed view. Whereas metaphors of feeling and listening which are more interactive might generate dialogue and conversation rather than maintaining a position of objective regard.

Despite the origin of narrow interpretations of evidence, metaphors are, of course, invoked in medicine. According to Mattingly (1994, p. 42), 'biomedicine [itself] is organised around several potent metaphors'. The way in which cancer is described using the terminology of warfare has been documented by Sontag (1977). Such metaphors serve to separate the person from the disease. The most significant biomedical metaphor is the metaphor of body as machine (Mattingly, 1994a). Foucault (1979) connects this view of the body to the objectifying 'disciplinary gaze'. In contrast, the noted pioneer of neuroscience Charles Sherrington (n.d.) has used 'as if' knowing to compare the work of the brain in weaving patterns of memory to that of a very different machine, 'an enchanted loom' (cited in Rose, 1998, p. 39). In these ways, the influence of metaphor in 'as if' knowing can be found across discourses of practice regardless of discipline. The significance of this way of knowing will be discussed later in the paper.

Given the fundamental differences between categorising evidence and making meaning, practitioners working outside the dominant paradigm try to preserve subjective ways of knowing in underground practices grounded in lived experience. Those phenomena that are complex, subtle and hidden underground are incompatible with reductionist systems where so called objective, measurable ways of knowing are privileged. Increasingly, professionals are encountering demands for simplistic (in the sense of measurable) outcomes in the protocols of government and non-government organisations. The prevalent interpretations of what constitutes evidence-based practice seem to demand a technocratic professional identity which belies complexity.

Yerxa (1988, p. 5) has explained oversimplification as 'the process by which inherently complex phenomena are reduced to parts or fragments which are more easily seen, understood and /or controlled'. More than a decade ago she cautioned that acute medical care, measurement and impressive technology could seduce the profession of occupational therapy into oversimplifying occupational therapy and urged therapists to preserve and nurture its complexity in practice, research and education. Gray, Kennedy and Zemke (1996) also draw attention to the paradox that 'the extraordinary complexity of human occupation compels and inhibits its study' (p. 297). The broad conceptualisation of evidence suggested in this paper supports Yerxa's earlier views on complexity.

Over twenty years ago Rogers (1983) highlighted the multiple levels of reasoning which underlie practice in occupational therapy. She has noted that the clinical reasoning process terminates in an ethical decision rather than a scientific one, and has described scientific, ethical and artistic strands at work in combination in the reasoning of occupational therapy practitioners. However, such multiplicity in reasoning may be submerged today in climates of economic efficiency.

Lived experiences of professional practice tend to be suppressed

The tendency in society generally to keep parts of life private can be exaggerated in situations such as pressured transactions taking place between health professionals and clients in out-patient clinics or emergency rooms where there is a high demand for professional distance. In institutional situations where professionalism is equated with a supposedly neutral practitioner then role distortion may impose unhelpful expectations of interpersonal distance and rigid behaviour, disrupting meaningful dialogue and empathic understanding (Lyons, 1997; Trysenaar, 1997). Consequently, both client and practitioner may experience therapeutic encounters in the late modern era as devoid of any meaningful intimacy and, ultimately, as unsatisfying (Grbich, 1999; Giddens, 1991).

However privately subjectivity is experienced, it is inevitably structured in ways which are drawn from the public domain, the socio-cultural milieu. Tensions between what practitioners discuss in case conferences and write in institutional files and what they actually do person-to-person in therapeutic situations mean that the relation of subjective and objective ways of knowing can be conflicted in contemporary work places. Maintaining a rigid professional distance can structure in unhelpful ways the relations between professionals and people seeking occupational therapy.

Because professional distance is highlighted in the prevailing climate of economic rationalism (Prowse, 1999; Rees, 1995), rethinking the personal-professional relation in the practitioner to integrate the multiplicity of the self (Melucci, 1996) and foster multiple ways of knowing is urgent. For more personal therapeutic encounters a new understanding of the connections between the lived experience of professionals is necessary.

Schön's studies of professional education in fields such as architecture, musical performance and counselling emphasised the need for practitioners to pay attention to what may be understood as the lived experience of their work, 'the indeterminate swampy zones of practice' (1988, p. 3). Originally, the time necessary for reflection was not highlighted in Schön's theory of reflective practice. Now, however, finding the time for processes of reflection is increasingly problematic in the time-starved climates of contemporary workplaces. In climates of economic efficiency and professional distance narrow constructions of evidence are typically demanded and phenomenological aspects swept aside.

Often, the meaning of 'professional practice', in the traditional sense that medicine, law and divinity are professions, does not fit with the experience of practices in emergent professions. Occupational therapy itself has often been regarded as a relatively invisible and under-theorised practice profession due, in part, to the 'unique but repressed history' of occupational therapists (Wilcock, 1998, p. 246). My reading here is that the creative, intuitive aspects of our practice tend to be under-documented because they are suppressed by economic and techno-rational imperatives. A decade ago, Cusick, Schofield and Twible (1994) personified occupational therapy as something hidden or in hiding with a silent, or rather silenced, history. More recently, Mattingly's doctoral research on the professional reasoning of occupational therapists linked her ground-breaking study of reflective practice within the occupational therapy profession to a general trend of reflective practice in the human-related professions (Ryan, 1998).

The term 'underground practice' (Fleming and Mattingly, 1994, p. 296) refers to the phenomenological aspects of people's lived experience – both practitioners and people seeking occupational therapy. Mattingly and Fleming undertook an ethnographic study of clinical reasoning with occupational therapists in a large American hospital.

This landmark study uncovered 'an unease at the heart of their practice. Most therapists were deeply ambivalent about the phenomenological aspect of their practice' (Fleming and Mattingly, 1994, pp. 296-7). However, working with the client and their lived experiences, rather than only with a person's physical body, was also what occupational therapists tended to value most.

The practitioners who participated in this study felt that, within the prevailing biomedical discourse, they could not openly acknowledge the emotional, social, political and symbolic experiences that routinely occur in therapy situations. They experienced ongoing dilemmas regarding professional ethics and professional identity due, in part, to occupational therapy being 'a two-body practice' (Mattingly, 1994b, p. 64). In other words, these occupational therapists were concerned with both disease and with illness experience, with both the physical body and the body in which a person lives and which they experience (Fleming and Mattingly, 1994).

At this stage of the development of occupational therapy in Australia, the symbolic level of practice, that is to say those richly imagistic ways of collaborating with clients using expressive media of their own choosing, for example, is more often part of an underground practice (Fleming and Mattingly, 1994). Hocking and Wilcock (1997) have concluded that description of the symbolic aspect of practice has not yet permeated the Australian literature. Their review of the professional writings of occupational therapists over forty-two years revealed the influence of mechanistic thinking on the way therapists perceive objects such as wheelchairs as functional tools devoid of subjective or symbolic meaning. However, there is an undeniable symbolic aspect in doing everyday rituals and in the use of objects which have particular meaning for an individual, but this level of practice has not often been articulated in the literature (Mattingly and Fleming, 1994).

The under-documented but unavoidable subjectivity of practice in occupational therapy values a sense of personal engagement rather than objective regard. Significantly, Crabtree (1998) does acknowledge the phenomenological aspects of reasoning in occupational therapy practice, in which Australian practitioners habitually generate a range of options for 'doing things', in concert with their clients, as typically involving imagination on the part of the therapist. This imagination is used to guide clients to envisage those life occupations they feel compelled to resume following some disruption to their lives. For example, choosing to plan and carry out an expressive project in the face of chronic illness. This everyday problem-solving process utilises a symbolic, imagistic thinking (Mattingly and Fleming, 1994; Fazio, 1992); one that, to be successful, needs to be empathic and future-oriented, with a focus on realising potential.

Ricoeur (1991) has suggested that we must look to productive imagination as 'the place of nascent meanings and categories rather than the place of fading impressions' (p. 82). Imagination may be regarded as highly desirable or as implying a lack of credibility, depending on standpoint. There is a spectrum of meaning in how the term is used. A perspective which restores the creative potential to images and symbols rather than being wedded to an understanding of imagination that is restricted to the sensory (Simpson and Weiner, 1989, Vol. VII, p. 669) is in stark contrast to the prevailing discourse of outcome measures and mechanistic, procedural ways of thinking (Clarke, 1999).

In this section I have raised issues now well documented in the literature (Clarke, 1999; Crabtree, 1998; Rees, 1995; Mattingly and Fleming, 1994; Ricoeur, 1991; Rogers, 1983). The work of all these authors shares links to considering the importance of creativity and metaphor when reflecting critically on professional practice within the context of acknowledging the lived experiences of our clients and ourselves in the present climate of regulated evidence in which we find ourselves as critical professionals.

Taking a phenomenological, hermeneutic approach to reflection

The second part of the paper will outline my approach to reflecting on figurative language in this particular case, in the context of a broader inquiry into reflection in occupational therapy practice. Phenomenological hermeneutics is a philosophical method of reinterpreting lived experience by a process of contemplating and re-framing the meanings embedded in language, a process that is inevitably subjective (Finger, 1988; Gadamer, n.d., cited in Blackburn 1996; Schleiermacher, cited in Blackburn, 1996; Valdés, 1991). I made use of a phenomenological, hermeneutic perspective when reflecting on actions and interactions in various domains and over various time frames in my Masters research. In this way I have come to a gradual reinterpretation of my lived experience as an occupational therapist through deconstructing selected literal and metaphoric language in my published writings (see Denshire, 2002 and Denshire and Mullavy-O'Byrne, 2003).

This paper reworks these earlier understandings of the role

metaphor can have in structuring professional practice. In this paper I will reflect on the figurative language contained in off-hand remarks made by a colleague. My reflections on these metaphors begin by citing the nominated metaphor in a sentence or phrase. The context of the recollection in which the metaphor was used is explained. I unpack the metaphor by describing in detail its meaning through recourse to a literal subject using the dictionary in the case of 'underground practice' to show the senses in which these words have been used historically. I reflect on values, beliefs and assumptions embedded in the literal and figurative meanings of each metaphor and question the metaphor's meaning by comparing its connotations with the life experience, knowledge, values and belief systems expressed in my writings in order to confirm (or deny) the meanings derived from the metaphor. And finally, I ask whether I now affirm these same assumptions, beliefs, values or understandings.

Reflecting on generative metaphors

In the third part of the paper three generative metaphors are unpacked using the method just outlined. These metaphors are related to hospital as an institutional setting, to myself as an occupational therapist and to dimensions of my professional practice. My reflections are entitled *Hospital as not a circus*, *Occupational therapist as Pied Piper* and *Practice as something underground*.

Hospital as not a circus

More than once a charge sister reminded me, 'this is a hospital, not a circus', when I requested space or other resources to use for art-making or performance by young people in hospital. Circus has performative connotations of noise and commotion, colour and movement, of the throng and the carnival, in contrast to the attitude that hospital is a still, solitary place of compliance and silence with no colours. Hospital staff can absorb institutionalised anxiety and then defend it through the controlling of resources (Menzies Lyth, 1988). Inadvertently, some staff may function as gate-keepers by suppressing the emotional, expressive aspects of practice. Although the speaker implied that there were established standards of behaviour in the institution and that requests for occupational resources did not fit these expectations, she was actually quite supportive of the Youth Arts Program as time went on.

At the old Children's Hospital, a place of children and youth, in contrast to other medicalised settings, there was an imprecise, nonclinical, spiritual dimension conveyed by the compassion of the brown-draped madonna of the Children's Medical Research Foundation and in the Australian fairytale paintings by illustrator Pixie O'Harris on the yellowing walls. There, the collective spirit was in evidence on Party Day with the transformation of each ward into something magic just for one day. To some extent, roles between patients and staff were blurred as in a carnival and the wards seemed more like carnivalesque, liberating zones with no division between performers and spectators on that one day (Vice, 1997).

More recently, the New Childrens' Hospital incorporates fantasy elements in its design and architecture with some recognition of the metaphoric nature of children's play. Melucci (1996) has considered questions of space, time and ritual magic in therapy despite the estrangement of the illness experience by technological apparatus. I wonder how such ancient beliefs can be reconciled with modern medicine and am reminded of the anthroposophical belief in the wisdom of fairytales (Grahl, 1970), something which arises in the next reflection.

Occupational therapist as Pied Piper
The old story of the Pied Piper (Marelles, 1977, p. 120), in which a charismatic stranger spirits away the town's children with music (after not being paid for ridding the town of rats) can be construed as being about the power of music to enchant (Bettelheim, 1976). But it can also have the more sinister connotation of the Piper deliberately leading away forever all the children of the town except the lame boy. After all, the Piper differed from the mainstream on a matter of principle. Perhaps, in this context, ridding the town of rats could be an oblique reference to the medical elimination of agents of disease. In this recollection I am being referred to as a fairy tale stranger by another member of staff. After all, I was colourfully dressed and worked collectively, rather than individually, with young people. I had begun my career by 'not rely(ing) particularly on my professional role or wear(ing) a uniform' (Denshire, 1984, p. 12). As I was bringing young people to or from the ward I had heard her say rather exasperatedly, 'that OT's a Pied Piper!'

Given that occupational therapy sessions with young people in hospital often took place in the youth centre across the road from the hospital, perhaps one interpretation for this rather evocative metaphor could be that as the youth-specific occupational therapist

I was regarded as someone unfamiliar, perhaps subversive, who took young people away to an unseen place, hidden from the gaze of ward staff who were often more attuned to treating their patients clinically. On reflection I now feel that being described as the Pied Piper could have attributed me with a disproportionate power over these young people. This metaphor could be construed as infantilising, precluding any sense of shared humanity (Muecke, 1997). The role as I recall it felt more like being a member of a travelling circus troupe, a gypsy nomad with magic at her disposal with which to restore institutional inequities between adults and young people, at least for a time.

My emphasis on peer group work and creative projects with young people who were regarded as 'occupational beings', that is as active, speaking subjects rather than as hospital patients, was not well understood by some medical and nursing staff in the early years of the program. Consistent positive feedback from young people themselves about their experiences of active participation, self-expression and collaboration with others was gradually constructed as evidence of the program's value. The alternative knowledges and ethical practices expressed through their actions and voices circulated publicly via displays of art works. For example, 'Great Escape Two', a Super-8 film regarded as instrumental in the campaign to open the adolescent ward was screened at Grand Rounds (Denshire, 1996), and sculptures made from recycled hospital equipment, such as wheelchairs and drip stands, by young people in hospital and art students were exhibited throughout the hospital during Postgraduate Week (Buckland, 1994). Gradually, the initial scepticism changed to overt support as the 'underground practice' became more public.

Practice as something underground
Dictionary definitions of 'underground' have a connotation of ideological action. Definitions and selected quotations of practice from between 1706 and 1969 also imply the existence of a degree of underlying doctrine in the political and philosophical senses of 'practice', even though this term is more commonly contrasted with theory. The hidden, covert nature denoted by 'underground' is conveyed in the selected dictionary definitions and quotations from between 1884 and 1962. There is also a notion of provision of alternatives, and a dissonance between what is reported and what is actually done.

underground **A** *adj.* = SUBTERRANEAN *a.*
   3.a. Carried on, taking place underground ...
   d. Adapted for use underground.
   1884 Knight *Dict. Mech.* Suppl. 911/1 Steven's underground engine.
   4. *fig.* **a.** Hidden, concealed, secret.
   b. Not open or public; concealed from or avoiding general notice.
   c. Designating (the activities of) a group, organisation, or its representatives, working covertly to subvert the aims of a ruling (often occupying) power. Cf. RESISTANCE I C.
   1939 [see resistance IC]. **1939** *War Illustr.* 9 Dec 392/3
Even in the completely occupied territory there was underground activity.
   d. Of or pertaining to a subculture which seeks to provide radical alternatives to the socially accepted or established mode; *spec.* manifested in its literature, music, press, etc.
   1962 *Movie* Dec. 4/2 Fuller is not an 'underground' director whose films actually *do* the opposite of what they overtly *say*.

practice
   c. *Philos.* The active practical aspect as considered in contrast to or as the realisation of the theoretical aspect.
   1969 D. CAIRNS tr. *Husserl's Formal and Transcendental Logic* 32 The distinction is after all a relative one; because even purely theoretical activity is indeed activity – that is to say, a practice (when the concept of practice is accorded its natural breadth).
   d. A Marxist term for the social action which should result from and complement the theory of communism. Cf. PRAXIS IC.
   1925 N. BUKHARIN *Lenin as Marxist* 17 If Leninism in practice is not the same as Marxism, then we get just that separation of theory from practice which is specially harmful for such an institution as the Institution of Red Professors.
   2. a. The habitual doing or carrying on *of* something; usual, customary, or constant action; action as distinguished from professional, theory, knowledge, etc.; conduct. (See also 9a, b, 10b, 11a.)
   5. *spec.* The carrying on or exercise of a profession or occupation, esp. of law, surgery, or medicine; the professional work or business of a lawyer or medical man.
   1706 PHILLIPS (ed. Kersey), *Practice*, actual Exercise, especially that of the Profession of a Lawyer, Physician, or Surgeon; the having of Clients or Patients.

170 critical psychology

In this way, the use of the term 'underground practice' can infer that practice cannot be separated from knowledge, and that the border between knowledge and practice is under question in the juxtaposition of 'underground' and 'practice'. This meaning of practice contrasts with traditional understandings of professional practice.

In my published autobiographic narrative and reflection on recollections from childhood and young adulthood I recall digging little sand caves 'underground' with a hole in the ceiling to let in the sun which could be construed as a concrete example of my early interest in bringing hidden realms to light (Denshire and Ryan, 2001). Although I do not use the expression 'underground practice' until my autobiographical narrative, the sentiment certainly recurs in my earlier writings on the underside of practice, the lack of funding, recognition and power, related to the perpetual innovation associated with using expressive ways of working with young people in an institutional setting. The insinuation of an 'underground practice' was particularly notable early in my writings on the need for self-expression by young people in hospital. For example,

> Working with adolescents in a children's hospital can sometimes feel like being part of a 'counter movement' in that working in the interests of an individual teenager may not be in the interests of the institution, wishing to maintain the status quo (Denshire, 1984, p. 12).

Fleming and Mattingly's (1994, p. 296) use of the term 'underground practice' refers to what I understand as the significant but informal parts of therapists' work that occur outside the standard documentation guidelines which are beyond narrow hierarchies of evidence. Yet there is an inherent tension in combining the terms 'underground' and 'practice'. The radical, hidden connotations of 'underground' offset the often public nature of conventional 'practice'. This juxtaposition of meanings echoes the dilemmas about professional credibility that have been reported by Fleming and Mattingly (1994) in their research. Game and Metcalfe (1996) remind us that 'although dictionaries are often treated as guarantors of literal meanings, lexicography has no privileged access to real meanings and can only codify the pattern of meaning it generates by juxtaposing each word's usages' (p. 45). So metaphors can significantly structure knowledge about practice – both underground and accepted practice.

The power of metaphor

In the fourth part of the paper I discuss the power of reflecting on generative metaphors to reach a deeper understanding of professional practice. Ultimately, characteristics of everyday ritual are revealed through the meanings I attribute to my engagement in occupation personally and professionally as an occupational therapist. Practising occupational therapy as an everyday ritual can be transformative (do Rozario, 1994). Ritual is not just empty repetition of social convention, but an active remaking of the world. An element of magic is common both to the experience of ritual and the play of metaphor to create new meanings (Game and Metcalfe, 1996). I understand ritual magic to be the ineffable, inexplicable processes of healing and transformation that self-expression can elicit, as illustrated in my reflections on a colleague remarking, 'this is a hospital, not a circus,' and referring to me as a Pied Piper. Now, my students create life course rituals and exhibitions in the occupational therapy subjects I teach. I have facilitated ritual behind the hospital walls, and community theatre (and performance) is part of my heritage, as shown in my autobiographical reflection:

> I remember at that time I did some corporeal mime for expressive rather than performative reasons. Then I saw the job at the Children's Hospital and applied for that (Denshire and Ryan, 2001, p. 155).

My reflections, which question the border between practice and knowledge, take us to the heart of how the literal and the metaphoric can be linked by a professional's 'as if' knowing. Duggan and Grainger (1997) have described drama therapy situations where 'as if' is given 'artistic form in the shape of a bridging presence, able to include idea and actuality within the same image. In other words, a metaphor' (p. 28). In this way, metaphors can be used as conceptual tools that can structure knowledge about practice by way of 'as if' knowing.

That metaphor can be used as a conceptual tool cannot be dismissed as irrelevant, even in the prevailing economic climate characterised by the new managerialism and narrow hierarchies of evidence. Beliefs, values and assumptions are inevitably carried in the metaphors we use (Deshler, 1990; Lakoff and Johnson, 1980). In this paper I have reflected on metaphoric and literal meanings ascribed and attributed to my 'underground practice' as an occupational therapist by analysing figurative language.

What is needed for deeper understandings of practice are

approaches which enable reflection through a combination of imagination and reason (Lakoff and Johnson, 1980). Metaphor can be used in this way. While we can never exist outside of language we can move within it. In order to come to a better understanding of the true extent of evidence we need to keep experimenting with ways of documenting occupational therapy practice. Foregrounding the metaphoric level is one way of doing this.

The underground practice of occupational therapy is something hidden. Yet it manifests itself through metaphor and symbol as in the case of ritual magic attributed to and experienced in the creativity-based practices of young people in hospital. Bateson (1996, p. 11) has called occupational therapists 'peripheral visionaries' who deal simultaneously with the many tasks of everyday life. Practitioners need to take responsibility for their actions by using congruent language that communicates the nuances and realities of a practice that celebrates the ordinary and yet important things people do in everyday life.

Gooder (1997) has raised significant questions about the identities of those who make claims about contemporary occupational therapy practice from inside and outside the profession when she asked 'who defines our practice?' On reflection, I had considerable professional autonomy in my work with young people. However, both tensions and considerable support from staff co-existed whenever young people were openly critical of the institution in the course of a particular youth arts project. For example, 'Great Escape 2', the Super-8 film already mentioned, directed by artist-in-residence Laura Hastings Smith, eventually served a political purpose in securing dedicated space for young people when conventional negotiations had failed.

Foucault (1975) maintains that the clinic reorganises what is seen and said, privileging the clinical domain and diminishing everyday experience. In this way, it is problematic for practices as different as occupational therapy and clinical medicine to share the same frame. This incompatibility has always caused a tension in my writings on working with young people in hospital. Initially, this was between everyday cultural and clinical domains and then, in later writings, between clinical and occupational interests. This excerpt from my life-writing describes my underlying motivation for working with young people in this way:

> The reason I stayed at Children's Hospital for so long was that I felt very strongly about making it a human place. It was very Dickensian archi-

tecturally, a very cold sort of place and I created change, that was quite a drive in me (Denshire and Ryan, 2001, p. 157).

Downplaying personal values of spontaneity and self-expression in my own practice is indicative of a broader professional trend towards suppressing the personal in climates of professional distance and economic efficiency. This theme of underground practice, of contested power and experiences that I am still grappling to understand is illustrated by an excerpt from my writings:

> I seemed to have this strong drive to make this hospital, as a territory better for them. So I did a lot of group work with young people. I got to know them really well. My practice was very relational. I was very much WITH them as a youth worker would be. I worked very informally, was very anti the clinical – yes – and did a lot of creative work about them finding their own voice and, in parallel, I was finding mine (Denshire and Ryan, 2001, p. 155).

I suggest the term 'underground practice' can still convey those vital dimensions of practice which are imaginative and imprecise. It can provide a sort of symbolic evidence to convey what metaphor theorists Lakoff and Johnson (1980, p. 193) have described as 'imaginative rationality'. The language we use to describe practice can have both literal and metaphoric meanings. For example, personifying the field of occupational therapy emphasises its 'silent history', and the 'Pied Piper' metaphor conveys the collectivity in my approach to working with young people as an unseen outsider in some sense. Such polysemy, that is to say one word with several senses, can unite reason and imagination.

Scope of this paper

While this paper is influenced by an approach which is phenomenological and hermeneutic, it is not of itself a piece of phenomenological hermeneutics, nor do I claim philosophical expertise in this area. Rather, I seek to make use of a phenomenological, hermeneutic perspective when reflecting on actions and interactions in personal and professional domains, looking back over my career and life. Similarly, my reflections on figurative language are those of a language-oriented occupational therapist, rather than those of a literary theorist. Writers who seek to be critical are still uncommon in my profession. Nevertheless, I trust that some aspects of my knowledge and experience as an occupational therapist which have been reported here may usefully contribute to resolving the dilemmas that we face as critical professionals.

Conclusions and implications

This paper has developed a matrix of literal and metaphoric descriptions which problematises the distinction through recollections of my practice as an occupational therapist with young people in hospital. Through 'systematising the informal', particular lived professional practices which tend to be undervalued within a highly regimented medical system have been brought to the fore. I have illustrated how metaphor significantly structures my knowledge of a relatively under-documented practice.

Generative metaphors of ritual magic which transcend the 'seeing is believing' vantage point typical of the scientific paradigm have elaborated some aspects of practice that I have felt and experienced rather than merely observed. My readings of the literature suggest that practitioners know implicitly about this phenomenon of 'as if'. Literal and metaphoric aspects of practice are constructed through a practitioner's 'as if' knowing. Empathy, that is to say being 'in the place of' another requires imagination, an ability to pretend 'as if' requires the capacity to connect our inner and outer worlds. However, often such ways of knowing are submerged or denied in the contemporary workplace (Clarke, 1999).

The artistry of practice comes into play where rules fade, and as patterns and frameworks emerge to replace them. Such a view implies creativity, room to be wrong, and regards theory as emerging from practice. Such a view holds that professionals can develop from inside (Fish, 1995). Seeing mystery at the heart of professional practices, embracing uncertainty and making time to reflect on the language of practice (in particular, on what others may say about the way in which we do our work) may be fundamental ways of being for practitioners at the beginning of the twenty-first century. Such ways of being may lead us to experience the challenge, uncertainty and occasional joy of professional practice in more fulfilling ways. Further inquiry into our lived worlds as critical professionals in the contexts of regulated evidence is recommended.

Acknowledgements

Thank you to Dr Jane Selby, Dr Suzy Gattuso, Dr Simone Fullagar and anonymous reviewers for instructive comments on earlier drafts.

Thank you to valued colleagues and young people associated with the Royal Alexandra Hospital for Children for your inspiration.

References

Bateson, M. C. (1996). 'Enfolded activity and the concept of occupation'. Zemke, R. and F. Clark (eds). *Occupational science: The evolving discipline*. Philadelphia: F. A. Davis. 5-12.

Belenky, M., B. Clinchy, N. Goldberger and J. Tarule (1989). *Womens' ways of knowing: Development of self, voice and mind*. New York: Basic Books.

Bettelheim, B. (1976). *The uses of enchantment: The meaning and importance of fairy tales*. London: Thames and Hudson.

Blackburn, S. (1996). *Oxford Dictionary of Philosophy*. Oxford: Oxford University Press.

Buckland, A. (1994). *Art injection: Youth arts in hospital*. Camperdown, NSW: Royal Alexandra Hospital for Children.

Clark, F., B. L. Ennevor and P. L. Richardson (1996). 'A grounded theory of techniques for occupational story telling and occupational story making'. Zemke, R. and F. Clark (eds), *Occupational science: The evolving discipline* (pp. 373-392). Philadelphia: F.A. Davis.

Clarke, J. B. (1999). 'Evidence-based practice: A retrograde step? The importance of pluralism in evidence generation for the practice of health care'. *Journal of Clinical Nursing*, 8, 89-94.

Crabtree, M. (1998). 'Images of reasoning: A literature review'. *Australian Occupational Therapy Journal* 45. 113-123.

Cusick, A., J. Schofield and R. Twible (1994, April 17-22). *Burning questions – No answers. The silent history of occupational therapy*. Paper presented at the World Federation of Occupational Therapists Congress Abstracts, London.

Denshire, S. (1984). 'How can teenagers fit in a children's hospital?'. *Interface* 9 (3). 11-13.

Denshire, S. (1985a). 'A comprehensive approach to youth needs'. *Contact* 83 (February). 10-12.

Denshire, S. (1985b). 'Normal spaces in abnormal places: The significance of environment in occupational therapy with hospitalised teenagers'. *Australian Occupational Therapy Journal*, 32 (4). 142-149.

Denshire, S. (1989). 'Labour report – The birth of Timothy by his mother Sally'. *Childbirth Education Association Newsletter*. 9-11.

Denshire, S. (1993). 'Work of art: Occupational analysis of a children's hospital youth arts program'. *Youth Studies Australia*. (Winter). 18-24.

Denshire, S. (1996). 'A decade of creative occupation: The production of a youth arts archive in a hospital site'. *Journal of Occupational Science: Australia* 3 (3). 93-98.

Denshire, S. (2002). 'Metaphors we live by: Ways of imagining practice'. *Qualitative Research Journal*. 2 (2). 28-46.

Denshire, S. (2004). 'Imagination, occupation, reflection: An autobiographical model of empathic understanding'. Whiteford, G. (ed.). *Qualitative research* as interpretive practice: Proceedings of the Inaugural RIPPLE QRIP Conference, Albury, 2003* (pp. 21-38). Bathurst: Centre for Research into Professional Practice, Learning and Education (RIPPLE).

Denshire, S., and D. L Bennett (1985). 'Have a say – Networking with teenagers in a hospital for children'. *International Journal of Adolescent Medicine and Health* 1 (1 and 2). 217-224.

Denshire, S., and C. Mullavey-O'Byrne (2003). '"Named in the lexicon": Meanings ascribed to occupation in personal and professional life spaces'. *British Journal of Occupational Therapy.* 66 (11). 519-527.

Denshire, S., and S. Ryan (2001). 'Using autobiographical narrative and reflection to link personal and professional domains'. Higgs, J. and A. Titchen (eds). *Professional practice in health, education and the creative arts.* (pp.149-160). Oxford: Blackwell.

do Rozario, L. (1994). 'Ritual, meaning and transcendence: The role of occupation in modern life'. *Journal of Occupational Science: Australia.* 1 (3). 46-53.

Duggan, M. and R. Grainger (1997). *Imagination, identification and catharsis in theatre and therapy.* London: Jessica Kingsley.

Fazio, L. S. (1992). 'Tell me a story: The therapeutic metaphor in the practice of paediatric occupational therapy'. *American Journal of Occupational Therapy.* 46. 112-119.

Finger, M. (1988). 'The biographical method in adult education research. *Studies in Continuing Education.* 10 (2). 33-42.

Fish, D. (1995). *Quality mentoring for student teachers.* London: David Fulton Publishers.

Fleming, M. H. and C. Mattingly (1994). 'The underground practice'. Mattingly, C. and M. H. Fleming (eds), *Clinical reasoning: Forms of inquiry in a therapeutic practice* (pp.295-315). Philadelphia: F.A. Davis.

Foucault, M. (1979). *Discipline and punish: The birth of the prison.* New York: Vintage Books.

Game, A. and A. Metcalfe (1996). *Passionate sociology.* London: Sage.

Giddens, A. (1991). *Modernity and self identity: Self and society in the late modern age.* Cambridge: Polity.

Gooder, J. (1997). 'Who defines our practice? Why does it matter? *New Zealand Journal of Occupational Therapy* 48 (2). 29-32.

Grahl, U. (1970). *The exceptional child: A way of life for mentally handicapped children.* London: Rudolf Steiner.

Gray, J. M., B. L. Kennedy and R. Zemke (1996). 'Dynamic systems theory: An overview. Zemke, R. and F. Clark (eds). *Occupational science: The evolving discipline* (pp.297-308). Philadelphia: F. A. Davis.

Grbich, C. (ed.). (1999). *Health in Australia: Sociological concepts and issues* (2nd ed.). Sydney: Prentice Hall.

Hocking, C., and A. Wilcock (1997). 'Occupational therapists as object users: A critique of Australian practice 1954-1995. *Australian Occupational Therapy Journal* 44. 167-176.

Lakoff, G., and M. Johnson (1980). *Metaphors we live by.* Chicago and London: University of Chicago Press.

Lyons, M. (1997). 'Understanding professional behaviour: Experiences of occupational therapy students in mental health settings'. *American Journal of Occupational Therapy* 51. 686-692.
Marelles, C. (1977). 'The Pied Piper'. Holme, B. (ed.). *Tales from times past* (p.120-127). London: Heinemann.
Mattingly, C. (1994a). 'Occupational therapy as a two-body practice: The body as machine'. Mattingly, C. and M. H. Fleming (eds). *Clinical reasoning: Forms of inquiry in a therapeutic practice* (pp. 37-63). Philadelphia: F.A. Davis.
Mattingly, C. (1994b). 'Occupational therapy as a two-body practice: The lived body'. Mattingly, C. and M. H. Fleming (eds). *Clinical reasoning: Forms of inquiry in a therapeutic practice* (pp. 64-93). Philadelphia: F.A. Davis.
Mattingly, C., and M. H. Fleming (1994). *Clinical reasoning: Forms of inquiry in a therapeutic practice*. Philadelphia: F. A. Davis.
Melucci, A. (1996). *The playing self*. Cambridge: Cambridge University Press.
Menzies Lyth, I. (1988). *Containing anxiety in institutions: Selected essays Vol. 1*. London: Free Association Books.
Muecke, S. (1997). *No road (bitumen all the way)*. South Fremantle, W.A.: Fremantle Arts Centre Press.
Prowse, L. (1999). Letter to the editor. *Australian Occupational Therapy Journal* 46. 74.
Rees, S. (1995). *The human costs of managerialism: Advocating the recovery of humanity*. Leichardt, NSW: Pluto Press Australia.
Rogers, J. C. (1983). 'Clinical reasoning: The ethics, science and art'. *Occupational Therapy Journal of Research* 3. 601-616.
Rose, S. 'You must remember this ...' *Sydney Morning Herald, Good Weekend*. (25/7/98). 38-39.
Ryan, S. (1998). 'Influences that shape our reasoning'. Creek, J. (ed.). *Occupational therapy: New perspectives* (pp. 47- 65). London: Whurr Press.
Schön, D. (1983). *The reflective practitioner: How professionals think in action*. New York: Basic Books.
Schön, D. (1988). *Educating the reflective practitioner*. San Francisco: Jossey-Bass.
Simpson, J. A. and E. S. C. Weiner (eds). (1989). *The Oxford English Dictionary* (2nd ed.). (Vol. 1-20). Oxford: Clarendon Press.
Tryssenaar, J. (1997). 'Clinical interpretation of "Understanding professional behaviour: Experiences of occupational therapy students in mental health settings"'. *American Journal of Occupational Therapy* 51. 693-965.
Valdés, M. J. (ed.). (1991). *A Ricoeur reader: Reflection and imagination*. Hertfordshire: Harvester Wheatsheaf.
Vice, S. (1997). *Introducing Bakhtin*. Manchester University Press.
Wilcock, A. A. (1998). *An occupational perspective of health*. Thorofare, NJ: Slack.
Yerxa, E. J. (1988). 'Oversimplification: The hobgoblin of theory and practice in occupational therapy'. *Canadian Journal of Occupational Therapy* 55 (1). 5-6.

Reviews

Let's theorise it better: a review of two introductions to critical (social) psychology

Laura Miller

B. Gough and M. McFadden *Critical Social Psychology: An Introduction*
Hampshire, NY; Palgrave, 2001

W. Stainton Rogers *Social Psychology: Experimental and Critical Approaches*
McGraw-Hill/Open University, 2003

Introduction

From its inception, social psychology has sought to be an agent of cultural change. It has explored complex phenomena from the benign (altruism) to the dangerous (prejudice) to develop understandings of human relationships on individual and social levels. Yet along the way it has been confounded, or so claim those engaged in a 'critical' project. Whilst studying conformity, social psychology has itself conformed to an academic culture in which particular forms of knowledge and method are reified and others are rejected. Scientific 'authority' has been invoked to institutionalise notions of gender difference that perpetuate patterns of domination whose origin is cultural (Kitzinger, 1987; Burman, 1990). Social psychology is accused of propagating the very prejudice it seeks to challenge through its unquestioning adherence to notions of 'race' (Billig, 1985; Wetherell and Potter, 1992; Ahmed, 2000).

In producing introductory texts on critical social psychology, Stainton Rogers and Gough and McFadden have attempted an almost impossible task – namely to create coherent and comprehensive guides through the dilemmas and debates that beset social psychology. As both books conclude, there has been no real accommodation between critical and traditional approaches: in fact, Stainton Rogers narrates an epic struggle between them, invoking the biblical clash between David and Goliath to portray an uneven and fierce struggle between intellectual cultures. Nor are those who challenge traditional approaches unified behind a particular agenda: the motivation of some is ideological; others raise epistemological questions. All share a concern with the individualistic underpinnings of traditional paradigms: in response, both books promote a multi-disciplinary ethos that emphasises the social and cultural basis of human experience.

Social Psychology: Experimental and Critical Approaches

Divided into ten sections, this book is the more basic of the two. Its aim is to bring together mainstream approaches and the critical, discursive and social constructionist paradigms that have emerged over recent years. This serves two purposes: it provides students with a foundation in mainstream approaches that enables them to appreciate the merits in critical ones; meanwhile, it creates a text for those who are interested in understanding critical social psychology from a traditional perspective. Despite the clash of cultures between traditional and experimental approaches, Stainton Roger's starting point is the same as it would be in any other introductory social psychology text. The question of whether social psychology is a science perplexed traditional theorists and generated debate amongst them long before being taken up by critical thinkers. It is answered according to epistemological orientation: whereas positivism and the desire for 'neutrality' are hallmarks of the experimental tradition, critical theorists point out that human behaviour can never be objectively measured. The social psychological project is an ideological one that invalidates claims to impartiality. Even if it was achievable, there are doubts that human behaviour can easily be quantified.

Having clearly and coherently argued the case against positivism, the book sets out an alternative perspective: social psychology is a complex endeavour and this fact must be reflected in the way it is studied and taught. Rather than launch into the 'topics' that grace most introductory texts, the second chapter continues to explore the philosophical and epistemological underpinnings of critical and experimental approaches. The distinctiveness of both is emphasised before illustrative studies are introduced; this is useful in highlighting the types of insight that are available from each. The student, thus oriented to the various paradigms, is presented with some of the methodological and analytical approaches that are associated with them.

Although less 'sexy' than many mainstream texts that embark on an almost immediate presentation of studies about group behaviour or attraction without much in the way of theoretical preamble, this opening section of three chapters provides an excellent guide to the debates that perplex and excite those with a serious interest in the discipline. Stainton Rogers devotes the remainder of the book to a discussion of some of the topics that preoccupy social psychologists: some sections focus on perspectives from within a particular paradigm; others set out the debates between experimental and critical theorists as they apply to a particular subject. Each ends with a guide to further reading and a number of provocative questions that are designed to challenge the reader.

Communication and language is the focus of chapter four: both are central to the work of critical psychologists who highlight how patterns of interaction shape social experience. This chapter follows easily from the previous methodological and analytic section and presents some of the most important work in the area. For those teaching critical or mainstream approaches, it provides a useful introduction to the role of culture in shaping language and 'meaning'. It includes experimental theories about non-verbal communication, highlighting how even this is culturally specific. As well as setting the scene for the following chapters, section four is important for students and lecturers who want to get to grips with intercultural communication in fast-changing professional and educational contexts.

Chapters five and six explore theories and research from within experimental social psychology. The ways in which we 'understand' the social world are presented through discussions of key theories on attribution, social cognition and the development of personal constructs. This focus on perceptual processes is central to mainstream academic tradition and has spawned some exciting theoretical developments within critical approaches as researchers begin to grapple with the role of language in creating social 'meaning'. Chapter six moves into a discussion of 'values' and 'attitudes', and their relationship to perception before presenting a cognitive model of persuasion: unlike traditional introductory texts, a cross-cultural approach is maintained throughout the account, providing a link between traditional and critical approaches that honours the aim of both.

Social constructionist perspectives are introduced in chapterSeven: these explicitly challenge the cognitive models discussed above. Stainton Rogers draws on research that highlights the way in which traditional psychological theory has created regulatory representations of mental health and identity and in so doing brings the focus to the key 'subject' of social psychology – the self. Chapter eight explores the way that critical psychologists have come to understand self and identity as discursive accomplishments. Throughout this and the preceding chapters, the book illustrates its points using examples that make theoretical perspectives accessible to the reader. Here, recent studies are cited that highlight how ideas from mainstream psychology have permeated our cultural and institutional lives, guiding the ways in which we live through promoting particular regimes and techniques of self-knowledge.

Almost exclusively, the focus of chapter nine is on experimental approaches to group identity and formation. This is important in highlighting that traditional methods *do* provide some basic understanding of the social forces that are at work in creating phenomena such as prejudice and aggression. The excellent guide to traditional psychological approaches to group processes shows how the individual is subsumed by social processes; yet there is something missing in the account: in the interest of 'balance' (between mainstream and critical approaches) important insights from within discursive paradigms are omitted. These are presented in the final chapter, which asks: 'where next for social psychology?'. Although it is clear that mainstream approaches have considered the role of the social in shaping individual experience, they do so in ways that are ethnocentric. It is difficult to see how an approach that alienates or disregards a proportion of the social world can be particularly meaningful.

The book concludes by encouraging a new generation of research and learning that challenges the 'institutionalised racism' that permeates social psychology. The importance of a social constructionist approach is emphasised, but Stainton Rogers concludes by providing a practical framework within which critical and experimental social psychologists can *try* to work together to juxtapose their insights in the hope of gaining better understandings of prejudice, sexism and other cultural ills that precipitated the birth of contemporary social psychology and permeate it. By ending on such an upbeat note creativity is encouraged in students and lecturers alike. This can only be a good thing.

Critical Social Psychology: An Introduction

In many ways, this is the more sophisticated of the two books – perhaps not so much an introduction as an exploration. Nor is the focus exclusively on critical approaches: their origin in traditional paradigms is set out, and some of the key theories that have established social psychology as a discipline are incorporated in the ten chapters of the book. Much of the text provides an exploration of the tensions and dilemmas *within* critical approaches. The book is written in a way that is immediately accessible to students and lecturers: as with Stainton Roger's text, it highlights particular information in boxes that draws attention to key dilemmas and studies. Meanwhile, the text itself is interspersed with reflexive exercises and each chapter provides references to relevant sources, directing students' self-study.

Gough and McFadden point out that it is necessary for mainstream psychology to teach critical approaches alongside experimental ones instead of marginalising them to specialist units. Following the structure of traditional introductory texts, this book enables easy comparison between different paradigms before exploring critical insights into the topics being discussed. In so doing, it provides the basis for an evaluation of critical and traditional approaches on the basis of their relevance to the subjects being explored. But whereas Stainton Roger's book attempts to be inclusive, Gough and McFadden make clear that their text is complimentary to those traditionally used in social psychology. It is, they argue, an attempt to promote a critical agenda alongside the mainstream one: to show how all 'knowledge' is a social production, including the taken-for-granted theories about group behaviour.

The first three chapters describe how theory and method are inextricably linked in social psychology. Highlighting the origins of critical approaches in a sociological social psychology (SSP) – as opposed to psychological social psychology (PSP) – the introduction explores the history of both: it contrasts them, exploring the ways in which each 'explains' or 'describes' social phenomena such as sexism and aggression. The authors explain that the divisions *within* critical psychology are a product of the academic traditions that have informed it (such as postmodernism or feminism) – just as they describe the source of conflicts within the experimental tradition. A cultural dimension is added to this narrative: the authors provide details of a rift between continental European thought and the development of a more cognitive North American tradition.

Chapter two ends with a critique of social-psychology-as-social-control. Interestingly, this is where Stainton Rogers (above) *concludes* her text on critical psychology; but in the case of Gough and McFadden's book, it is an important framework for *introducing* it. This warrants a focus on language, communication and the analysis of 'text' in chapter three. In contrast to experimental methods, the authors advocate ethogenic approaches that have a multidisciplinary ethos (Harré and Secord, 1972): these guide the choices of text for analysis and the way that their content is interrogated. The relationship between theory and method is one that is seldom explored in introductory texts, and the way that Gough and McFadden approach it is invaluable.

It is the straightforward manner of their explication of critical psychological research methods that makes this book ideal as a second-year text: it provides a comprehensive introduction to qualitative approaches in a theoretical context. The notion of 'action research' is used to describe how scholarship can be an agent of social change. The need for reflexivity on the part of the researcher is emphasised; this is not only detailed as a criticism of experimental methods – which, earlier in the book, were described as placing the 'subject' in situations that they had no control over – but as a manifesto for future research.

From here, it is an easy transition into chapter four, which provides experimental and critical interpretations of 'the self', building on earlier arguments about the way that traditional approaches form part of our everyday 'knowledge' about who we are, which – itself – is regulatory. Multicultural identities are discussed to show how notions of selfhood are grounded in social contexts that are seldom tackled in mainstream accounts: the phrase 'death of the "subject"' is coined to describe how traditional conceptions of the self fall away in the light of everyday realities. The examples given in the text are accessible to students: notions of ethnicity and diversity that are familiar parts of intercultural discourse are invoked in ways that are directly meaningful and relevant; a new kind of 'subjectivity' is created (Henriques et al, 1984).

The importance of 'social influence' in defining and refining our sense of self is outlined in chapter five. The authors draw on traditional accounts of social cognition: in so doing, they provide an important interconnection with mainstream psychology whilst showing its limitations. The chapter ends with a citation of research that reworks mainstream conceptualisations of conformity and obedience to highlight how identities are discursively accomplished: meanings are subverted and reworked in ways that resist control. Against the backdrop of this more critical research, the authors provide students with a way of understanding the complexity of human experience in ways that are overlooked in traditional accounts.

The range of research that is cited is vast and it is carefully interspersed into the account to provide a comprehensible and well argued critique of mainstream approaches before setting out alternative paradigms and conceptualisations. Thus, chapters six and seven describe how traditional formulations of gender-as-biological have established stigmatising norms in traditional research. This account provides students with robust feminist and postmodernist critiques of the way that gender and sexuality has been made to signify in mainstream psychology. The discursive approaches that were discussed in previous sections provide the framework for this critique. Foucault's work on the history of sexuality, and its corollary – 'Queer theory' – are subjected to scrutiny towards the end of chapter seven: it omits the question of gender, however. Similarly, challenges from black academics to the white hegemony within critical perspectives are cited to provide an illustration of the ways in which patterns of domination are transmitted – even within seemingly liberating approaches.

The clarity with which these debates are discussed in this text is exceptional and it is with an awareness of the problems of unitary explanations of social phenomena that the authors move into chapter eight – an account of theories of aggression. Drawing on traditional theorists as diverse as Freud and Bandura, the authors present the traditional canon on theories of violence. Recent debates about the affects of media violence are discussed to highlight the complexity of the phenomena associated with it. The authors cite the more 'surprising' instances of female aggression to highlight that it is not necessarily as masculine a phenomenon as theorists traditionally assume. They make good use of the concept of narrative to suggest that representations of violence are culturally specific. Such presentations of recent research are invaluable in providing a basis for challenging the relatively simplistic approaches borne out of traditional paradigms.

Prejudice is one source of aggression – physical and emotional – and as such has provided a focus for a substantial amount of social psychological research. But as the authors point out in preceding chapters, mainstream (and critical) theories are littered with prejudice and so chapter nine provides a means of exploring the various layers of understanding that have been developed from within different social psychological paradigms. In many ways, this chapter is the argumentative climax of the book: it highlights the extent to which we are social beings whose patterns of behaviour are culturally mediated. An exploration of 'new' racisms – i.e. those who conceal their ideological pedigree behind rebuttals and seemingly liberal discourses – is conducted in this chapter by drawing on groundbreaking research (Billig, 1988). The centrality of language is emphasised as the chapter (and indeed, book) draws to a close: warrants for violence and discrimination; constructions of identity and selfhood; relationships with others and conformity – as the research cited suggests – are all discursive accomplishments. The formative theories of social psychology (and indeed the critical alternatives) are culturally embedded and reproduce, to varying degrees, patterns of power and domination. It is at this point that students are left to draw their own conclusions about the power of social psychology to provide valuable understandings of the world in which we live. Chapter ten finishes with a caution: critical psychology, itself, should never become 'sanitised' or 'institutionalised' to the extent that it is simply 'another discipline'. It should remain – they argue – a reflexive space: on that note, they cite publications and forums that remain open to new research that engages with such a project.

Concluding comments

One of the most impressive aspects of both books is their painstaking attention to the problem of teaching critical approaches. Far from being didactic texts, both encourage reflexivity in the readers, requiring them to engage with complex questions to explore the topics under discussion. Strategically interspersed with questions, the texts provide the techniques of critical thinking that they advocate. Rather than patronise the reader with barely relevant practical work that 'proves' a particular theoretical perspective, these reflective exercises encourage an engagement with the dilemmas and debates that are outlined in each chapter. Both books contain excellent glossaries of the terms of debate that provide a useful resource to students who are uncertain of the meanings and use of academic language. If students were never to read a mainstream text alongside either of these, they would still be well versed in the traditional perspectives in a range of topics that are relevant to the mainstream psychology curriculum. But clearly, they are not simply alternatives to other introductory texts: they move beyond them to encourage the development of approaches that fulfil the original aims of social psychology.

References

Ahmed, B. (2000). 'The social construction of racism: the case of second generation Bangladeshis'. *Journal of Community and Applied Social Psychology* 10: 33- 48.

Billig, M. (1985). 'Prejudice, categorisation and particularisation: from a perceptual to a rhetorical approach'. *European Journal of Social Psychology* 15: 79-103.

Billig, M. (1988). 'The notion of prejudice: some rhetorical and ideological aspects'. *Text*. 8: 91-110.

Burman, E. (1990). *Feminists and Psychological Practice*. London: Sage.

Harré, R. and P. F. Secord (1972). *The Explanation of Social Behaviour*. Oxford: Basil Blackwell.

Henriques, J., W. Hollway, C. Urwin, C. Venn and V. Walkerdine (1984). *Changing the Subject: Psychology, Social Regulation and Subjectivity*. London: Methuen.

Kitzinger, C. (1987). *The Social Construction of Lesbianism*. London: Sage.

Wetherell, M. and J. Potter (1992). *Mapping the Language of Racism: Discourse and the Legitimation of Exploitation*. London: Harvester Wheatsheaf.

Notes on contributors

Irina Anderson has lectured in social psychology at the University of Birmingham and is now Senior Lecturer at the School of Psychology, University of East London. She teaches social psychology and critical psychology to undergraduates, and supervises postgraduate students on social, critical and qualitative issues. Her research interests include issues in sexual violence, discourse and conversation analysis, and attribution and attitude theories, particularly in relation to rape.

Eva Bendix Petersen is a lecturer in the School of Teacher Education at Charles Sturt University, Australia. Her research focuses on academic culture, subjectivities and discursive practices.

Lise Bird teaches and researches difference/diversity and critical educational psychology at Victoria University of Wellington. She is co-author (with Wendy Drewery) of a critical book on human development, widely used in Aotearoa/New Zealand, which includes multiple voices from diverse and indigenous cultural perspectives.

Jane Callaghan is a lecturer in psychology at the University College Northampton. She is a South African psychologist, and has worked as both a lecturer and a psychologist in that context. Her research interests include professionalisation and professional 'development', and the history and practice of psychology.

Sue Cornforth is a Lecturer in Counselling in the School of Education, Victoria University of Wellington, New Zealand. Her doctoral work is in ethics and counselling/psychotherapy.

Bronwyn Davies is a Professor of Education at the University of Western Sydney and co-ordinator of the research concentration Narrative Discourse and Pedagogy. She is currently researching the impact of neoliberalism on subjectivities at work, and the transformation of subjectivities in educational contexts.

Pippa Dell is a Principal Lecturer in the School of Psychology at the University of East London, where she teaches critical social psychology on the undergraduate programmes and contributes to the qualitative methodology course for the Doctorate in Clinical Psychology. Her recent publications focus on embodiment and women's health from a feminist poststructuralist perspective and current projects include women's experiences of hysterectomy and domestic violence.

Sally Denshire is currently lecturer and honours coordinator with the Occupational Therapy Program at the School of Community Health, Charles Sturt University in Australia. She has 28 years experience as a practitioner-researcher in youth health, mental health, childbirth education, area health services and curative education. Sally established the Youth Arts Program at Royal Alexandra Hospital for Children in Sydney in 1984 and entered academia in 1995.

Duane Duncan is a doctoral student in feminist and cultural geography at Monash University, Melbourne, Australia. His doctoral work contributes to disciplinary engagements with gender, sexuality, and embodiment.

Kerry Frizelle is a lecturer in the School of Psychology at the University of Kwa-Zulu Natal, Howard College Campus, Durban, South Africa. She is a registered psychologist and has a particular interest in HIV/AIDS in the South African context. Kerry trains HIV/AIDS counsellors and lectures on an HIV/AIDS service-learning course that involves training students to run sexuality discussion groups with local high-school learners.

David Harper is Senior Lecturer in Clinical Psychology and an academic tutor on the Professional Doctorate in Clinical Psychology at the University of East London. He is interested in critical and social constructionist approaches to research and therapeutic practice in mental health.

Laura Miller is currently teaching social psychology to undergraduate and postgraduate students at UCL. She has worked with Lisa Blackman on a project exploring the constructions of selfhood in popular cultural forms and the way that these reflect regulatory notions of 'the psychological'. Her current research explores educational discourses and the forms of selfhood that are made possible in a pedagogic context.

Shirley Roberson is the Programme Coordinator in Allied Mental Health at Victoria University of Wellington. Her doctoral work is on young people's talk about their violence. She has presented papers on the challenges of critical research, and has published and advocated on behalf of graduate students.

Jane M. Selby is a clinical psychologist in Australia and former full-time academic. Her published work includes papers about indigenous Australia, infancy and young people, all within a context of understanding the links between 'individuality' or 'identity' and the politico-cultural contexts within which we live and thrive.

Paula Smith is Vice President of the Institute of the Sisters of Mercy of Australia, a 1700-strong group of Catholic women religious living and working in Australia, Papua New Guinea and Pakistan. She is an educator with backgrounds in secondary and tertiary education. Paula's commitment to feminist research over the past 20 years led her to the investigation in feminist poststructural theory and analysis that was the framework for her doctoral research.